AFTER MONTAIGNE

AFTER MONTAIGNE

Contemporary Essayists Cover the *Essays*

EDITED BY DAVID LAZAR AND PATRICK MADDEN

The University of Georgia Press
Athens and London

© 2015 by the University of Georgia Press
Athens, Georgia 30602
www.ugapress.org
All rights reserved
Designed by Melissa Bugbee Buchanan
Set in Adobe Garamond Pro and Cronos Pro
Printed and bound by Thomson-Shore
The paper in this book meets the guidelines for
permanence and durability of the Committee on
Production Guidelines for Book Longevity of the
Council on Library Resources.

Most University of Georgia Press titles are
available from popular e-book vendors.

Printed in the United States of America
19 18 17 16 15 C 5 4 3 2 1

Library of Congress Cataloging-in-Publication Data
After Montaigne : contemporary essayists cover the essays /
edited by David Lazar and Patrick Madden.
pages cm
Includes bibliographical references and index.
ISBN 978-0-8203-4815-5 (hardcover : alk. paper) —
ISBN 978-0-8203-4817-9 (ebook)
1. American essays—21st century. 2. Montaigne, Michel de,
1533–1592—Influence. I. Lazar, David, 1957– editor. II. Madden,
Patrick, 1971– editor. III. Montaigne, Michel de, 1533–1592. Essais.
PS689.A37 2015
814'.6—dc23
2014045430

British Library Cataloging-in-Publication Data available

To Seigneur de Montaigne,

our inspiration,

and Étienne de La Boétie,

his inspiration

Bees cull their several sweets from this flower and that blossom, here and there where they find them, but themselves afterwards make the honey . . . so the several fragments [one] borrows from others, he will transform and shuffle together to compile a work that shall be absolutely his own.

I never speak of others, but that I may the more speak of myself. . . . these are my humors and opinions; I offer them as what I believe, not what is to be believed.

MONTAIGNE, "OF THE EDUCATION OF CHILDREN"

Contents

Acknowledgments

The editors heartily thank our essayists, for their engagement with the reimagination of Montaigne we asked of them. We also thank our students and teachers (it's nice to see the cart before the horse sometimes).

Much gratitude to Sydney Dupre and Walter Biggins at the University of Georgia Press for their extraordinary support.

Patrick Madden would like to thank his family, near and far, young and old. They are participants in and witnesses to his unwritten essays.

David Lazar would like to thank his lucky stars, since it's about time. Friends and family gathered under them, and were kind.

Steven Church's "Of Idleness" was first published as "On Loitering" in *Rumpus*, May 16, 2013, therumpus.net/2013/05/on-loitering.

Lia Purpura's "Of Prayers" originally appeared in *Ecotone* 8, no. 1 (Fall 2012).

AFTER MONTAIGNE

Introduction

Montaigne . . . to whom, down even to our own day, even in point
of subject-matter, every essayist has been more or less indebted . . . /
. . . is an immense treasure-house of observation, anticipating all
the discoveries of succeeding essayists. / He has left little for his
successors to achieve in the way of just and original speculation on
human life. Nearly all the thinking of the [succeeding] centuries, of
that kind . . . is to be found in Montaigne's *Essays.*
ALEXANDER SMITH / CHARLES LAMB / WILLIAM HAZLITT

What do the Beatles' "Twist and Shout," Aretha Franklin's "Respect," Elvis Presley's "Blue Suede Shoes," Jimi Hendrix's "All Along the Watchtower," and Ike
and Tina Turner's "Proud Mary" have in common? They're all cover songs, songs
originally recorded by other artists (the Isley Brothers, Otis Redding, Carl Perkins, Bob Dylan, Creedence Clearwater Revival, in these cases), then borrowed,
modified, flavored in new ways by new musicians. Covering is a long and proud
tradition in music, especially popular music in the last half century, and if you
think about it, before recorded music, most performances were covers (of a
sort). Recording a cover is a way of paying homage to a respected forebear while
simultaneously asserting newness and individuality. In some cases, a cover song
achieves greater popularity than the original. In some cases, people don't even
realize the cover is a cover.

For 350 years, almost every essayist paid homage to the creator of the essay
form: Michel de Montaigne. While there were precursors of the essay—cognates
and close influences—Bob Wills and the Texas Playboys (great stuff!) are not
Chuck Berry. But even Chuck Berry didn't *create* rock 'n' roll. Montaigne stands

virtually alone as having introduced a new form of writing: the 107 essays contained in books I, II, and III of the *Essais*, published in 1580, 1588, and 1595.

Essayists and aficionados of the essay will please excuse a few reiterations of the basics: Montaigne, who lived from 1533 to 1592 and was raised by a genteel and progressive father, led a life that was politically engaged in troubled times. He witnessed plague, wars of religion between Catholics and Huguenots, and personal tragedies: the deaths of his beloved friend Étienne de La Boétie, his younger brother (from a tennis ball that hit him in the head!), and all but one of his children in infancy. But Montaigne stayed engaged with life, with ideas, and, most important for our considerations, with the creation of a form that he called the *essai*, coining the term from the verb *essayer*, to try or attempt, which started and sustained an innovative, playful, experimental edge to prose.

Those doing the math at home will have noticed that 350 years doesn't quite get us to the present. This is our observation, one that sparked the creation of this book: that what was once so blatantly obvious—Montaigne's greatness and influence—has become less acknowledged. His formal inventiveness, disarming intimacy, and rhetorical complexity, which were once the essential tracks for anyone listening to the essay or listening to themselves trying to understand what an essay might be, are often simply ignored or are considered quaintly traditional. Some newcomers to the essay seem to have trouble hearing Montaigne's orchestral brilliance just because he is "old." It's like being unable to keep hearing how radical Louis Armstrong is. New students in MFA and PhD programs calling themselves essayists arrive (and sometimes even leave) without having read a single essay by the writer to whom they are inextricably indebted. Their curiosity about the tradition of the essay doesn't seem to reach very far back in the essay's history. This is a great shame, a disgrace. So much that's vital about the essay seems uncannily present, explicitly or in utero, in Montaigne.

This anthology aims to modestly correct that trend and reassert Montaigne's centrality. We asked more than two dozen of the most exciting essayists writing today to give us their take on a Montaignean subject. Like an album of cover songs paying homage to an influential band or composer, these essays attempt to reenvision Montaigne's topics through a contemporary sensibility. Each one uses Montaigne's original title (or an inspired variation) and begins with an epigraph from Montaigne, ending with a coda explaining the process through which the essayist translated, transfigured, reimagined, or rethought some of the essential ideas, figures, and motifs in Montaigne's original.

In between the quoted and critical apparatus are the essays, the heart of the heart of the matter. Each writer in the anthology attempts to find a way to revise and connect with Montaigne's original essay. We mean "revise" in the sense of "re-create," not "fix" or "correct." As impassioned as we are in our love for the master of the form, we don't see the *Essais* as museum pieces. They're living works of prose; they're multifaceted; they breathe; they have complex structures, and occasional *longeurs*. In short, they're brilliant and imperfect, which is probably why so many generations of writers have cleaved to them so closely, from Bacon to Hazlitt, Emerson to Woolf, Flaubert to Cixous, Sterne to Baldwin. Some wrote essays using the same subjects and even titles as Montaigne. One could argue that writers have been covering Montaigne, more or less, all along.

Montaigne is the ur-essayist, the essayist essayists have started with and returned to, like writing upstream, but his essays are both approachable and inexhaustible. As Hazlitt said of Shakespeare, it would be vulgar to create a godlike figure out of Montaigne. Our essayists, essayistically, play with his essays, because he gives us room to enter, engage, and think for ourselves.

Once you've enjoyed these new essays, or *while* you're enjoying them, we urge you to read the originals. You can start at www.aftermontaigne.org. Then we hope that you, too, will feel inspired to write essays after Montaigne.

1

To the Reader, Sincerely

DAVID LAZAR

Non men che saver, dubbiar m'aggrada.
DANTE, *INFERNO* XI

For it is myself that I portray.
MONTAIGNE, "TO THE READER"

Come here often?

We've both been around the block a few times. In fact, I think I may have even seen you loitering in my back pages. I don't hold it against you. It's like the old joke: we're both here, after all. My apologies if that sounds slightly salacious. But just as Montaigne wished he could appear naked, and worried that he'd be cast into the boudoir, it's that desire to be raw and that need to cook, wanting to blurt out everything and wanting, too, to be discreet, that creates the maddeningly necessary friction for essays. It's that thinking about what you think you thought. Raw rarely wins.

I want something from you and you want something from me, and I'm not trying to just be chivalrous when I say I know I owe you a good time, in the broadest sense. What I want from you is more complicated, reader. You're mostly doing a great job of giving me what I need just by being you. I know that sounds hackneyed: "Just be yourself." And of course, to a certain extent, you're my invention, whether you like it or not, the monster to my Frankenstein—or "steen," depending on my mood. Potato, potahto. But if we call the whole thing off, we must part. Keeping all of this in mind, I think it's fair to say you can read me like a book. But even as I'm imagining you, you're (with a little help) imagining me. Which is to say, dearie, old pal of mine, that the thing about whistling in the dark is, "You just put your lips together and blow."

Reader, I divorced her. And she me. And perhaps I'm looking for a surrogate, a perfect other, perchance at least a friendly friend to while away the hours conversing with. After all, I spend so much time talking to myself, writing little concertos of prose in my head, that after a time, having spent too much time walking around the city and thinking in concentric loops, layering idea upon idea only to have them evaporate like the lightest of brain soufflés, it seems to make sense to write them down. I try to tell myself that the story I tell is real, but really, what would that really mean, other than that I really mean what I say? Nevertheless, I think, I've always thought, that intention counts for something. Isn't that recherché? Wasn't intention nine-tenths of the law in some places?

I'm sincere, in other words. Whether or not I'm honest is a judgment that shouldn't be self-administered. I'm sincerely sincere. I've always loved the song in *Bye Bye Birdie*, "Honestly Sincere":

> If what you feel is true
> Really feel it you
> Make them feel it too
> Write this down now
> You gotta be sincere
> Honestly sincere
> Man, you gotta be sincere

If I didn't have a dash of modesty, I'd be entirely and wholly sincere! I'm even sincere about the things I say that are slightly less than sincere, but which I try to sincerely slap myself around a bit for having been insincere about. It's one of the ways I can show you that I'm being reasonably honest. It's also a sincere display of how flawed I am. Look, if I told you I was thirty-nine, and then told you I was fifty (don't roll your eyes), you'd think I was a bit of an idiot, but at least you'd know I had a self-correcting mechanism. But I'd take everything I say with a grain of salt if I were you. And I mean that sincerely. I'm fifty-six, by the way. You could look it up.

If I really just wanted you to like me, I'd tell you a story. It would be a story of adversity of some kind, and I would be the protagonist. It would arc like crazy, like Laurence Sterne on Ritalin, and I'd learn something really valuable from my experience. But who knows where an essay is going to go? Really. I'd be a defective essayist if all I did was tell stories. Sincere stories. Like the one about walking out of my house yesterday. I was feeling my age as summer bled into fall on a day that was really too nice for such a metaphor. A guy who was working on installing a new wrought iron fence outside (I love wrought iron— partly because I love the way it looks, and partly because of "wrought") told me he liked my style. "Thanks!" I said, thinking I was so smart to have bought that '50s vintage jacket online last week for fifteen dollars. Then the fine fellow said, "You look like Woody Allen."

I was taken aback. I had never been told I looked like Woody Allen. I'm not sure I want to look like Woody Allen. I don't mind sounding a bit like Woody Allen. It comes with the territory: Brooklyn Jewish, and he was an enormous influence on me. But, *look*? So I said, "I'm sorry, did you say I looked like Errol Flynn?" And he said, "Yeah, that's right, but not from *The Adventures of Robin Hood* but from *The Modern Adventures of Casanova*, in 1952, when he was dissolute."

I made that last part up. Forgive me? He really did say I looked like Woody Allen.

For the last few years everyone I've met has been telling me I look like Lou Reed. I don't see it. I was in one of my favorite bars in Chicago, the Berghoff (essay product placement), and a man was staring at me. He finally made his way to my table and said, "Excuse me, I don't mean to bother you, but are you Lou Reed?" I said, "No, I'm John Cale." He said, "Who's John Cale?" I mean, how can you possibly know who Lou Reed is without knowing who John Cale is? It's like walking up to someone and saying, "Are you Oliver Hardy?" "No, I'm Stan Laurel." "Who's Stan Laurel?"

In any case, I wasn't even sure of how I felt about that. Lou Reed was great looking, although a bit older than I; he was getting a bit weathered . . . and do I have to look like a Jewish New Yorker in the arts? What's the connection between Woody Allen and Lou Reed? Who's next? Mandy Patinkin? Harvey Fierstein? Hey, what about Adam Brody?

Look, reader, I'm sincerely not trying to look for things to complain about, but part of bedecking myself is the confusion and profusion of identities "I" shuffles through. Surely you have some version of this? Don't you have some walk-in closet of self or selves? I do have some version of a Fierstein shirt, a Patinkin suit, I suppose, especially when I'm being shticky. When my persona is shticky. When it's less so, I like to think I'm closer to

Me and my shadow
Strolling down the avenue
Oh, me and my shadow
Knock on the door is anybody there
Just me and my shadow

You might call me a self-made man. Hello to the essay Lazar, goodbye to the talker-walker Lazar. The former has inscribed the latter, imbibed the latter, put him through a meat grinder, and feasted. I'm self-immolated, a phoenix. Rise, he said. Or: Monty Python: I write rings around myself, logically, if not impetuously. (Don't you wish John Cleese had written essays?) The spirit of Whitman is in the essay: we enlarge ourselves even as we're talking about our pettiness, our drawers, our moths, our doors. The "I" that takes us along (remember that terrible song "Take Me Along"?—bad songs stay as long as delightful ones) does so because we're attracted to the way it vibrates or concentrates, clicks or skiffles. The essay voice is a boat that can carry two.

And no voices are alike—my own jumpy, interruptive style, which might not be to everyone's taste, will be seen as a flaw or a defect by some, and by others as the only dress in my closet. But let me tell you that I think that I, like most essayists, want to be known. That this "created" voice you're hearing (created voice, creative writing, creature of the night!), this persona, this act of self-homage and self-revelation, occasionally revulsion, frequently inquisition or even interdiction, actually is tied very closely to the author. Since I'm frequently my subject, to say the "I" who is writing isn't quite me is slightly fatuous; which "I" is the more sincere, the more honest self? That one? The ontology of essay writing involves a conversation with oneself, and one, after a while, exchanges parts back and forth so that writer and subject become bound, bidden, not interchangeable but certainly changeable. I become what I've created, and want to be known as that.

For Montaigne the wanting to be known was partly due to the loss of his soulmate, Étienne de La Boétie. At one point Montaigne offers to deliver his essays in person. I like that idea, reader. We've lost the telegram, after all. Wouldn't you like to open the door and have Mary Cappello or Lia Purpura hand you a personalized essay? "Essay, Ma'am," might just enter the lexicon. I'd write you one. I could come over and read this one to you, if you like. Like Montaigne, I think I'm in search of company, and I talk to myself in essays as a way of finding it. So you're really very close to me. A matchbook length, a cough, a double-take away.

At the end of his invocation "To the Reader," his introduction to his *Essais*, in 1580, Montaigne bids farewell. It's a double joke. He's saying goodbye because, in an extension of the modesty topos, he has urged the reader to not read his vain book of the self, his new form: the essay. He is also bidding adieu to the pre-essayed Montaigne, the one who isn't self-created, self-speculated, strewn into words and reassembled, if so. A playful gauntlet. And he is invoking the spirit of his death. To write oneself is to write oneself right out of the world. It's the autothanatological moment: "when they have lost me, as soon they must, they may here find some traces of my quality and humor."

Montaigne says his goal is "domestic and private," and so it may have been, at first, though Montaigne's literary ambitions start seeming more and more clear as the essays lengthen and grow more complex, as Montaigne takes more risks with what he offers of himself. And my own, I ask myself, in the spirit of Montaigne. What are they? I'd say they're twofold: (1) to write the sentence whose echo doesn't come back; (2) to be known, in some essential way, without sucking the air out of the mysterium.

Montaigne's address to the reader occurred when doing so was still a relatively new, a reasonably young rhetorical move. According to Eric Auerbach, Dante seems to have been the first writer to establish an intimately direct poetic address to the reader. Dante then plays with this form, using it a structuring device, tossing off asides. And Montaigne quotes Dante in the essays. This dynamism is epistolary, liberating and seductive. *Sotto voce*. Let me whisper in your ear. It's just the two of us. Come on, you can tell me. Or rather, it's okay, I can tell you. The confession. After all, I'm writing about myself, and my subject is really important, right?

Except: Reader, she says—grabbing me by the shoulders, telling me that what she needs to tell me is more important than anything that's ever been told—I married him. And you thought *comedies* ended in marriage? In my triad of great addresses to the reader (meaning me, in the place where you are now), Charlotte Brontë's direct address will always be for me the most stunning, the single most relational moment, perhaps, in literature. "Reader." And for the moment it's your name. *Call me Reader.* And as a male reader, and as a male adolescent reader, my response was always: You should have waited for me.

Addresses to the reader are not, you see, just about intimacy. They're also secretly about infidelity.

Reader, comrade, essay-seeking fool, blunderer upon anthologies for whom the book tolls, when I said, "I divorced her," I'm sorry for the lack of context, but really what I wanted to talk about here wasn't her and me, that was a bit of a feint, but you and me. You know I've been missing you. Since we last met, across a crowded essay, I've really been thinking about nothing but you. Well, you and me, and me and you. Let's go for a little walk, shall we? Flaneur and flaneuse, or flaneur and flaneur. I might even let you get in a word or two.

Baudelaire must have breathed Montaigne. And his "Au Lecteur" or "To the Reader" (also the title of Montaigne's invocation) is almost like Montaigne inverted, Montaigne through the looking glass. Actually, Baudelaire and Charles Dodgson were contemporaries, which makes a kind of perverse sense. If you look at some of the language, some of the phrasing of "Au Lecteur," you find a Montaignean sensibility, if not a Montaignean tone: "In repugnant things we discover charms"; "our souls have not enough boldness"; "Our sins are obstinate, our repentance is faint." But whereas Montaigne is only suggesting, via a modesty trope, that his readers may be wasting their time (not really), Baudelaire is saying (Hey, you!) we're going to hell in a *panier à main*, which means, ironically, that we need to listen to his brotherly jeremiad. "Hypocrite reader, my brother, my double"—the antithesis and the brother (and sister) of Montaigne's and Brontë's addresses. Theirs are seductive in their close (reading), one-on-one asides to us, just us. They need an intimate, we feel, and so appeal to our need for intimacy. We need what they need. But so does Baudelaire, because who else would dare say that to us? Hey—you! Yeah, I'm talking to you! I remember being shocked by that, the audacity, someone daring to say that to me. He would have to . . . know me pretty well. My brother, my double? Push, pull.

Depending on my mood, I could tell you that there are better things to do than reading essays—going for a walk, watching a movie, throwing a rubber ball against a stoop. But at other times, perhaps when I'm treading across Charles Lamb's "A Bachelor's Complaint of the Behavior of Married People" or Eliza

Haywood's *The Female Spectator*, Nancy Mairs's "On Not Liking Sex" or John Earle's *Microcosmographie*, I feel like telling you that there may not be anything better to do, that in fact you're wasting your time reading novels, or going to plays, looking at art (I can't ever speak against the movies—I just can't), or doing the things you do to keep yourself alive. You should just read essays and live on the delight. The delight of Stevenson, Beerbohm, M. F. K. Fisher. But modesty tropes are worthwhile, so part of me wants to tell you: Go for a walk.

So, reader. Reader. Darling reader. There's something I want to tell you. It's a story, but it's more than a story. It's what I think about what's happened to me. To us. And where I might be headed. We might be headed. It involves movies, books, walking around if it's not miserably cold, and your occasional willingness to laugh at my jokes. Together, we might be able to cobble together an essay. We can assay! I'd love it if you really thought you knew me.

CODA

Montaigne's "To the Reader," less than a page, contains much of the internal friction and frisson of the creation of the essay's persona. It's full of play and a theoretical masterpiece in miniature. "To the Reader" has been my inspiration, and has inspired and intrigued essayists for 435 years. So I wanted to join Montaigne's along with a couple of my other favorite readerly salutations and try to let them breathe in my own question mark as lasso out to whoever might find or be looking to find that note of connection in the voice of reader and writer, writer and reader, who in the essay play a game, at times, of musical chairs.

2

Of Liars

E. J. LEVY

Lying is indeed an accursed vice.
MONTAIGNE, "OF LIARS"

I forget. Birthdays, appointments, the names of close friends, even the day of the week of late. I blame it on midlife pregnancy, on a long Latin word my friend Camille told me last week—a fancy phrase that I've forgotten.

I used to have a photographic memory, which always felt vaguely as if I were cheating on my college tests. Now I am happily disburdened of such guilt. Now I remember haphazardly, idiosyncratically. I remake the past to suit myself, a crazy quilt of recollection. I unnerve acquaintances by recalling intimate details long ago revealed—an erotic fantasy, a favorite book, an ungenerous opinion— but ask me what I ate for lunch the day before, and I am defeated.

"To err is human, to forgive divine," we say, so what better means to facilitate godlike generosity than a lousy memory? "Forgive and forget" gets the matter wrong, backwards, for nothing heals faster than poor recall. Forget—and all is forgiven.

This memory loss has been long in coming, and I know I am not alone. Bad memory is our national habit, allergic as we Americans are to history. There are others worse than I. My friend Cheryl, not long after marrying her second husband, found herself seated among strangers at a literary dinner in Portland where, to her horror, she found she could not recall her *new* husband's name. She remembered only that of her first, which understandably would not do.

We bemoan our poor memories, but would any one of us really prefer perfect recall, the hyperthymesia that, since 2006, has officially plagued our human race? Officially, only a few dozen of us suffer from it, recalling in exact detail all events, conversations, and feelings from decades ago, swamping the present moment. No wrong ever forgotten, no betrayal softened by time, no chance of forgiving and forgetting.

But memory is a necessity, if we're to navigate our days. Increasingly I out-source mine. My iPhone is my memory. At night before I sleep I note there what I'm to do the following day—meetings, e-mails, phone calls—then promptly forget them all. Trusting it to remember for me. Like a butler in charge of what Augustine termed memory's many-roomed mansion, my little friend reminds me each morning, afternoon, and evening what I need to know. What I cannot afford to forget. (But will.)

There is a certain insouciant charm in forgetfulness, in a fallible memory like mine. Memory lapse can inspire courtesy as well as complaisance (who will argue a point they can't remember?). Marcus Aurelius was said to have ad-dressed in flattering terms strangers and intimates equally, as my partner does in imitation of that great man: my beloved greets men as "Big Guy" and calls all women "Beautiful," he explained to me early in our courtship, in case he can't recall their names. It seemed a charming gallantry, until he took to calling me "Beautiful."

Perhaps the greatest gift bestowed by bad memory is the inability to lie: *if one cannot recall the truth, how can one be said to dissemble?* As Montaigne notes in his essay "Of Liars,"

> grammarians make a distinction between telling an untruth and lying.
> They say that to tell an *untruth is to say something that is false, but that we*
> *suppose to be true*, and that the meaning of the Latin *mentiri*, from which
> our French word for lying derives, is to go against one's conscience, and that
> consequently it *applies only to those who say the opposite of what they know*.
> (italics mine)

All of which makes an honest woman of me.

But such etymological defense does not relieve me of my suspicion that honesty is overrated in our age, as in the past. "I cannot tell a lie" is a watchword of

American schoolchildren weaned on fibs about our national history—Washington's cherry tree, honest Abe. But, honestly, what could be duller? Give me the exaggerated compliment, the embellished tale. Hardly anything is as uninteresting as earnest honesty in companions or in conversation.

Honesty in regard to the receipt of gifts is merely an excuse for boorishness or worse (a petition for a better gift). And would anyone *really* want a thoroughly honest spouse assessing one's enduring appeal over decades, one's lovemaking, or relative physical charms vis-à-vis the delectable young thing across the room? "Do you love me?" is, after all, a question most often asked when the listener is least inclined to answer in the affirmative.

When friends praise a book I have written, I do not wish for more frank assessment, a more honest evaluation of my intellect or talents. I want the lie that binds.

Honesty is said to be the best policy, but it is surely not the most interesting. (And the saying itself may be a lie. "The truth shall set you free" is after all not true if you are Bernie Madoff or Nixon or any of a number of liars one might name.) Literature is filled with fascinating liars from Iago to Lady Chatterly to Raskolnikov. For a good story, God give me a liar any day.

So why all the praise of honest men in our dishonest age? We tap the phones of friends and foes and citizens alike, call war-waging "peacekeeping," give the dullest of names to that most dreadful of weapons, the unmanned drone, and claim it does not kill civilians—in short, we lie. As NSA whistle-blower Edward Snowden makes clear, an honest man is a despicable thing, a pariah, a blight on our nation, showing us up for hypocrites, spies, undemocratic as those we would convert to democracy.

Truth takes its toll after all. While lies may fuel conflict, wars are almost always fought in the name of truth, that unbending tool of the ideologue, the tyrant. Set aside the smug certitude of that word and most campaigns would crumble. Without truth on our side or its proxy, God, whom could we justify killing?

As a child I was painfully honest and had few friends. My fealty to frank honesty left me vulnerable. I was tormented for decades by the memory of a false accusation that I had cheated on a difficult exam, because my score was perfect, a possibility our science teacher could not imagine, but a score I'd nonetheless honestly achieved, as I regularly would in math and science until I discovered this was an unsociable habit and gave up both in my junior year in favor of the lie of popularity. I wonder if, as with the exaggerated heterosexuality of queer kids in my youth (of which I was one), those most attached to honesty in youth are those least inclined to practice it later in life. We understand that truth—like sexuality—is a performance rather than an absolute.

Truth and lies—like sex and death—each have their place in life, their charm. The virtue is in knowing which to embrace when. We look to facile absolutes (seek rules in regard to lies) to shade us from a harsher truth: we must assess, discriminate, consider occasion and proportion. A lie told to spare a friend's feelings is no wrong done ("I'd have invited you to dinner had I known you were in town!") when compared to unflattering candor ("We feared you'd drink too much and hold forth on 9/11 conspiracy theories"). Like children, we want to be disburdened of the obligation to discriminate, to weigh, *essayer*, decide for ourselves and take the consequences, when it comes to truth and lies. The question to ask perhaps is this: *Whom does the lying serve, oneself or others?* It takes an honest man or woman to know the difference and answer truthfully.

Common locution may illuminate the matter. One need only consider colloquialisms to discern the relative merits of each: "stretching the truth" has a capacious, generous ring, whereas "brutal honesty" does not; one "confronts the truth," whereas the perfidious "tells a little white lie," reminiscent of Mary's lamb . . .

The necessity of incessantly stating the case on honesty's behalf itself calls the practice into question. Like millennia of laws against sodomy that attest to homosexuality's enduring appeal, injunctions against lying ironically bespeak its charms. We think of lying as an injustice to others, but in many cases it serves the common good; the lubricant of lies creates a gentle buffer in an overcrowded and increasingly surveilled world.

What we mean, when we esteem the truthful, I think, is *don't lie to me*. Or rather, *don't deceive me in a way that will do me harm*. In business and politics, honesty should arguably be the enforced norm, even as it is worth remembering that it is often not the lie that harms but the actions concealed thereby. I couldn't care less about the false rating of bad loans, but the bilking of the poor to line the pockets of the rich really tees me off. It is the theft—not the lie—that wrongs. And should be righted.

Dostoyevsky was right: lie to everyone but yourself. "The man who lies to himself . . . cannot distinguish the truth within him, or around him, and so loses all respect for himself and others."

A lie, even the smallest lie, grants the liar a capacious cloak of privacy. In an age of increasing surveillance—our era of technological hyperthymesia, in which each tweet and call, each coming and going, every street crossing and red-light run may be recorded and kept in permanent archive—lying may be the last hope of the individual, offering a shelter in which the self may know itself in solitude, unobserved, creating a space into which one can retreat to contemplate one's life, one's thoughts, *unknown* to others, the last refuge of honest men.

CODA

One of the reasons that I return to Montaigne's essays time and again is for the freshness of his thought, his frank and often surprising reappraisal of the familiar—whether friendship, smells, or thumbs—which makes the matter under consideration, and my own thoughts, new to me again. A rare exception is his somewhat disappointing essay "Of Liars." While the opening of that essay delights with its extravagant, almost hubristic claim that his is the worst memory ever ("There is no man so unsuited for the task of speaking about memory as I am, for I find scarcely a trace of it in myself"), when the piece takes a turn toward its titular subject, Montaigne mostly reiterates cant. He seems—rare vice for him—to rely on the tried and (un)true claims of others in regard to the much maligned practice of lying. So I offer this response in homage and as gentle corrective to that noble adventurer in thought, if not exactly in praise of lying, then at least, I hope, in complication of its contemplation.

3

Of the Education of Children

BRIAN DOYLE

> But, in truth . . . the greatest and most important difficulty of
> human science is the education of children. For . . . after that which
> is planted comes to life, there is a great deal more to be done, more
> art to be used, more care to be taken, and much more difficulty to
> cultivate and bring it to perfection. . . . it is no hard matter to *get*
> children; but after they are born, then begins the trouble, solicitude,
> and care rightly to train, principle, and bring them up.
>
> MONTAIGNE, "OF THE EDUCATION OF CHILDREN"

*To the young woman who approached me last year after one of my muddled and
peculiar readings and told me she was about to have twins, which I wasn't going to
say anything about even though she was incredibly vast in the uteral area, but one
thing you learn at Guy School is to never ever comment on what seems like a pregnancy unless you see a leg sticking out where you shouldn't be looking anyway, which
reminds me later to discuss name tags and how they are always exactly at the breast
level where you should not be looking no matter what; and who said also that she
and her husband had a two-year-old child already, and she knew I had once been in
her position, as a parent of one small agent of entropy with two more imminent, and
did I have any advice for her?*

I never yet saw that father, howsoever headlong and spillacious his son or
daughter, or later surly and sneering and vulgar with his or her mobile phone
permanently glued to his or her palm even if it is dinner or a wedding, who
would disown that child, although to be honest I have often *thought* about disowning most of my children, and I know many a man who has contemplated

16

this also; and I would guess many a mother has been in similar position, with the distinction, subtle but telling, that this headlong or later surly child actually *lived inside her* once upon a time, down by the kidneys and the spleen, actually attached to her by a long tube rather like the tubing that you use when you distill whiskey. I am no obstetrician, as yet, but the fact that children live inside the mother, like tenants in an apartment building but without the rent and utilities and security deposit and maintenance man who just will not for heavenssake fix that thermostat, and then eventually, again like tenants, are forcibly ejected or evicted and must seek for new accommodations, is endlessly interesting to me, and not something, I feel, that we celebrate enough for the sheer whopping oddity of it. I mean, we could be born in so many ways, for example calving from the larger corpus of the mother, or hatching in a skin pocket and eventually being released, or becoming flesh from her morning thought or evening dream, or being laid as eggs in clear rushing water and then being fertilized by the father swimming by; but this image is so amazing to me, as my dad hated swimming and the very idea of him in his dark suit and gray overcoat and fedora hat and cigar desperately paddling down to the gravel nest that my mom made at the bottom of the river before the neighbor dads came over to see if they had a chance at it, that we had better move along finally to the second paragraph; remembering that Montaigne, bless his soul, also often began and ended paragraphs anywhere he damn well pleased, as if paragraphs were carriages to be driven any old distance, for example from Saint Michel de Montaigne to Paris, which is more than three hundred miles.

Not only have I pondered disowning my children, but in one case I actually no kidding thought about selling him via an ad in the newspaper, *Teenage Boy for Sale, Clean, Runs Well*, but his mother, my lovely bride, in whom he lived for a time, down by her spleen, with his twin brother, the two of them seething and elbowing each other for nine months in the epic glad bag of her amniotic sac before emerging startled into this world to continue the battle, adamantly refused to allow me to place the ad, even though she would have been cut in on the profits fifty/fifty, or I was ready to go to even seventy/thirty to her advantage, considering she had to carry him around inside her like a passenger on a bus for nine months, which I didn't, which thank God for that. One great thing about being a guy is that you never have anyone living inside you down by your spleen, and have to endure a moment when you are just sitting there happily smoking a cigar and watching the Celtics hammer the oily smarmy arrogant oleaginous cocky tinny prissy self-absorbed Lakers when suddenly a person inside you takes it upon himself to *punch you in the bladder* for no discernible reason. There are many difficult things about masculinity, most of them having to do with insurance forms and ear hair, but being punched in the bladder by a person the size of a cod living inside you is not one of them, I am happy to say.

I happened the other day upon this piece of fortune; I was pawing through the epic piles of paper and letters and notes and exam papers and cards and test papers and et cetera that I have saved from each of the three children that the Coherent Mercy placed inside my lovely bride, right near her bladder, until they emerged mewling and spitting and in one case grabbing for the shiny scissors with which the doctor had cut the umbilical cord, and I stumbled across a sheet of foolscap on which I had written hurriedly THINGS MY CHILDREN HAVE SAID THAT THEY DO NOT KNOW I KNOW THEY SAID, and among those things were these lines: "Pretend you have been sleeping for two days, and you tied me with a rope, and I woke up and *shot* the rope, with the gun in my toes, and the rope turned out to be an elephant, and then it got married to an *eagle* and then we went upstairs and had soup!" and "I told dad I did my homework but the teacher *didn't give us any homework today* so the joke is on dad!" and "If you really like jello, and you really like mayonnaise, then you should be able to have a jello and mayonnaise sandwich, and dad is *wrong*!" and "I know I said I would be home at midnight, but *I* am the one who said that, so when *I* decided to not be home at midnight, I was not actually late, because *I* can change my mind!" and "If dad dies, mom has to marry his next younger brother, and if *he* dies, she has to marry Tommy, because he is the last brother, but if *Tommy* dies she is an unrestricted free agent," and other things like that, and even more amazing remarks, and I think you will agree with me that having children is lunacy. It is a species of madness. It is a fool's errand. There is no training for it. There is no licensing program. There is no real oversight or decent tutoring other than gnomic advice from your own parents, which they murmur between hysterical fits of vengeful laughter at the fact that you are now sentenced to being the parents of a child just like you. There is little serious outcome assessment and the only evidence of accomplishment is anecdotal, which is to say immeasurable. Financially, unless your child is going to be like my poor son Joe who all his life has had his father sit him down and stare him in the eye and say *Why are you on this earth, son?* to which the poor lad has had to reply, since he was age five, *To*

take care of you when you are old, dad, and ideally get wealthy enough to buy you one of the smaller Hawaiian islands, educating your children is an undeniable money pit into which you throw pretty much every iota of your cash and energy in exchange for things which again cannot be measured except anecdotally, amorphous and ephemeral things like love and pride and a sort of shivering feeling you get sometimes when they are asleep and they look cooler and more beautiful and more astonishing than anything else in the history of the universe, or when they say something so piercing and haunting and honest that your heart suddenly grows a new chamber, or when they do something with such intent creative independent zest that you sob suddenly in the stands at the basketball game and have to pretend you have a terrible cold to explain the profligate moisture. I suppose in the end the coolest thing about the education of children, and the thing that keeps you going through nights when everyone has the flu, or when they curse at you as teenagers, or when they lie about the car or their homework, or when they are surly and sneering and rude and vulgar and you contemplate selling them as crew to a tramp steamer in Malaysia, is that finally, if you are lucky, they educate you, rather than the other way around. I am much more humble and edified and easily elevated to tears now, after twenty years as a dad, than I was before I was a dad, in the years when I was myself a surly teenage, and then a careless and reckless and selfish young man. The best things that ever happened to me are the subtle joys and stabbing pains inflicted upon me by my children; in a real sense my children have been extraordinary universities from which I hope to never graduate, not even when I breathe my last; I am one of that breed of men who hope very much to afterwards be an attentive spirit, and so be able to laugh at my grandchildren giving their parents grief, and to weep when they weep in the fastness of the night, and to protect their divine spirits as much as I can, in a bodiless and probably incommunicative state, and throw my energy, in whatever form it assumes, against the darkness when it reaches greedily for my children and grandchildren; and perhaps they will feel a spin in the wind, and think of me; long gone but not gone at all.

"'Tis the custom of pedagogues to be eternally thundering in their pupil's ears, as they were pouring into a funnel, whilst the business of the pupil is only to repeat what the others have said," writes old Michel. "I would have a tutor to correct this error, and, that at the very first . . . put it to the test, permitting his pupil himself to taste things, and of himself to discern and choose them, sometimes opening the way to him, and sometimes leaving him to open it for himself; that is, I would not have him alone to invent and speak, but that he should also hear his pupil speak in turn."

Amen to that, brother, I would say, if we were sitting together in his study and I was gently razzing him for how his countrymen, in my opinion, invented only two glorious things in all of French history, to wit the bra and the Etch-a-Sketch, whereas my countrymen invented jazz and basketball, so that, in my opinion, we are totally winning the creativity game, all due respect, but then I would say something like you are exactly right, Mike, about letting kids find out things for themselves, and eat new and strange foods, and find their own way, partly because that appears to be the best way to learn, and partly because kids don't listen to sermons and homilies and lectures and remonstrations and instructions and diatribes, they just don't, and believe me I know what I am talking about here.

And were we sitting in his study, he would be on his own home ground, and comfortable, and relaxed, and willing and able to be as garrulous in person as he certainly is on the page—you never saw a more long-winded guy than Michel—but for all his wandering and constant sudden quoting of Latin writers, he was a perspicacious man, which is why so many love and read him still, even though he was French, and probably, if we were sitting in his study, he would suddenly say, just as I was about to launch into an incredible litany of the million ways my kids have never listened to me at all not once, "What is it that you have taught them? What was it you wished to teach by lesson or example? What is it that you think crucial and holy about the education of children?"

And I would hem and haw for a moment, and resist the urge to make jokes, and then say something like, "I would not have their spirits cowed and subdued, to quote, dang it, you. I would wish that their independent creative questing spirits be supported when young so as to be firmly rooted against the storms that will come and howl and batter upon them. I would hope that I gave them some instruction and example of endurance and patience and mercy and laughter and kindness as the bedrocks of joyful existence. I would hope that it registered somewhere deep in their souls that love is bigger than mere romance and it has to do with reverence and celebration and witness and sacrifice and empathy and honesty and tenderness, tenderness above all. I would hope that they would overlook my fits of temper and my lazy hours and my shortcomings and note and remember and cherish some shards of the inarticulate love I bear them.

I would hope that they would understand somehow deeply that I would die for them in a second without the slightest hesitation even as I snarled about homework and chores and cleaning their rooms once every decade whether they thought that was necessary or not. I would hope that they understood that while they would remember very little of their school lessons perhaps they had gained some more permanent lessons in diligence and in the shaping and sharing of the creative impulse. I would hope that they would understand that their greatest teacher was their mother, who never hesitated a second to give of herself so that they would be happy and healthy and joyous as much as possible in this one and only life. I would hope that they realized that to be rich in friends and family is to be richer than any billionaire in flimsy dollars. I would hope that they would teach their own children the sweet wild prayers of laughter and music and mercy and tenderness, tenderness above all, and their children would in turn teach their children those lessons, and so on and so on down the years, and so my love for them, and their mother's love for them, would never die, persisting long past the dissolution of our bodies, even their mother's body, which almost certainly will last another hundred healthy years in this form, because she is pure of heart and drinks wine moderately and no longer smokes those horrifying unfiltered Camel cigarettes, how anyone could smoke those foul vulgar things is a mystery to me, my god, when she started that old car of hers and lit up a Camel you couldn't tell which was issuing more dense clouds of epic smoke, the car or the driver, but that was long ago, and far away," and Michel would lean back in his chair, and scratch his balding pate, and look at me with amazement and concern and awe at such cheerful madness, a look I have seen very many times upon the shining faces of my beloved children, which seems to me an excellent place to conclude an essay on the education of children. So I do.

CODA

I admit with a smile that I am that rarest of essayists, one who does not and never did adore Michel de Montaigne; what for other readers is the great pleasure of his perambulations and wanderings and jaunts into parenthetical statements, his constant quoting of his heroes, his obsessive self-analysis, his epic swerving away from the topic as if he were Kobe Bryant terrified of the awful prospect of having to throw a pass to a teammate, is for me essentially frustrating to read, though pleasant to pick through for riveting lines and passages, as you would paw through Emerson for aphorisms, while shrieking at the received wisdom that he too is a fine essayist, which he is most certainly not; and believe me I know the irony of this statement, for no man ever enjoyed the nonlinear narrative path more than the undersigned. Yet this essay of Montaigne's hits home for me more than any of his others, for he did have children, five or six daughters, depending on what source you trust, and while most of them died young, he clearly did spend a great deal of time and effort thinking about their independent spirits and energies, and how those lovely souls should not be trammeled, and I admire that, and aspire to that as a dad, and think highly of Montaigne for it, for I can only imagine the pressure in his time and class and culture to stuff Principles and Discipline into his children as if they were empty sausage casings rather than wild holy beings never before in this world and never to come again. It seems to me he saw that, and tried to act on it, at least by the evidence of this essay of his; and so it is this essay I have chosen to dance with—to my benefit as a dad, I hope.

4

Of Prayers

LIA PURPURA

> It seems, in truth, that we use our prayers as a jargon,
> and . . . we count on their effect depending on the texture,
> sound, or sequence of the words, and on our bearing.
> MONTAIGNE, "OF PRAYERS"

It was a quilt such as the kind I know to be in most U.S. hotel rooms—synthetic and scratchy on the underside where little pills gather from rubbing, and snags from rings (diamond, engagement, upright in that very impractical setting) make a constellation of lines. Time marks blankets and towels with thin spots, blinds with frayed slats, a toilet seat with a chip. Rust stains a sink, water marks a nightstand. Quilts of this kind withstand a lot—our antics and rest, much shaking and straightening, rough cleaning—all forms of the passage of time.

It was an early spring day, but likely the AC in the room was on. He'd have thought of the sound as *muffling*, a small calculation any mind would make.

Mine would.

I'd think of that.

Maybe he fixed on the single word "muffle" and repeated it a few, then too many, times. Any word, under strain, will collapse into nonsense.

There's a store manager in this, too, you might recognize. Imagine him at the new Crate and Barrel, a few blocks from the hotel. Just hired, proud of his clean and bright unit, a step-lively-and-much-can-be-yours kind of guy, with promise, energy, smarts. Here, when you buy a knife, they wrap it securely in sturdy paper, which indicates they run a safe ship, no bows or gift wrap for the cutlery. They seal such things with a wide strip of tape and let it be your problem getting it all undone at home. How could he know, the manager-taper, that he had his hands on something terribly wrong? That another hand, a hand he touched—showing the balance of hilt and blade, passing the pen to sign the receipt—would act in ways so unthinkable that he himself might feel implicated? Sometimes I touch my dollar bills, especially the fifties, and think what bribes they sealed, what drugs they scored, and run in my head DNA tests on all the microbes, stories, economies I'm passing along in the purchase of onions, sliced turkey, and cheese.

Likely the manager asked a question, a simple one—"Is this a present?" And perhaps his customer said, "Yes, it is," very fast, as a way to throw the manager off the trail. And maybe that there *was* a trail, that he himself was building it, became clear for the customer precisely *then*, and for the first time. It's possible, too, that such a trail might have been shifted by the simplest statement, the way a weatherman might transform a gray morning by saying, "A beautiful light rain is falling on the city . . ." This happened to me recently and I was, all day, grateful to have my mood reconstituted by a brief phrase. How willing I was to assent to *a beautiful light rain* once it was suggested. Whole strings of decisions could have been altered, the more instructions a chatty manager gave at the register, if it was slow, if he was good at building "relations," as in "Be careful with this, it's wrapped well for now, but if you intend to post it or gift it . . ." (The verbing alone might have startled the buyer: how weird, *to gift*! how archaic, *to post*!) And what about "To wash this knife, you need not submerge it . . ." (The phrase "wash this knife" alone might have done it.) The more time shared at the register, where one man was working the hip/bright store and the other planning the murder of his family, the more some internal diffusion of light, a breaking of clouds, a breakthrough, a breakdown, a falling-to-knees and trembling sort of scene, a right and good rending—violence done in the name of healing, like breaking to reset a bone—might have halted things. I'd like to believe that more chat, the right words, the weight of them, would have shoved a wedge in and filled the hole in the air before him—emptiness in the chest, rent in the logic—wherever the unthinkable kept firming up and was starting to feel inevitable.

It's a quilt with a busy pattern of grays and browns, or various blues, either way dark-toned to hide the stains you very much don't want to think of—from, say, couples not waiting and tearing into each other right there on top of such quilts, or from bedbugs, spilled drinks, muddy street shoes.

The quilt, rolled and kicked. Bunched on the floor. Dampened. Stepped on. Trampled, balled, twisted.

That quilt.

There it was. That's what I saw on this brisk fall day. It came unbidden, the way so many things, as I'm walking, come in—on stippled light (or gray light, or very bright sun), landing and piercing.

In its place I tried to install quilts *I've* made. Three altogether. One for a boy who cared nothing about quilts, which my mother watched me make as I listened over and over to *Jesus Christ Superstar* for weeks one summer. *Fervently*, I'd say, singing into the belief of others but not, myself, possessing anything like their strain of it. The second quilt was for a friend who did appreciate it and who gave more to me than I could accept at the time. And the last I made for myself. I still have it, pieced mostly from little dresses, kerchiefs, and smocks my mother made for me. I recall with ease, by way of these colors (late-summer-sky blue, sunny yellow flowers), an old atmosphere: deep snowy mornings when I'd stand on a chair and look out the kitchen window a long while. The trees at the front of the house were just planted, and because I was young too, I felt we understood each other. The quiet hummed. It was before the world was up, my box turtle crawled around in his tank, and the far-off flagpole in the park was a very dark gray against the brighter, snow-packed sky. I became aware of distance then, by feeling the plot of a day hovering and the space where I stood, a central point. Standing still, I could collect what it seemed the day was trying to say.

In that famous photo of workers eating lunch on a crossbeam high over New York (it's 1932, they're immigrants, mostly Italian and Irish, sitting like kids on a riverbank, legs dangling) it's the *beam* I fix on. How do you stay upright on a beam that high and narrow—the sixty-ninth floor of what's going to be the GE Building—and eat and chat as if on a park bench? They must have each found a still point to concentrate on, no watching pigeons swoop and settle in Ionic roosts, no twisting around to catch their iridescent shine in the sun. Thus to do their job, they tethered themselves to a task and a place.

Thus I let the quilt come in.

I locate the pockets and dips, deep valleys for terrible pools and rivers; in patterns, streams swell, spill and seep. I let the puddles rust in air.

To be in the business of letting the blood come.

We each have our fields. The word "field" is capacious—a place to be turned, planted, worked. Gathered from. Field of light, field of inquiry, field trip, field of—and here I'm getting closer—*battle*. One man's, with his soul, and he lost very completely.

Explanations fail.

Plenty don't murder who you'd expect might.

A man with no hope acts like a knife. Failed financial schemes act like a knife. A sham is a knife. Shame is a knife. Fear is a knife that cuts a caul of darkness out and hangs it over all of us, like—once I saw in a restorer's hands—a sheet of gold leaf lifted on the edge of a blade, struck up like a flame, and laid over the hem of a wooden saint, then rubbed to a shine with a blunter blade. A knife, like a pillow, can snuff a life out. Knife like a drowning. Quilt like a vessel, mop, body bag, grave. Snarled. Fretted. Bogged. Consigned and corrupted. He'd brought his wife and younger daughter to visit the older daughter at college. She came that afternoon to the hotel, and when it got late and she hadn't returned, her roommates called. Her father answered and said not to worry, she was going to spend the night with the family. At which point he'd already killed them all. Soon after that, he turned the knife on himself.

The girl went to the university where I teach. She was, as I learned, much loved by her friends. She was kind and had plans, exams, parties upcoming.

A bed. A wardrobe. Pencils. Soap. Socks.

The day after the tragedy, when the story broke, we heard the breaking. Hearing it made the sun incongruous. Made me try to say something into the beauty, warmth, light it kept giving (poor sun, always shining on everyone, brightening all events in its path). In one of my very best classes—where soon, at the end of the semester, one student was heading to China, one into the army, one to teach at an inner-city school—what I said about the tragedy wasn't *nothing*, it was just the best I could do. Given my limited. Since I hadn't known. Which is better than nothing, but still weighs very little. I said something like: Though you might not have known her, she was part of your day. A presence you passed as you crossed the quad, an ambient laugh you heard and took in, and in that way she colored your stubborn loneliness. She brushed crumbs off the table before you sat down. She exhaled as she passed, and air held the breath you drew into your body. You caught her cold. You swallowed her sigh. You picked up the penny she dropped, thinking, "Hey, lucky penny." And just as she gave proof to *your* day, you gave *hers* shape, made her afternoon buoyant with color, sound, presence.

The quilt reddened. The quilt twisted and fell. The funerals were separate, the girls with their mother, the father apart, and yes, people did attend his. How would he feel, I remember thinking, floating above his body (where, for the sake of this thought, I put him) and seeing what mourners made, best they could, of the wreckage he caused. How they forced the persistence of goodness to live. Made themselves hold opposing forces, admit there *was* good, there *had been* in him, and allowed that mystery to compel them to come. Or they were obliged because they were family, and that's what you do.

All loss is weighted with disbelief. All homage seeks to make something to keep, to make loss mean, to give the fissile core of grief some shape. The quilt bore the weight of the act, of the bodies; and since such fabric isn't given to absorbing, it must have made *channels*, and there the blood pooled. There were *runnels*. And *chambers*.

Words very like "muffling" kept coming: fleet, shocking, precise and unspoken.

When I suggested we take a moment of silence, all of them, every single student, bowed their heads and prayed. What rattled me, though of course it shouldn't have, was that they seemed to have a prayer *ready*, that they knew what to say, had something on hand (this being a Catholic university), while I had to make up something on the spot about breath and pennies and each of us being assumed into another's day.

And what *did* they say?

I asked a few of them this fall, now a year and a half later, if they remembered that moment and what they were thinking. One said she created a silence around herself and asked, she didn't know who, the force she was used to calling God, for comfort and healing on the family's behalf. Another, with no go-to prayer either, recalled the sensation of bowing her head with everyone. I told her I feared that I, alone, had no prayer. She said she'd always suspected we bow our heads to hide our faces, to keep from each other how ashamed we feel in the face of grief. For another, the Prayer of the Faithful Departed came first, and then a rush of fear: if no one saw this coming at all, what if I, too, can't see? My father was out of work that year, she said. What kept *me* from being *her*? The last one I asked—I think of him as especially adept at matters of the spirit—didn't recall what he thought or prayed. But he said that after her death nothing was the same. One day he was a kid, working, hanging out, and the next, all was changed. And when another classmate died this year and he found himself repeating the steps—go to the mass, go to the grave—that shook him: the familiarity. After that he no longer wondered how adults always seemed to know what to do.

Why does she come back now, in fall?

I'm walking the same path I walk every day. I had no intention of recalling her—but stories overlay the land. Leaves-losing-color, then trees-losing-leaves, that's an old one: Demeter's loss of Persephone.

The land must have always looked very like death when the blooming ended and nothing grew for months on end.

One naturally mourns a girl in fall.

Though I have no fixed date upon which to recall her. Nothing like All Souls' Day, when, ten years ago now, my own friend jumped to her death. It was a particularly bitter Warsaw winter and, climbing the stairs to the top of the building, I'm thinking now, she'd have worn a coat. *Why*, though? Why, at the end, bother? And the heavy door to the roof—why wasn't it locked? (Though I used to go up to the roof with my friends all the time in New York, at night the lights of the city like codes, like necklaces along rooftop bars, the sky finally vast from so high up, and none of *those* doors was ever locked.) Was there a moment when the wind hit and she cringed? Did the force of that chill, just for a moment, trigger the instinct to stay warm and alive?

Every year since, each thirty-first of October, a new piece of that scene fills in, suggests itself, makes a bid for inclusion. As if—though nothing can be changed—imagining better might bring some relief, and precision upend disbelief. This year it was the top step, whitewashed but with scuff marks and grime in the corners. Last year was a twig broom and ash can. In years past, lines of tar sealing cracks in the roof, a silver bucket with frozen wash rags, a wobbly handrail, a switchplate's stiff toggle at the foot of the stairs.

One year, nothing came (that was a dark time) and the cold itself had to suffice.

Once the scent of the stairwell came forth, a meaty/sour dinner smell overlaid with stale smoke, damp boots, and coal dust. When the smell dissipated, the ash, boots, and black dust over everything remained. Insisted. Asserted. Oh strange and constant spring.

CODA

I've always imagined that Montaigne sat down in the morning, boldly scratched a title at the top of his paper, and began writing. The ensuing meditations would then take off in all directions of course, veering, wandering, leaping, redoubling, contraindicating, and spinning centrifugally out of orbit—but the wild, astonishing venture would have started with a rooted intention. I work very differently, beginning in chaos usually without much tethering. Montaigne's method was a tonic to me, nonetheless.

My essay "Of Prayers" was originally titled "Quilt," referring to an object at a crime scene, a still point in what was a horrific incident—the murder of a student at my university by her own father, driven to despair by shadowy financial dealings. By way of meditation on the object, my essay, too, veered and found its byways and, as it went along, a wholly unexpected center firmed up. I knew the title wasn't right from the start, but it was unobtrusive and allowed me to keep roaming. Reading Montaigne's essay of the same title helped me discern the beating heart of my piece, its most essential, core inquiry: What is prayer, in what forms does it come forth, how do others—and how might I, who have had no training at all in the practice—pray?

To create a sense of freedom, writers often fool themselves, divert their attention from "goals" in generative ways, skirt the true subject so as to remain open and receptive, and to ratchet down the scope and weight of conscious intention. Montaigne's method, or bravery, or tic, his ability to assert a subject and have a go at it, gave me the impetus to name my subject as if I had every lucid intention in place at the start. Though applied in hindsight for me, the title provides a point of discovery for a reader to anticipate and read toward. And privately, the title serves as homage and as a mark of gratitude to a great voyager and unfettered soul—a mind adept at working its way free of conventional thought patterns and the corrosive effect of good manners.

5

Of Thumbs

MARY CAPPELLO

> In Sparta the schoolmaster punished his
> pupils by biting their thumbs.
> MONTAIGNE, "OF THUMBS"

Isaac Newton thought the thumb alone proved the existence of God.

Pliny attests that the right thumb of a virgin can cause a fallen epileptic to recover.

The classicist Anthony Corbeill relates "the most awful authority of the *pollex*," for this is how the ancient Romans called the thumb, with their word for strength, thus distinguishing the thumb from the rest of the hand for its power: "In Roman practice the thumb lived up to its etymological reputation. It could both bestow and withhold favor, grant and deprive life." In antiquity, "the gesture of *infesto pollice*, in particular, which seems certain to refer to the erect thumb, was indecorous for the orator and demanded death for the gladiator." Scanning the crowd for thumbs thrust skyward, like so many middle fingers, the "editor" interpreted the will of the mob: whether a gladiator should slay or spare his opponent. The defeated fighter, in turn, conveyed his request for mercy by raising the index finger, usually of his left hand.

Though "extant evidence . . . indicates that the Romans were unique among Indo-European peoples in identifying at an early stage of their language's development the thumb's singularity as a digit," no direct line of influence can be traced between the current American application of thumbs-up to indicate approval and the Roman use of the upturned thumb to signify certain death. It is believed that thumbs-up as a signal of joyful camaraderie, win-win, yes-vote, or victory was introduced into Italy by American GIs during the Second World War, though they could also have been saying "fuck you" in broken Italian.

For both cultures—ancient Roman and contemporary American—the up-turned thumb augurs the death and birth of civilization. For both, the thumb yields to the will of the rabble, each thumb conferring on man the right to his own opinion as supreme.

In Yogic practice, the thumb represents the Parmatama or Supreme Soul. When a yogi brings together the tip of the thumb with the tip of the index fin-ger, she is creating the seal of wisdom. In palmistry, the examiner heeds a short or thick, long or well-formed thumb as indicative of an essential trait belonging to the person who sports such a figure; she attaches a different virtue to each of the three phalanges.

It is said that children who suck their thumbs will grow up to be gourmands, whereas children who suck their fingers will grow up to be dilettantes. Children who put their whole fists in their mouths will grow up to be hit men.

"Occasionally I crush one with my thumb on an impulse and go back to cooking my potatoes." The American poet David Ignatow describes a lonely man's relationship to baby cockroaches who come to greet him in his apart-ment's kitchen thus. As for the larger cockroach parents, he says they are "long as the first joint of my thumb" when he turns on the light at night and watches them in anger. This may be what is meant by "rule of thumb," since other ori-gins of that phrase have been disproved: for example, its apparent reference to a law in eighteenth-century England by which a man was allowed to beat his wife so long as the stick was no bigger in diameter than his thumb. The thumb is the standard either for the length of a cockroach or for the girth of the man entire, the ground zero of his essence, an idea that entered naturally into the minds of Jonathan Swift's Lilliputians as they attended Gulliver:

> Then they measured my right Thumb, and desired no more; for by a mathematical Computation, that twice round the Thumb is once around the Wrist, and so on to the Neck and Waist, and by the help of my old Shirt, which I displayed on the Ground before them for a Pattern, they fitted me exactly.

The thumb makes possible industry and therefore sloth. I have noticed that for each pluck of the Seven Deadly Sins there are seven corresponding thumberies.

Sloth: to twiddle one's thumbs
Greed: to put a thumb on the scale
Pride: to stand out like a sore thumb
Lust: to suck one's thumb
Wrath: to thumb one's nose
Envy: to stick a thumb in someone's eye
Gluttony: to put in a thumb and pull out a plum

A thumb is a sort of finger and yet not a finger at all.

Fingernails are modified hairs.

The same device that men used to torture their fellow men—the thumb-screw—was applied in the eighteenth century to women's fingers to elongate them and thereby make them more elegant.

Rose petals, now that I think on it, are in every way shaped like thumbnails struck from their thumb, but we would never venture to call a rose by the name Thumbed Beauty, or Pink Thumb of Paradise.

When the yogi brings his first two fingers under his big toe while pressing the thumb on top of the same toe, the power of the thumb is felt in full force. So, too, when Moe of the Three Stooges pulls Larry around the room by gripping his nose between his thumb and forefinger.

Without a thumb, the white man has no handshake, and thus no means to seal the deal.

No thumb, no fist.

There was a man of my acquaintance who had lost his thumb in his father's pickle factory. The father, who had been a member of the Communist Party, was cut out of his family's pickle-business fortune as a result of his siding with the factory workers when they went on strike. Thinking he could still run a business and remain true to communist principles, the father opened a factory of his own. Somehow he left the son unattended to do what any boy at the age of ten might do: this boy proceeded to play with the pickle slicer, and in the midst of his play, he lost his thumb. The father, awash in remorse, immediately closed the factory, and the son grew into a man who resented his father for having him read books all his life rather than, he said, taking him to the circus as other boys' fathers had done. The boy's name was Harris, but after a visit to an ashram, after a search for Joseph Campbell, after EST training, and after a beating of drums with groups of men in the woods of upstate New York, he changed his name to Joel. Whenever I shook his hand, I experienced the feel of what remained—a tiny bone—like a pang.

In this our twenty-first century, the unpracticed touch of my thumb to my iPhone renders me suddenly illiterate, but like all those who, deaf and dumb, live outside the law, this only leads me to notice what the well-thumbed cannot see: how, in summer, it is common for a girl's large toe to cross over the second toe while she uses her thumb to text; how, in elevators, young men, their thumbs athwart a device, gird themselves for dear life: head buried, the thumbs move with such diligence and speed that the head is forced to sink into the neck like a turtle's while the thumbs strain and strut, ostrichlike, upon a cramped glass. If, in an earlier era, hunting and pecking upon a typewriter was a sign of manliness, now men's and women's thumbs move just as dexterously to telegraph their thoughts.

According to e-Hand.com, the Electronic Textbook of Hand Surgery,

> Contrary to popular opinion, humans—*homo sapiens*—are not the only primates possessing opposable thumbs. Chimpanzees and monkeys can oppose the thumb to the index digit. What makes the human hand unique in the animal kingdom is the ability of the small and ring fingers to rotate across the palm to meet the thumb, owing to a unique flexibility of the carpometacarpal joints of these fingers, down in the middle of the palm.

Thumbed, I grope, grip, diddle, pick; I strum, I steer, I stir. Pawed, my cat bats, pats, presses, swats. She regularly stretches; she opens, and extends.

Leonard Nimoy was able to splay his fingers in such a way as to introduce a gap between the third and fourth finger, with the second glued to the first and the fourth glued to the pinky so as to make a V. Not all humans are capable of this, the Vulcan greeting, but I admit a certain pleasure in imitating it while miming the mantra "Live long and prosper."

Thumbs are as ugly as penises are beautiful.

Unlike the penis, the thumb neither dangles nor dribbles; it does not wait on ceremony; it never mocks the man with its flaccidness or size. I hardly need will it, and it stands erect and for as long as I wish. The big toe is more like the penis than is the thumb, for its stupidity. The big toe can hardly hold a candle to the thumb. While the penis lies idle, the thumb is a figure of industry: it maketh erect structures more enduring than mere flesh and bones.

We err when we look to the thumb for a sign of manliness, but are perhaps no better in hoping to find in our thumbs our humanness.

There is no other part of the human body to which the thumb may be compared, though like my anal sphincter it releases and grasps. There is no part of the body that the thumb is like, even though we try to make it resemble the chin and lower lip of a face in a literal hand puppet. I should like to request that it sing "You Are My Sunshine."

If there is a way to experience the world from the point of view of a Thumbelina and a Tom Thumb, I should like to know it. The thumb, for our part, affords us an ocular advantage: it allows us to hold what beguiles us up to the light and project it betimes like a third eye upon the surface of reality. Others might consider the thumb's greatest virtue the ability it affords man to precisely squash a louse until it bleeds, for I live in the age of the hostile thumb, an age in which knowledge is got by tapping and pointing, an age in which a knowledge seeker uses his device to ask whether it takes the same force to bite through a finger as through a carrot.

There was a period of time when my thumb stuck in place. It appeared at the break of day like Gregor Samsa's cockroach, but in my case I awoke to my thumb immovably bent. When I asked my physick about it, he gave it a name and suggested it was a product of age. Recently a friend presented with a similar condition in her second toe. In the middle of the journey of my life, bereft of a Virgil, I must cultivate the pretense of movement the more frozen I become. At a time such as this, I come to appreciate the beauty of the ballpoint, a far finer invention than the iPhone as companion to my trade. I have no truck with those pens that ask that we turn their barrels, but am awed by the elegance of the retractable spring whose button anticipates my thumb and my pocket, wakefulness and sleep, darkness and light, life and death, gravity and ink.

Thimbles (etymologically, "thumb-stalls") were melted down during the Second World War. This must explain the derivation of the now ubiquitous thumbs-up on American soil: I picture the soldiers' gesticulations to the Italians now to mean "We have given our thimbles for your lives!" In the Netherlands, American tourists leave in disappointment when the Dutch natives fail to identify the dike that the boy in the folktale was supposed to have plugged with his finger (some say his thumb) in order to keep the waters from swallowing the country. The Dutch legend was invented by a nineteenth-century American named Mary Mapes Dodge for inclusion in her fantasia *Hans Brinker and the Silver Skates.*

What difference does it make, with my finger upraised, whether I beg mercy from my opponent or from the officiating judge? Inside the cleft formed by my thumb and forefinger, I rest my chin—just as my quill has a pot in which to charge, to rest, or to reside.

I have discovered that writing that aims to guard its writer against being pricked—writing as thimble—is no writing at all.

Corbeill reports that "unlike the rest of the hand, the thumb disdains rings and other forms of luxurious ornamentation." Another source evidences that the earliest known thimble was found in Pompeii.

Writing has made my fingers knobby and protuberant, and lately I have discerned a spur inside my thumb from the repeated pressing of my pen upon these pages. In this way my writing has altered me, if not the world I hope to sound with it.

During the Victorian era, schoolteachers hit the top of a disobedient student's head with an iron thimble.

CODA

Montaigne's "Of Thumbs" is one of his (very) shorts, and I call it this while acknowledging its part in the making of a larger body from which it cannot be detached: the voluminous *Essais.* Like a Wikipedia "stub," but less in the interests of completion, an essay like "Of Thumbs" wishes for more contributors, just as the voice of so many of Montaigne's essays asserts and invites in equal measure.

I tried to "channel" Montaigne—to honor his example while reserving the right to sing his song in my own way. I tuned my writerly voice to meet the pitch of his, from perfectly deadpan to suddenly sexual to counterintuitive. Sticking to his subject du jour, thumbs, I tried to emulate his quirky essayistic formula, from knowledge through hunch toward foible, in order to expose some essentially strange nugget of our shared humanness. I have always been moved by the frankly lewd or nakedly physical in Montaigne, and, following his lead, I wanted to work with the body as sign and custom, as gesticulator and articulator. I tried to keep his essay's physics nearby (where we presume equivalency, we find asymmetry), as well as his aesthetics (where we assume substitutability, we find mis-fittings or grotesquerie).

My essay is one part research, one part accident (based on what fell into my line of vision while I was composing it), and one part invention. I had the most fun trying to find thumbing counterparts to the Seven Deadly Sins. Usually we think of inquiry leading to invention, but in creating a Montaignean "cover," I enjoyed the pleasures of a countermovement: I could feel the extent to which my inventions helped me to inquire. Examples, etymologies, copious quotations, untoward juxtapositions: in Montaigne, they never merely serve to demonstrate or prove, and I hope I've met that challenge here. Can we run counter to custom while also celebrating the customary? Montaigne and I agree that this is a question worth asking the essayist. Last but not least, I had to find a way to respond—truly to play—rather than simply react to the gendering of the thumb in the original: the extent to which the thumb in Montaigne's essay is explicitly, implicitly, and tacitly, literally and symbolically, male. We'll recall the one place reserved in the essay for the female thumb is as comic relief, as if to suggest the only significance available to his otherwise encyclopedic view of "thumbs" as they apply to the female body is for the part they play in giving a man a hand job: "*Sed nec vocibus excitata blandis, / Molli pollice nec rogata, surgit*" (Neither sweet words of persuasion nor the help of her thumb can get it erect).

But what do I know? I know that I don't know. That's what Montaigne's essays always teach me. I give you "Of Thumbs" as a partial contribution to the infinite play of non-knowledge.

6

Of Smells

WAYNE KOESTENBAUM

> My mustache, which is thick, performs that
> service. If I bring my gloves or my handkerchief
> near it, the smell will stay there a whole day.
> MONTAIGNE, "OF SMELLS"

I told my boyfriend, "Smell this paper." Customers came to our apartment to drop off handwritten manuscripts, which I converted, via my IBM Selectric, into presentability. One client's pages—untyped rough drafts—stank of Stilton and Sobranies. I wanted my boyfriend to smell the paper, its malodorousness a freak show. He said, "No! Please! Don't make me!" He ran away. I was behaving like Klaus Kinski in *Nosferatu*: agent of olfactory torture.

Montaigne mentions hairy armpits as particularly blameworthy. Several times I've googled the connection between body hair and odor; the results are never conclusive. Crotch follicles stink, one website said. Fact? Mentioning hair makes me a stinky speaker.

Blindness: I smelled it in a pine cabin where a blind flutist lived. I was her accompanist. That summer, I attempted masculinity by using Irish Spring soap. A trumpet player with hairy armpits (I idolized him) also used Irish Spring: he looked like John Davidson (costar of *The Happiest Millionaire*) crossed with Roger Federer. Throw in Franco Nero, who, in *Camelot*, had roundelay hair: a shag, songful and circular.

Montaigne mentions incense. Barbara, the first girl I'd heard confess that she loved masturbating, invited me to a Buddhist temple in Berkeley, but my parents didn't approve. (I was fifteen.) Maybe LSD dominated the temple, a cult epicenter, where I could be kidnapped. Barbara, who gave me a copy of Baba Ram Dass's *Be Here Now*, burned incense. At her Buddhist temple, I might have met men who placed sex ads in the *Berkeley Barb*, sold outside Carol Doda's strip parlor, its va-va-voom neon twinned with beatnik espresso.

Montaigne mentions perfume. I'm trying to cultivate distractibility, to fray the edges of consecutive thought. Smell is a privileged highway for destroying punitive logic-rivets. Travel the Smell Highway to leave behind your ideas.

The blindness nebula of the piney cabin, amid redwoods: the cabin's boards—if indeed they were pine—smelled flat, hard, tonic, like *The Bad Seed*. And there I arrived, with my salubrious, cheeky Irish Spring, as if with Franco Nero's Lancelot urge to triangulate, to pierce, to flash monogamy-defying curls.

Incense, you were packaged in triangles, gray or umber, which slowly turned to ash. Incense, you resembled canned pet food, resistant to the human mouth. Incense, in your solid form, unburnt, you were like tropical-fish food, or doggie biscuits, or human throat lozenges (Sucrets?) that were not candy but medicine—a distinction that my mother preached and that I still practice. Civilization depends on these rivalries. Candy versus medicine. Raw versus cooked. Men's bathrooms versus women's. The stink of a corpse versus the sweetness of perfume: Absynthe, by Christian Lacroix. I appear to be waging a holy war between perfume and death.

I ran away from home—at seven years old—and sought shelter in a Safeway supermarket. I stole a roll of Certs: nourishment for the prodigal. Upon my return home, my father served me Campbell's tomato soup, which smells indelibly flat, like blindness in cabins. Tomato soup's cardboard odor doesn't tremble into a Debussy-style cloud. Certain pale reds—as they edge toward pink—are horizontal smells, like under-ripe members of the nightshade family.

My great-aunt Alice worked as accountant at a tomato canning factory. At a workday's end, we picked her up—in our buttermilk Rambler—from the factory. Hello to Tante Alice, as she emerges at dusk, like cigarette girls in Carmen's Seville. By the factory doorway, the tomato odor blooms in its flattest guise, as if the tin can had communicated Martian depthlessness to the soup within.

Yoplait on the tongue has the flatness of that tomato cannery's smell at workday's end: you want the flavor to ripen but it remains unaccommodating, like a yard-duty I knew in first grade. Around her neck she wore a whistle, an instrument to conclude recess and to arrest malefactors. She looked like the butch secretary Jane Hathaway (played by Nancy Kulp) on *The Beverly Hillbillies*. Nancy Kulp, you were a shining force for good! Our yard-duty smelled (as Montaigne put it) "of nothing." Better to smell of nothing, Montaigne says, than to stink. I had kiddie odor, the stench of a boy exploring a supervised yard.

I wonder about the texture of Montaigne's mustache. Was it straggly or thick? Odors, according to Montaigne, remained in his mustache for days. The mustache was Velcro to visiting aromas. Did the mustache proceed seamlessly into his nostril caverns, or did he enforce separation? I hope for French literature's sake that he shaved a Maginot line between mustache and nostril.

Walt Whitman: "the scent of these arm-pits aroma finer than prayer." He boldly refuses unnecessary words between "arm-pits" and "aroma." The head-on collision between "arm-pits" and "aroma"—alliterative—intensifies the blasphemous assertion of B.O.'s sacredness.

Toward what goal do I aspire, ever, but collision? Always accident, concussion, bodies butting together, "arm-pits" and "aroma" colliding. Smell amplifies collision. By collision I also mean metaphor and metonymy: operations of *slide* and *slip* and *transfuse*. I want to press my forehead against a flat surface, like a foam wall. And if the surface—whether door or page—smells like Yoplait or a tomato cannery or piney blindness or neon topless incense, so much the better.

Laundry odors, though seductive, may be poisonous. I surrender to the possibly toxic perfume of Bounce sheets, those questionable yet addictive leaves tossed into the dryer to prevent unspecified damage. The most romantic moment in my childhood might have occurred during a Cub Scouts camping trip, when I brought a towel and soap to an alpine creek for morning ablutions. My mother had packed the towel in my rucksack: maternally laundered towel, aroma finer than Ruby Keeler's return to the Broadway stage singing "I Want to Be Happy."

My pal in fourth grade had stinky feet, I discovered when sleeping over at his house. Maybe he bragged, "I have stinky feet," and suggested that I smell them to verify; or else I came to this conclusion myself, and taunted him with the verdict. His feet were large, as were his cheekbones; our mutual competitiveness was large, as were our growing stamp collections. Doggishness suffused his feet, though he didn't own a dog. The concept of "another boy's house" came with "dog" built into it, and therefore "turd." Onto the feet of a young Christian descends (in my Jewish brain) an abject avalanche. Twice, we fell into foreplay. Our erotic incidents took place in a bathroom and involved a cup and a rug. Did I insert my penis in the cup? Did I command him to lie on the rug? Did he sprinkle talcum powder on his rank feet? Was I the ringleader? Did I have a plan? Was I inspired by *And God Created Woman* on Channel 36, a UHF frequency from distant Stockton? Did our foreplay interrupt tournaments of Battleship and Clue and other board games, like landscape-feigning jigsaw puzzles overlaid with Kissinger-style statecraft-in-utero?

Smell is syntax, is grammar, is the copula, the "is," the copulating verb, the intercourse sign of =, the stink of equivalence, the stink of enforced likeness and its pleasures, whether fecal or ambrosial. Anywhere I go with smell (and we can go *everywhere* with smell) I owe to the permissive powers of the copula, the "is," the stick-shift-in-neutral power of olfactory suggestiveness. We could therefore call smell "the whore of grammar." Or "the fall into false closure." Or "the rapid departure into cloud consciousness." Or "a sudden dilapidation." Smell locks us into words but also helps us to escape them.

CODA

From Montaigne, I took hairy armpits. I took mustache. I took the desire *to smell of nothing.* I took perfume, incense, seasoning, gender. I took brevity. I took casualness. I took a tourist's tone. I took sex. Sex I can take from anywhere; I don't need Montaigne for sex. But I'm glad to find it in his sentences. From Montaigne, I took disgust: sex's doppelgänger. From Montaigne, I took randomness and decisiveness. I took easy movement. I took permissiveness toward *in medias res.* We enter an idea in its middle. We leave before the idea can reach completion. We lean into the idea from above or below. We don't greet the idea directly. Ten cents a dance with the idea. Toward the idea we express reverence but also eventually dismissiveness. We don't allow the idea to tire us, and we try not to ruin the idea by pressing too hard against its vulnerable surface.

7

Of Cannibals

LINA M. FERREIRA C.-V.

Notice what you eat, and you will find
in it the taste of your own flesh.
MONTAIGNE, "OF CANNIBALS"

The very second I laid eyes on a placenta, I wanted to put it in my mouth.

I stood by Dr. Santillan as she placed a purple-gloved hand gently over it, just like someone covering another's mouth, and sank her scalpel into the afterbirth.

Meat, vein, and blood. Four intersecting cuts, a little fibrous cube of dark red pulp you could have easily stuck a fork into and pulled right out, bite sized and dripping.

If I were to write, "The first thought in my head was to eat it," I'd be lying. There was neither skillet nor skewer in the thought. No "Peas and a nice Chianti." No, imagining someone else's muscle and fat sloshing around in my mouth, taste buds alive in the red of another human's flesh. There was no "thinking the moment through," because there was barely the pulse of a thought in the impulse to drag my tongue across the red-velvet flesh of the sliced organ. My eyes met the gaping red of a mid-dissection placenta. Snap. Red, wet, lick, rip, swallow.

And it was that, red. Red-red. Deep red. Red, and veined, and fresh. Mere minutes before, it had been happily tucked inside a woman, between uterus and fetus, negotiating nutrients and toxins and life between them. And then, contractions, and then screaming, and then a call to the University of Iowa Maternal Fetal Tissue Bank. A red yoke lying flat on our slab—all surface tension and invitation—which Dr. Santillan sliced and separated into small plastic containers usually reserved for grocery store salsa and lasagna on sample days.

My college and later grad school summers were, as these things go, a haphazard arrangement of resumé-confusing short-term employment experiences. The anything-goes mélange of income supplementation that rarely gets mentioned in CVS and job interviews.

I worked as an early morning custodian, I planted shrubs, I delivered dentures, "designed" a website for a literary society, wrote infomercials for a weight-loss-shake pyramid-scheme company, and "guest starred" on an episode of "Learning Spanish with Friends!" I clerked, I delivered, I lifted, I baked. And I rode my bike between tutoring jobs to sliced and diced placentae in a dingy lab in Iowa.

The very first time I saw it happen, I went from leaning against the door frame to standing directly behind Dr. Santillan to resting my elbows on the counter to being nearly tucked under her arm as she cut into the tissue—without so much as noticing myself move. I leaned in closer, pointed at the meat with a gloveless finger, nearly put my finger through the cube-shaped hole in the placenta. "What is this? And this, and this, and this? What is this called? What is that? How is this different from that over there? Why in little cubes? What happens to the rest when you're done cutting?"

I was originally slated to work as clerk for Obstetrics and Gynecology, as I had done the previous summer, though even the word "clerk" may present a glorified version of my actual duties. Mine was the realm of the quasi-redundant and the barely non-negligible. Beige days of color-coded schedules, paper clips, staples, and the very rare day when all the secretaries were simultaneously swamped and I alone was left to order bagels for the weekly infant mortality and morbidity meeting.

But then something came up or someone fell through, and I was asked if I might not mind working in the MFTB research wing instead.

"Is there any difference?"

"Like how?"

"Like, any difference?"

"Money?"

"Sure."

"Not really. Might be more interesting, though."

On my first day I was led by Dr. Santillan from OBGYN to MFTB through

fifteen minutes' worth of hallways, passages, and elevators so he could deliver
me to his wife, Dr. Santillan. "This one only goes to these floors. That one to
those." Down one elevator, up a ramp, and into one of the oldest, mustiest,
and quietest wings of the hospital. "This one connects to Inpatient, that one to
Chemo, that to the morgue. Take this one, don't take that one. The stairs lock
you out." All the way down a long corridor with semi-abandoned labs on either
side. I walked through looking from one side to the other and back again, moving my head from left to right every two steps like a mechanical wind-up toy.
To my right a desk stacked with dusty papers, to my left a room full of liquid
nitrogen tanks. To my right a lab full of broken lamps and empty boxes, to my
left a room full of freezers, right full of freezers, left full of freezers. Room after
room of freezers packed and lined against the walls, below another floor, below
another corridor, below yet another set of rooms with another set of even deeper
and colder freezers, the vast vaults of tissue and gore of the vast research projects
of the University of Iowa's medical research wing.

At the very end of the hallway of half-empty labs, by the emergency exit,
there was a long sort of closet with dirty frosted windows, an old computer, and
a flimsy scanner. "This is you," I was told and handed a stack of papers. "Scan
and save."

"That's it?"

"That's it."

"Scan and save."

"Scan, save. Enter into the Excel sheet."

"Easy."

"Super easy."

Straightforward, clerical. More than a thousand paper consent forms of
redundant, tedious, and comfortable work. But then one day I stood in the
doorway watching Dr. Santillan cut up a placenta, and I moved without noticing, and I nearly stuck my finger inside the cube-shaped hole, and everything
changed.

Dr. Santillan furrowed her brow and put her scalpel down, finally making me
realize how close I had been standing. She looked at me with a face that seemed
to dare the universe to impress her. Lines around eyes as if drawn on the sand,
wide and tired and entirely accustomed to the smell and spill of human flesh on
a white countertop. A tall woman, with glasses and a slightly nasal voice, who
spent nearly all her days, every day, writing and rewriting grant proposals inside
the paper-stack fort lining her desk. A busy woman, of silence, and science, and

research, with absolutely no time for the menial monotony of consent-form digitization and placenta dissection.

"It doesn't bother you?"

"What?"

"The smell . . . blood?"

"No."

"Not squeamish, then?"

"Not really."

"Hm."

The placenta is the most incredible un-alive thing I've ever held in my own two hands. Within twelve weeks of hearing the chemical call of procreation it has calculated the length of blood canals, the width of uterine walls, the number of tenants to host and feed and keep and grow. It stitches itself up between the walls and corridors of a fertile body—opens its own way, pulls its own bootstraps, parts its own seas. It is its own god, it makes itself in its own image and then expels itself from uterine paradise onto dirt floors, metal basins, soiled sheets, and splattered shoes. Ending, in this case, in my blue Styrofoam bucket.

Along with the transfer came a series of unexpected responsibilities, the first being that for an entire summer my every workday would begin with a "placenta run." A text message: *3 names. Durbervilles, White, Bomb. Can u pick up?* Always the same. Number, names, and *Can u go?*

Yes. Always. I'd walk the length of the hospital, past pictures of Rosa Parks and Martin Luther King in the hall of African American Leaders. Past the smallest of the hospital's Java House coffee stands and the baby grand piano that sometimes played itself. Past the NICU, the children's wing, and a picture of the Illustrated Pig ABCs. *A is for Apple, B is for Big Pig Litter.* All the way to Obstetrics and Gynecology for blood samples, and to Labor and Delivery for the organs themselves.

I walked through waiting rooms and hallways holding my bucket awkwardly, sometimes at my side and sometimes against my stomach because it had no handle and seemed oddly modeled after Winnie the Pooh's honey jar. Occasionally I'd catch a reluctant glimpse of myself on the shiny metal of an elevator door, swimming in a spare oversized lab coat belonging to Dr. Santillan's husband, Dr. Santillan. Black sneakers and shorts, enormous white lab coat, and a blue honey-jar bucket full of ice packs and someone else's gore.

"Do you want to try it?"

"Try what?"

"This."

"The cutting?"

"You don't have to."

"Could I?"

"Why not?"

When I pointed out to Dr. Santillan that my background in science did not ex-
tend beyond the average *CSI / Law & Order* subdural-hematoma-subcutaneous-
lesions vocabulary, she didn't even look up from the magnifying glass as she removed organs from a dead mouse. "It's not really necessary. It's more, if you can,
you can." I glanced at her mouse, a cross between a painting of the Crucifixion
and instructions on how to make a kite. Forelegs and hind legs and muscles
and skin from the tip of each paw to the tip of each opposing paw, outstretched
and taut and pinned down with needles. A belly like a confession, all truth and
transparency and entirely surprising in all that surface can hide.

"I can."

"Then we'll have you watch a few. Then you can do it on your own."

"A few?"

"Yes."

"How many?"

"Not sure."

"Two? Ten?"

"Three, I think."

It seems both hard and unnecessary to explain why this was as exciting as
it was. Maybe something restricted, maybe the starkness of clerical contrast,
maybe the possibility of digging fingers into human flesh separated only by the
thinness of latex. It was not excitement, however, that remained as I walked away
from Dr. Santillan's mouse-kite spread, but the neon noise of should-be-obvious
realizations suddenly flickering on.

First, mice have placentae too. Tiny ones. Which scientists extract regularly, not just in the University of Iowa's MFTB but all over the planet. Men and
women—probably this very minute—lean over magnifying glasses and extract
them carefully like grains of sand stuck between the gears of a pocket watch.
Second, even more basic and obvious, somewhere in the bowels of the University of Iowa hospital there was a room full of mice awaiting organ harvesting
season.

Sometimes, while I watched the three required dissection observation sessions, some cluster of veins would resist the blade and Dr. Santillan, or Brenda the lab technician, would have to saw her way through the tangle. Brenda told me that the first time she ever saw a placenta, she felt her stomach was trying to climb out her throat. "And I've seen lots of things, lots and lots. Been here a long time. But there is something about these things. Don't know what it is, you know?"

What it is, is human. The stuff of eyeballs and knees and lips and shoulder blades, reconfigured. A bit messy and sloppy, but very much very human. What might make the stomach turn is the circuitry lighting up too slowly, the cognitive dismemberment that separates the images of little chicks in an Easter basket and a bucket of KFC. "We give the title of 'barbaric' to everything that is not in common use in our own country," in our own walls, in our own kitchens. It's hard to stomach another's stomach. If you think about it, anyway. "I'm okay dissecting them now, but for a while— Well." The key is not to think about it.

There may be a chance my enthusiasm and strange capacity to stomach the gore is the only reason I was allowed to do such work. There is also a chance I was an unexpected but welcomed relief effort. "You know what I think? A lot of it is the smell. It's like, I don't know." Within two weeks I was dissecting nearly every placenta to come in, missing only a couple, and only because deliveries refuse to follow nine-to-five schedules. "But it's also a bit about the look, it's like nothing else, you know? No heads or tails."

Brenda is right. A heart is a mystical shape, lungs have a sort of nobility. Kidneys are hilarious, and the liver is long-suffering, but placentae are bulbous and grotesque. Red-dead and dead-red. A scarlet jellyfish with one thick white tentacle protruding from its center. "Yeah, something about it. Just turned my stomach."

Brenda is right, again. There is something about it, and something about the turning too. Something reliable. Impulses, like vomit and scream, ignore convention. They never represent things as they may be, but rather as they appear right then and right there, perfectly anchored in the second of sight and sound and smell. *The rustling is a lion, the smell is poison, the dark is abyss.* There is something in the honest whispering of impulse—vomiting, weeping, running, gouging, and gorging. Especially in public. "Put that in your mouth, there are nutrients in the red." Moral relativism and nutritional objectivism. I want to chew on an umbilical cord.

"Ready?"

I was sitting in my closet-office testing different methods to scan and save a document—which by the end of the summer I believed I had perfected—when Brenda came knocking. Pastel shirt, pastoral smile, leaning against the door frame while her ID badge swung gently from her neck. "If you want, one just came in," she said, "one" meaning a placenta and "if you want" meaning you-cut-and-I'll-watch. "Only if you are ready."

"Definitely."

The room where the nurses left the placentae for pickup was relatively small and poorly lit. A sink, a counter, a mini fridge, a large chest freezer, and a sign with a cartoon frog over the soap dispenser that read, "Ruuubit Ruuubit."

Brenda walked over to the counter where a good-sized placenta lay flat on a bed of gauze and plastic, my very first placenta. Red and full and slick and dripping still with all the spilled fluids of birth. "Okay, this is it." It barely fit in my honey-jar bucket, meat poking out of plastic corners, which I tried to cover with my hand as we rode the elevator with khaki-pants-wearing families, and it took up nearly half the counter when I set it down back in MFTB.

"All right, you know what to do."

I made an incision for the "whole" sample, cutting through the entire placenta, membrane and meat, which I would later beat into a solid strawberry paste, mix with a preserving solution, and place in a liquid nitrogen freezer for storage. Easier watched than done. I cut an uneven cube but somehow failed to cut deep enough and had to fetch the tweezers to finish the job. I pressed the lumpy cube between the levers, pulled, and felt it pull right back, fibers and tangled bits of membrane stretching and reaching. "Just get them with the scalpel." I did as Brenda instructed, played them like violin strings with the blade, and they snapped back into the inner walls of the excision. The cube-shaped hole filled slowly back up with blood, a lethargic, uninterested blood drip. Nothing pumped there, nothing beat, nothing pushed blood in any direction—no direction left after birth. "Now the amnion." I pulled on the sides of the placenta. If one does not know what to look for, it might all seem like one solid crimson shapeless shape—a hefty bag full of cranberry juice—but the placenta has hidden compartments. Pull on the membrane's sides and it returns to its original design, a sac, a baby container, a pliable spaceship with complete atmospheric control. "Now peel it back." There are actually two membranes there, one inside, the amnion, the other out, the chorion. "That's right, the one on the baby side." Before we are pulled out into the world, we float in amniotic fluid and kick at the amnion walls, where our feet slip and our fists slide, because the amnion is thin, like bat wings and eyelids, but slimy and slippery like wet soap and custard.

And it was like nothing else I'd ever seen before. Pink shrink-wrap, melted latex, coconut-pomegranate jelly. And running my tongue against the inside of my cheeks was all I could do to keep myself from slipping some into my mouth. When the phone rang and Brenda left me alone for a few minutes, I took a handful of amnion and closed my fist. Shiny slivers of membrane slipped out between my fingers while I imagined their texture with my tongue, cutting through the viscous shine with my incisors and chewing it to bits—silk rubber and red milk skin—interrupted only by the click of a phone being hung up in the adjacent room.

"Now the decidua." The decidua is my favorite of the cuts, though it's a pretty tight race. It is the meat of the beast. The deep of it, the thick of it, the thing that bleeds and speaks. It filters nourishment and waste, communicates in nutriment and chemical, mediates between tenant and landlord. When Dr. Santillan walked me through the first dissection, she slapped it like a baby's bottom and it made a deeply satisfying wet sound. "This is what's on the mommy side," she said in one of the least scientific tones I've ever heard. Then she showed me how to cut it, and I watched carefully, repeating the steps back to her as if I were learning to conjugate verbs. It's always like this, like saying and imagining is the same as having and doing, but to do it yourself is always something else entirely. The strange surprise, which continues to surprise me, is how easy it is to slice through the formerly alive former flesh of a person recovering in a room only a few floors away.

When I made my first cut, the scalpel slid effortlessly into it, like a crayon moving across a hot pan, as if melting down and disappearing into the decidua. The fibers put up no resistance and oiled the blade with black blood. Then I plucked the sample with the tweezers, squeezed hard to feel the threads of flesh being crushed between the metal levers.

"Almost there. Careful with that; don't ruin your shirt."

Last comes the cotyledon, right beside the decidua—a cut not really relevant to any of our studies but a sample another lab, on another floor, has requested. So, one I extract with a certain level of feigned resentment. *You wanna piece of our placentae? Wanna jump on our subjects' mommy sides? Wan' us to cut it up real nice for ya, eh?*

"Are you sure you don't want to do something in the sciences? You'd be good, not getting grossed out or anything."

I wondered, quietly, if it might be reduced to that. Not the skill to do something few can, but the inability to react as most do.

"Is there something where they would just let me do dissections?"

"Not 'just,' I don't think."

When I was finally allowed to cut unsupervised, I took my time. I picked up the umbilical cord and tied a knot in it like I'd seen Dr. Santillan do once. It was smooth white wax rope made of melted cartilage and artery mesh, but stronger than I'm able to describe. You could have tied assailants' hands with it, sails with it, harnesses, mattresses atop cars and trucks. You could have replaced bungee cords and knitted bulletproof vests with it.

I pressed it between my thumb and fingers, felt the tightly woven lattice of veins and stem cells and connective tissue, and I squeezed a blood clot out like crimson toothpaste until I was left staring at a thick raspberry jam slug in the middle of the table. I poked it, half expecting it to recoil like a real slug would, but it only continued to deflate, as if exhaling, as if sinking, and slowly white cells and red cells and stem cells dissolved into the gauze.

"It's all surface tension and clotting. If they let the moms stay in one position a long time, they bleed all in one direction and it pools. The blood clots can get really big."

"How big?"

"Oh, I don't know. Pretty big."

The size of a medium-sized rabbit, at least. I know, I saw one. I ran my hand along its back as if there was a spine beneath, as if it might be capable of pride, rivaling the placenta in girth and weight, and I wanted nothing more than to crush it with my fist or forehead.

Dr. Santillan told me that preeclampsia is the most common of the most serious complications an expectant mother can encounter during pregnancy, and then she handed me a box full of jars with bits of mice floating in formalin like the last few Cheerios in a bowl.

"Why's preeclampsia so scary, then?"

"If it happens before the third trimester, it really increases the possibility of death for the baby and complications for the mother."

I held the box against my stomach and felt the tiny plick-plick of small skulls hitting the glass walls of the jar.

"You'd think we'd get more funding, right?" she said. "Women being fifty percent of the population and all."

"Is that what we do, then? Trying to cure preeclampsia?"

Dr. Santillan raised her eyebrows, defiant lines on the sand. Something, I thought, to do with the forces behind grant funding and hoop jumping. "We're making progress. We could do more."

I held a jar up to the light, pretending I could see the signs of preeclampsia in the floating pieces of mice, and pictured the lab techs doing their autopsies on these red blobs and long-toothed heads with bits of skin and fur still attached.

"If you hurry and get back in time, you can come help me feed the mice."

There is a disease called kuru, found only in Papua New Guinea. I read about it on my lunch break. The infectious agent, a prion actually, burrows through the stomach, swims through the bloodstream, and crawls into the brain like a worm tunneling through the soft flesh of a ripe peach. It wriggles, squirms, and chews through the gray circuitry, shutting off and shutting down whole houses, blocks, and neighborhoods of thought and function, until the brain is a map of flashing scattered islands on a darkened sea. The word *kuru* means "shivering" or "trembling," because that's what it does, it shakes the sufferer like a maraca, like a rattle, like a baby that won't stop crying. And at first it is only a quiver, a shudder, but soon enough the infected cannot walk, cannot talk, cannot even so much as stand on their own. It reduces men, women, and children to a solitary year propped against a wall or face down beneath a tree, trembling, shaking, weeping, and bursting into manic bouts of involuntary laughter, and then it kills them.

It lives and feasts on the human flesh of those who live and feast on human flesh. The direct result of ritualistic funeral endocannibalism. A man dies, and his family eats him to keep him alive in them, and he lives in the illness inside them, and the illness kills the people who loved the man, who kept the man and his illness alive inside themselves. And the people who loved the people who loved the man eat those people, to keep them and the man they loved alive in themselves too. And the man continues, and the illness continues, and people continue to eat, to live, to shake, to laugh, to die.

In a slightly sensationalistic documentary I watched later, a British reporter in khaki cargo shorts and matching shirt interviewed the "last known cannibals." A suspenseful manufactured clicking noise and intermittent shots of savage jungle. "Did he—" the British man stuttered nervously while the translator and the cannibal watched. "Did he enjoy—" An obvious strain visible on his face, the enormous effort to repress shock and the more obvious question bubbling to the surface. "Was it a good taste?"

I watched Dr. Santillan pull a mouse from a group of three others and drop it into an identical but empty cage. She measured and scooped out food from a large container as I wandered through aisles of mice-cage walls.

The mice scurried and piled one atop the other, pressing fur and face and feet against the transparent cages arranged against long tubes connecting each one to a watering system reminiscent of Mayan irrigation canals. That's where I learned, amid the drowned echoes of screeching monkeys and honking birds, that I was wrong. Not one room of mice awaiting the scalpel to makes bellies bloom claret red, but entire hallways of rooms stacked to the ceiling with clear plastic cages.

I walked the length of the room past mostly sleeping mice until I noticed one holding its companion's head in its mouth. Not really chewing or attacking or grooming, but rather like some impulse had taken over without so much as knocking before walking right in and making itself at home. And they both seemed equally surprised, this one to find a mouse's head in its mouth, and that one to find its head inside that one's mouth.

I tapped on the plastic like I've been told a million times not to. The mouse whose head was partly engulfed blinked sleepily, and Dr. Santillan pried two more mice apart in another cage.

"So what are we doing, then?"

"Feeding and separating."

"Why?"

"Why what?"

"The separating part."

"If the little ones get big enough, the big ones sometimes eat them." She counted the mice in one cage and scooped out more food from the large container while the sleepy mouse pushed halfheartedly against the other's face. The cannibal mouse neither pushed back nor loosened its jaws.

"Why do they eat each other? Instinct? Territory? Hunger?"

She dropped a scoop of food into the final cage and snapped the lid back on the container. "Well, it's not hunger."

Hester Swane, Josie Swane. Mary Redglen, baby Redglen. Mel Jones, Cora Jones. Maria Iriarte, Juan Iriarte. I digitized consent forms and updated Excel spreadsheets by date, by birth, by number, trimester, and name. *Maureen Wilde, Max Wilde.* Typing mechanically and timing my progress as I tried to triangulate the minutiae of productivity. *Hazel Green, Rob Green. Marge Garner, baby Garner. Baby Prin. Baby Tull. Baby Stone. Baby Ramsey.*

"How come some of these babies have names and some don't?"

"Hm? Oh. Indecisive mothers."

"Ah." *Baby Ames, baby Bennet, baby Bundren, baby Pilgrim.*

"And sometimes, if the babies don't live, the parents don't name them."

"Ah." *Baby Baptiste, baby Raycos.*

Are u able to pick up placenta?

Ice packs in my blue Styrofoam bucket and an oversized lab coat. *Yes.*

One name, maybe already delivered. Check n pick up?

I noticed the blue plastic on the counter before I'd checked the mini fridge for blood samples. These things become mechanical, no thought of the hundreds of gears between steering wheel and street. The steering wheel turns, the car turns. No distance between thought and place and motion. *This is my counter, this is my counter to the right of the sink where my placentae are left, for me to pick up. This is for me to check and take.* Blue plastic on the counter, to the right of the sink, I check it.

In retrospect, it is clear that I should have realized right away that nurses never went to the trouble of covering the placentae with such care, but rather plopped them flat on the counter, gauze, plastic, and gore. At the very least I should have noticed how carefully and neatly the blue plastic was tucked around the small shape on the counter. No blood, no drip, nothing spilling into the gauze or peeking from beneath the blue sheet. But I didn't notice, I simply walked over and lifted it, no pause, no thought, no placenta either.

And I would like to say that I did so gently, or with some type of finesse, but it would not be true. I just lifted it, one motion, like the lid of a pizza box. No placenta. No clots, no blood samples. No blood at all. Just a small body. Tiny, in fact. Minuscule, miniature human almost translucent, eyes closed, fingers outstretched, soft and new and with the marked features of prematurity. But this is all one instant. My hand went out, a turn of the wheel, the car turning with it. Before I could stop myself I felt the plastic stick to the still moist skin, the baby's forehead and fingers. I heard the plastic leave his forehead, like a soggy Band-Aid worn too long. I saw it pull on minute fingers, extending them briefly into a familiar gesture, like *stop*, like *hello*. Then the stickiness gave out and the hand returned, stillness and softness and inertness.

I felt the floor through the soles of my feet, through my ankles, my knees. And never a notion to move across the room, out of it, from this place to that, only three or four quick paces, a straight line, and a metal door before me. I did not think, *I should go*. Did not think, *I shouldn't be seeing this*. I don't remember the thought, at least, or any thought, really. Just that sort of direction, pulseless impulse. *Cold, blue, quiet, dead. Be somewhere else.* And then I was at the door, with my face millimeters from the cold metal and a hand on the doorknob.

But I didn't turn it. Instead I turned around to see a quiet baby untucked on the counter of a poorly lit room, and it didn't seem right to leave, or leave it like that. So I walked back, careful steps, like a man approaching an edge. The immediate impulse is to keep the body warm, to reach for a blanket, to take one's coat off, though the child on the counter is only shell and vacancy, and the dead don't mind the cold. The impulse remains and it takes some effort to overcome it.

Occasionally, walking past the NICU and through the interconnecting corridors of cancer units and admissions, you will see a child in someone's arms with tubes like tentacles emerging from noses and mouths and arms and abdomens, something out of a science fiction novel. And those parents, and grandparents, and uncles and aunts hold them so close it's like they want to form a cage around them, fashion their own knuckle and muscle and skull into parapets of protection, turn themselves into exoskeletons and incubators. So frail, so easily pierced and made to bleed. But there is also something powerful in the medical aegis—intravenous, inorganic, mechanical, and intelligently designed. Layers and distance, and a squirming child in a parent's arms. Simultaneously approaching and resisting extinction.

But a body cannot serve two masters or forever travel in opposing directions. One will prevail.

I approached the counter slowly. The body seemed to lie untouched, almost out of reach, almost unharmed, and smaller than I'd ever seen before, or have since. Pink and gray and literally breathtaking. It took effort to will oxygen back into my lungs and myself the rest of the way back to the counter. I looked only a second before reaching for the plastic, covering the body up again, and whispering, "I'm sorry." Not entirely out of superstition, but also because that's what you say when you open a door you weren't meant to open.

I walked back to MFTB more slowly than usual, stopping by the cancer ward when a bald girl waved at me from her wheelchair. *E is for Electric Fence. F is for Fight. Z is for Zzzzzzz.* I waved back and thought about the only placenta that had ever turned my stomach. A small, yellow, brittle thing that fit comfortably at the bottom of my bucket and left plenty of space for blood samples and ice packs on top. I remembered that when I tried to pull off the normally pliable and oozy amnion, it peeled off in strips, like yellow wallpaper from a moldy wall. Necrosis has a unique smell that even my underdeveloped senses can easily pick up. It wakes up the cells, makes them jumpy with some olfactory recognition of decay and mortality and cellular vulnerability. It makes you want to turn away from it. It knocks the oxygen out of the air, leaves it dry and hollow. *I is for Ice. J is for Jerks.* It took me four tries to get a decent sample, and one question to understand the problem.

"Why is it like this?" I asked Dr. Santillan, covering my nose with my sleeve.

"Mom's a smoker."

I tried to imagine life inside that rotten sac. Brittle walls, constriction, and haze. It's not possible, to unimagine back to the limits set by a fetal brain, but the notion remains, and it comes back to me in the undigested sludge of dreams. Something stiff tightening around me, shrinking as it rots, and choking as it shrivels, yellow and fetid.

"The babies are always very small, the placenta just can't do its job right."

The little girl turned to the television where a man was jumping hurdles, and I turned to the Pig ABCs. A black-and-white pig scrunched his snout and furrowed his brow as a thought bubble floated above him—a pig's head on a platter, lettuce beneath, apple in mouth, ready to be served. *N is for Nightmare.* I stared back at the child in the wheelchair as she maneuvered around the waiting room corners, and then at the Illustrated Pig ABCs again. A pig danced from frame to frame and letter to letter until he stumbled into T and was swallowed by a large black-and-white snake. *T is for Tragedy.*

The body on the counter was not necessarily the result of anything done wrong, intentionally or unintentionally. Whatever was done, or came undone, whatever preventable unpreventable, one way or another, it is the result of the placenta's failure. Its raison d'être: to bring to term, healthy and well.

The heart pumps our blood, makes our red cells red, oxygenates, refills, refuels. Our kidneys filter for us, lungs replenish for us, livers process for us, but they do it for themselves too. Their lives tethered to the ship, sailors and sails all at once. If the heart could think, it would think: *This blood is my blood, these ribs my ribs. Behold the marvel of engineering built around* me, *to keep and protect* me—*my exoskeleton-planet.* If it had a choice, the heart would pump for itself, to maintain itself. The lungs would inhale for themselves, to maintain themselves. The liver, the kidneys, the brain, the pancreas. But not the placenta. The placenta lives for a fraction of a moment of the life of most organs. It lives to bring to life, and then it extinguishes its own life, having completed its mission.

"Did you bring the blood back?"

When I arrived back at MFTB I realized I had forgotten every piece of standard procedure I'd been diligently learning for the past few weeks.

"Don't worry. I'm a scatterbrain too. Just go on and get back here soon."

A white lab coat—even an oversized, blood- and coffee-stained lab coat worn over shorts and sneakers—will make anyone invisible in a hospital. The nurses never stopped me, never so much as spoke to me, asked me where I was going, what was in the bucket, or why I had returned so quickly from wherever it was that I came from. They simply continued chatting in whispers at the reception desk while I walked past empty delivery rooms, empty wheelchairs, and empty clear plastic incubators until I reached the room and stopped just outside, letting the seconds collect between my body and the metal door. Waiting, I think, for some sign that what I knew was inside wasn't, or at least wasn't there anymore. And then the image of all the post-dissection placentae in our lab, wrapped and stuffed in various freezers across various hallways. How, after we had stripped them for easy-to-store research parts, we would fill a couple of Walmart bags with their mutilated remains and dump them in a chest freezer for the biohazard crew to later pick up and incinerate. And I thought about turning back again, telling Brenda there was no blood, or that maybe someone had accidentally taken it, and that's when I heard voices.

I turned the doorknob slowly and found two doctors standing over the body, speaking in hushed tones. The more experienced doctor, a woman maybe in her forties, guided through whispers a younger woman, who I imagined might be an intern. "You have to be very careful, with something so small." She maneuvered little arms and legs, with her instruments, into what looked like an all-white hand-knitted outfit. She was incredibly precise and delicate. She said "child" and "parents" and "baby" and "these kinds of situations," and not a single ounce of gallows humor or callous language. Not a word above a whisper as she explained to the intern that parents who had suffered similar losses often donated boxes of clothes with little cards for group meetings and emergency contacts. That's where the box had come from, she explained, the little sweater too. So the intern nodded and watched her mentor pull a hand gently through a sweater sleeve like a thread through the eye of a needle, as I pulled blood samples from a mini fridge as quietly as I could, pretending I really was invisible and could slip through the doorway as delicately as the doctor could untangle a tiny finger from the miniature sleeve of a miniature sweater.

Good morning! We have 3: Charlotte n other 2, Ammeer n Grisette looks like delivered this a.m. Can u pick up placentas?

When I cut into the placenta I noticed, for the first time, the uneven clumsiness of my incision. A combination, I imagine, of the stark contrast, the surgical precision with which a small body can be dressed, and how late I'd stayed out the night before. I parted the amnion with my scalpel, nonetheless, bursting vessels, slitting veins while picturing a dead cat. From the sight of the gray body of the stillborn on the counter I'd driven home to find a dead cat in front of my apartment building. It was not quite full grown and not quite a kitten either. Something in between, mixed age and breed, with bluish gray underbelly fur and a scrappy orange coat.

I leaned in, my face only about an inch from the placenta, trying to steady my hand and blade. *Lean in, see red, cut carefully.* A deliberate move unlike those that made up the previous night, when I nearly ran over the stiff body of the small cat. I screeched to a halt, got out of the car, and found myself kneeling beside the sun-dried body before even realizing I'd taken off my seatbelt. I could feel, as I sliced through the flesh on my table, the scent of fresh blood rising and scant warmth dissipating into the room. Placentae always seemed so alive to me, even now, in memory. Exhaling blood, inhaling razor blades. Red, and raw, and ripe. So I leaned in closer still and didn't notice my hair tie sliding off until my hair began to fall forward toward the dissection table. The night-before cat had looked almost alive too, could-be-alive alive, check-for-a-pulse alive. One of its eyes must have been popped out like a button on impact, or else something had come later and pulled on it until the thread had given out. But apart from this, it was whole and almost untouched—and so like a cat to sleep on a frying-pan summer pavement.

I pulled away from the counter just in time and brushed my hair out of my eyes with the back of my hand, only to have it immediately fall again. It had occurred to me, when I noticed the tip of the cat's tail barely touching the rubber of my car's front tire, what would have doubtless happened if I had been a little more tired, or distracted, or careless. The last slow-motion moment of a favorite breakable thing knocked over before ground and gravity and gravel break and breach and burst.

The enormous weight of a Honda Accord on a very small cat's very small ankles and knees and head. Dead as those ankles and knees and head may be, the thought seemed somehow profoundly offensive. That anything or anyone might damage the shape of former life, of something so slight and delicate and soft. So I got up, popped the trunk, and pulled out a box left over from helping someone move.

I brushed my hair behind my ears with my knuckles, inadvertently leaving a streak of blood on my cheek. I buried the cat in a friend's backyard. Two friends brought out shovels and flashlights and drinks and food, and we ate and drank and dug by the light of the car's headlights. I changed my gloves and tied my hair, I leaned right back into the placenta and steadied my hand, hair back behind my shoulder and scalpel back into the red. Four intersecting cuts, deep and sure, all the way through membrane and meat, and without giving it much thought, I licked my lips and tasted blood.

CODA

By some odd stroke of luck I happened to talk to Patrick Madden just around the time my work with the University of Iowa's Maternal Fetal Tissue Bank was coming to a close. So, naturally, I told him about the placentae and the blood thirst and how, if you think about it, meat can't get any fresher than that.

My mother warns me about candor. She informs me that there are "accept-able thinking things" and "acceptable saying things" and that cannibalistic fan-tasies are neither.

Here a note: Dr. Madden, who introduced me to both Montaigne and non-fiction, is a very lovely, gentle family man with very earnest, educated and con-sidered views on life and writing alike. He also is, or at least was then, deeply disappointed in me.

"And you didn't take at least one bite?!"

I imagine that, on some level, this must be an attempt to get back in his good graces.

On another level, "Of Cannibals" seems to me to touch on something basic and repeated numerously throughout Montaigne's work. It is at its core, to me, an exercise in empathy. The very essence of what I love best in Montaigne's essays. Not to simply resist the natural tendency toward prejudices, precon-ceptions, and biases, but to try to see another in the light of his or her own torch. An apparently simple idea, often intellectually discarded for this seeming simplicity. But the idea is neither irrelevant nor truly simple. It is both easy to conceive and difficult to apply, and harder still to sell to those who seem most entrenched in their own personal hegemonic perspective. But Montaigne, he tries, over and over, essay after essay. He is a creature of great empathy, for the living, for the dead, for friends, for enemies, for cannibals, for monsters, and even for the barbarous "trouser wearing" self that, faced with the deep red of another's blooming abdomen, might instinctively lick her lips and meet herself for the first time—or one of the many first times when we truly meet one of our many selves.

8

How the Soul Discharges Its Emotions Against False Objects When Lacking Real Ones

DANIELLE CADENA DEULEN

What causes do we not discover for the ills which befall us!
What will we not attack, rightly or wrongly, rather than
go without something to skirmish against?

MONTAIGNE, "HOW THE SOUL DISCHARGES ITS EMOTIONS
AGAINST FALSE OBJECTS WHEN LACKING REAL ONES"

The blind hallucinate. In a story I heard on the radio, one blind man could hear his eyes singing to him. I was driving and pulled over to listen. The guest neurologist explained that the brain is a glutton for sensation; when one sense goes out, the brain turns on itself, just as it does when a limb is severed, and haunts the site of its severing—*phantom pain*. Loss also causes hallucination: The Pythia of Delphi each lost their names, their bodies, before they were worthy of Apollo's breath. Some say the volcanic pneuma beneath the shrine, built at the axis of two fault lines, caused their oracular hallucinations. Some say they could speak the god's chaotic will because they were pure, they were lonely. The radio show ended and I pulled onto the road, the name of the street as blank inside me as my knowledge of the engine beneath the hood of my car, that richly oiled machine fretting against its own parts. On a billboard above me, there was an image from the Pompeii exhibit on display in the city museum: a human form, thrown down by the weight of ash, faceless, details erased, a solid, untranslated secret. Sometimes I hold the box of old letters I found written in code, a cipher

I invented with a girlhood friend to conceal our secrets, though I can no longer read the symbols and that girl whose hair once fell across my face is lost. There's no one left to utter the signs, no priests to mediate the meaning. As a child, I was always a passenger in a car, left to watch the gray city shifting around me without any knowledge of where I was led. At intersections, I'd look into the windows of other cars, wonder where they were going, why I didn't know who they were, though they looked familiar, though I might have mistaken them for someone I knew, like Mrs. Blue, who after her husband's death called each passerby by his name. He was stabbed by a thief in their front-yard garden and lay down in the cool, loose earth. She'd lived with him for sixty years, and in the months between his death and hers, she wandered through our yards in her wrinkled dress, weeping on our porches, already a ghost. All the neighbors shook their heads in pity, though they never opened their doors to her, because that kind of grief is contagious. I never saw her after she died. I don't have that gift, that curse. But that winter I had a fever so high it made the walls shimmer their terrible light, the floors buzz with longing. I felt the earth's breath possess me, let me see through its surface, and even after the fever broke, for months I was haunted by the shapes inside it: mandala, ouroboros, spiral, eye, everything shifting beneath the stunted veneer of sight—what Cassandra must have seen the moment she tried to rise from Apollo, who only wanted her again and again; it was too much. Some say when she refused to sate him, he scorned her, made everyone think she was insane, as if otherwise everyone would have listened. That onerous vision of an army in the belly of a horse—who would have believed it wasn't a symbol, a sickness in her, but a gift on the eve of a fall?

CODA

Of all Montaigne's writerly virtues, what I admire most in his work is the architecture of his thought. His rhetorical trajectories are often complex, if not downright inscrutable, moving by association rather than logic, and his assaying might incorporate anything that piques his curiosity: political gossip, classical literature, philosophical rumination, biblical allusion, moral instruction, and myth alongside personal reflection and even, at times, confession. There's looseness in Montaigne's essays, a willingness to accept mindful deviation as essential to central subjects, which makes them so delightfully bizarre. In responding to Montaigne's "How the Soul Discharges Its Emotions Against False Objects . . ." it seemed right to me to begin with hallucination and end with vision—both supposedly projections of the soul and extreme manifestations of the brain's attempt to understand the inexplicable. In between, I tried to remain as open as Montaigne might, allowing in the deviations and even the possible dead ends that might nevertheless contribute to the piece as a whole.

9

Of Constancy

NICOLE WALKER

> The Peripatetic sage does not exempt himself totally from
> perturbations of mind, but he moderates them.
>
> MONTAIGNE, "OF CONSTANCY"

Emeritus marketing professor Theodore Leavitt lectured his students that "the reason the train industry could not compete with the automobile industry was because it failed to recognize that it was not in the railroad industry but in the transportation industry." But how can you expect the train industry to forgo its iron beginnings? The heavier the rails, the faster the train, that was how it worked then. It's the opposite thought to current-day featherweight travel. Fiberglass and superlight aluminum—that's the domain of the transportation industry. The train industry knows what it's good at. Ruts. Lines. Permanence.

An online, less-reputable-than-the-OED etymology website says that "rut," meaning "narrow track worn or cut in the ground," was first used in the 1570s, probably taken from the Middle English word for route. The OED finds this "improbable." But perhaps it is the OED that is in a rut.

Every day I wake up at 6:55. I make my kids' lunch: pepperoni, rice, yogurt, grapes, pretzels, carrots, juice. I eat an English muffin, then check Facebook, Gmail, work e-mail. Then I check work e-mail, Gmail, Facebook. I grade student-essay one, check e-mail, essay two, check Gmail, essay three, Facebook, essay four. I hold office hours. I tell students that their Spanish courses will fulfill their cultural understanding block. I teach. I tell students that the difference between dissociation and distance in a narrator is how willing the narrator is to be obviously broken. It is better to be broken. You can see yourself better, like when an arm breaks through the skin and for the first time ever you see your inside, now out.

I come home. I make dinner—tacos. I have a glass of wine. I watch a show called TV. I go to bed at 10:00. I wake up at 6:55.

I am in a rut, but it's okay because I'm a lover of routine. No disrespect to the OED, but I love my route. A well-worn route is a rut. A well-worn routine is a life capable of heavy lifting. You can do the work of a thousand boxcars. You are iron track, trains running along the back of you. A rut-lover is a conveyer of speed. My life is going so quickly. My rails are on fire.

People, like my husband, Erik, or his parents, try to convince me to travel. I'm conflicted. I want to go—Napa sounds beautiful. I like wine. I don't want to go. It's far away. I'd have to take an airplane. It will disrupt my route. A self divided. My father-in-law set up a trip to Napa. Three days of wine drinking at Far Niente, Chateau Montelena, Caymus. "We'll get the rooms," he said. "You just have to buy your plane tickets and the wine tastings." Cost: $99 companion tickets, $99 a tasting, $99 a dinner. The transportation industry is not always a bargain, but $198 per day plus $198 to get there and back is not bad for two nights, three days in Napa.

We forgot, Erik and I, in our calculations, to include the cost of traffic. It took us three hours to drive fifty-five miles. That night, a tangle of stop-and-go nerves, I lay awake in bed. Too much wine and a too-fluffy pillow triggered trains of thoughts: the flight attendant's eyebrows, the waiter's glasses, the definition of "tasting," plastic water bottles, recyclable or not, the surreptitious reuse of other people's water bottles, contagion, the avian flu, flu shots versus flu mist, wondering if I am a bad parent to say okay to flu mist for one child, a shot for the other, and if I, that same bad parent who left her kids with a babysitter and who is not sleeping in the middle of Napa, sated and spoiled and a little bit drunk, should give up and get up.

I go outside. The vineyards layer in rows. The bad parent walks between the vines at five in the morning. It is fall, and the leaves of the Cabernet turn yellow like the leaves at home in Flagstaff. I take some comfort in this—I am missing red leaves equally, everywhere—although comfort is not the same as sleep.

In the 1940s a front company for General Motors called National City Lines began dismantling light-rail-based trolley lines in big cities. In this GM (or Great American) Streetcar Conspiracy, the rigid rail lines were replaced with flexible, bendable, turnable, car-able roads. No longer did the city worker have to abide by the strict rules of predetermined tracks. If the worker wanted to take A Street to work, he took A Street. If he wanted Lexington, he took Lex. If he wanted to turn around and go home, he could circle that car in the middle of any intersection, at least in Utah where the U in Utah means freedom to go in circles forevermore, thy will is thy command.

I'd rather drive than fly. Driving is more familiar. I do it every day. My car is nicely beige—a color as comforting as sand. If I am driving, I can stop to pee at any convenient Shell station along the way. I try not to stop at Texaco because if there's one constancy in my life, it's a prejudice against Texas. The other constancy, because constancies should multiply, is the persistent belief that Shell oil comes from kinder oil places than Texas. I shouldn't drive or fly at all. Global warming. Perhaps I should take the train, except Amtrak is the only game in town. Because Amtrak runs on tracks owned by freight train companies like Burlington Northern, they often must give way to freight trains. It takes forever to go fifty-five miles on Amtrak. Freight trains are as numerous as prejudices and persistencies. Perhaps, instead, I will stay home.

Like prejudices and persistencies, ton-miles add up. In the United States, in 1975, freight trains carried 750 billion ton-miles of freight. By 2005 that amount had doubled. Transporting cargo by rail releases far less carbon than transporting cargo by plane: the train releases 0.0282 kg of CO_2 per ton-mile, whereas the plane releases 1.527 kg of CO_2 per ton-mile. Transporting people by car releases about 1.2 kg of carbon per passenger mile. Transporting people by train releases 0.18 kg per passenger mile, making rail transportation one of the most carbon-economical ways to go. Planes go farther and higher, making the plane the most dangerous to the air. Planes are also most dangerous to routine. When I am on the plane, I need to sit on the aisle. If I don't sit on the aisle, I weep. Mostly for my bladder. Sometimes from my bladder. If there's one thing I must do, it is feel free to pee on a regular basis.

Unilaterally, my friend Rebecca won't fly. In 2010 she took the train from Los Angeles to New York City for her art opening at Ameriger Yohe. She boarded the train at 10 p.m. Having booked a bedroom, she unpacked her pants, her shirts, her dress, her books. Bedrooms are for two, and she was traveling alone. Plenty of room to make herself at home. Plenty of time, too. It would take three days to cross the country. Three days if all went well. Time enough to establish a routine.

To take the 4 Southwest Chief from L.A. through Flagstaff and Albuquerque and onward to Chicago takes forty-four hours and costs $1,931. Then you still have to transfer to, and pay for, the 48 Lake Shore from Chicago to Albany to New York. At five o'clock that evening she called me. She had only made it five hundred miles in nineteen hours. I was in downtown Flagstaff, walking through the square on the way to dinner at Karma Sushi's. We always walk around the block when we go to Karma's. We stop at Mountain Sports and Aspen Sports and Babbitt's to look at Northface and Patagonia gear that we never buy. Max, my son, tries on a hat that reads, "Life is good." Zoe, my daughter, asks if she can have a flashlight shaped like an iguana. Rebecca calls me. She's in the station. I wave to her through the walls of the store, across Route 66, through the metal of the sleeping car. She can't get off to say hello. There has been a delay. A woman walked in front of the train. The train could not, as it never can, stop in time. I tell her, they do that, in Flagstaff. Walk in front of trains. I picture the woman, long blue coat, hair flying out behind her. I picture her pushing a stroller away from her. I don't know if there is a stroller, but I see one. Maybe in my imagination, she's pushing her better self away. Maybe she's wishing that she could send the happy part of her to go on and on while the unhappy part could be stopped by the poor train conductor's heavy load. What a great human achievement, even surpassing the invention of the transportation industry, to divide routine from despair.

But Rebecca is stuck with both routine and despair and is thus stuck on that train and there is no way around if she wants to make it to Chicago.

She waits so patiently, since patient is the only thing you can be on a train that goes only one direction on tracks that turn only toward Chicago. Despite her patience, she misses the transfer. To make the show on time, she is forced to take a plane. O'Hare to LaGuardia in an hour and a half. An hour and a half to defy death. To withstand the unnaturalness of flight. To put aside the fear that you're tearing through God's cloak of safety. Now she's done it. She's changed her mind. Her policy. Her beliefs. To change your mind is to kill your former self. Rebecca is anything but suicidal, and yet here she is, torn in two.

I am suicidal. All my friends are dead. Or dying. Or will be dead one day.

My husband, when I said that I couldn't go on, thought I said, "Do you want chicken for dinner?" I didn't correct him, but the poor chicken is dead too. My husband kisses the top of my head. Internal, eternal war: There is purpose in death but better purpose in dinner. I will make fried chicken, chicken cacciatore, chicken fricassee, chicken and dumplings, chicken tacos, chicken in a can. There is purpose in life again. Then, the chicken burns. I want to die. I turn on the radio to hear Maggotbrain's "Can You Get to That?" They sing, "You're going to reap just what you sow."

Sow. My daughter and son swing together in concert. There is order and balance in the universe. Life is good and even.

Reap. My daughter, older, jumps off the swing, sticks the landing. My son, before I can stop him, follows suit. He falls to the ground. Cracks his chin open. I should have stopped him, should have stopped them. I have no power. There is no justice. I sowed. He reaped. I remain resolved. I will live. I will die. From the cherry tree, the blossoms fly off into summer heat. They count one more day, one more day. I have never been so happy to be alive. So sad. I shall fight myself no more forever.

What would Leavitt have had the railroad industry do? What does he mean, they failed to realize what industry they were in? Who is the *they* here? Robber barons like Vanderbilt and Harriman and Gould? Does Leavitt mean the railroad industry should have started building cars, divided itself in two? Should have expanded to absorb all transportation—automobile, aeronautical? The trains should have become cars? Or should they have become more themselves? Is there a way the railroad industry could have kept the trains on the tracks? Is there an America that could have been tracked, where the individual would not want to make his left turn at will, her U-turn at random? Could America have been America crisscrossed by railroad rather than held up high by overpasses and bridges? The railroad industry failed to become the automobile industry. Adapt. The times. The fossil fuels will be gone soon. Use them while you can. We seem willing to abide the plane that goes only to the stops already determined, sometimes making us lay over for hours in some place we distinctly do not want. We recover by getting off the plane and quickly finding a taxicab, a Town Car, our mother in her Prius to pick us up at the curb. The train speeds by, empty.

I love my routine of hours but I hate the routine of morning. Same soap. Same contact lenses. Same hairbrush I bought in Portland, Oregon's Aveda when I was pregnant with my daughter and traveling my first time to read to students—at Evergreen State. I was pregnant with the new. Traveling didn't seem so hard then, even though I slept on a cot at my friend's house in Portland. Even though I was put in my host's bedroom, in a bed so redolent with graciousness (who can sleep in their hosts' beds while the hosts sleep on the foldout?). I slept. Everything was a first time and I crashed into it. Life was a bucket of sleep and I soaked in it, but now my pants are so old and my shirts are so old and I'm tired of drying the water off from behind my knees. This face I've looked at before with these old eyes and the old thoughts are dull as a doorknob. I don't want to die. I want a new brain. A neural net with pathways ungrooved. I want some new pants.

The war with the self is the most brutal war. Is there anything more heavy than the re-collection of track by the industry that laid them down? Railroad ties resold at the local nursery as landscaping tools. Spikes melted down into wheelbarrows. Tracks themselves pressed into service as dumpsters and graffiti canvas. A railroad industry cannibalized by a transportation industry. Pulling up tracks is sentimental. Can you turn old business into a new garden?

After the latest oil crisis, after Iran, Iraq, Syria, Hurricane Katrina, and the Gulf Oil spill—after the world continued to be its inconstant self—gas prices rose so high that it became less expensive to ship freight by train than by semi-trailer. Stopped at the crossing, as I check my e-mail, Facebook, Gmail, brush my hair, the boxcars flash by, as do flatbed cars topped with trailers normally attached to semi trucks. Boxcar after boxcar speeds by. Rubber-tired trailers, filled with freight one gasoline-fed engine at a time, bounce on top of steel wheels, going forward, mostly gas-free. Maybe there was forethought. Or slow thought.

The railroad industry is doing fine. They say they're going to build a train from L.A. to Napa. It's a straight shot. Save a lot of gas. Someone in the railroad industry in an industry that doubles as the transportation industry chose that straight line because taking every available turn sometimes gets you nowhere, especially in California, where no one ever wants to die, unless they're trapped in traffic.

Here's a new thought for another trap: Roads are asphalt train tracks. You're still driving where someone else is telling you to go. A new neural net can't be paved. How do you make a new thought? You have to move. It's worse than travel, I know. The packing and the goodbye-saying and the finding a new grocery store. But you have to go. The tulips you saw in Michigan are not the same tulip you see in Phoenix. That tulip, eaten by a javelina, will break your mind. Inside that broken mind, on the edge of a gnawed tulip, you will find a reason to live. It's called yellow. You have never seen a yellow like this before. Keep looking at it until you have to move again.

Or maybe you have never seen a tulip. Maybe you should get out of your car. Leave it by the jangling railroad stop. The noise will go away soon enough. The other cars will find you. You'll be surprised how smooth the ground next to the tracks is. Don't worry. You won't trip. The tracks are dangerous, but the weeds alongside never are. It's a route that's been taken a million times, but never once by you. You might think it's suicide for a flower to grow along this route—from Flagstaff to Los Angeles is mostly Mojave. But the Utah penstemon grows there. You're from Utah. It survives. So can you. Indian paintbrush survives everywhere, even here, in between the oil-dipped lumber and the steel spikes, between the Turtle Mountain Wilderness and Barstow. You are willing to take note. You take comfort in color. Even desert dandelion seems surprising, in the desert, even though it looks as routine as the ones stuck in your hard dirt at home. Desert larkspur is as blue as your coat, and owl's clover is pink for the owl that is calling you to go ahead. This rut is less of a route. You're going so slow you might actually get somewhere.

CODA

"Of Constancy" is one of Montaigne's most contrarian essays. Often Montaigne begins with an anecdote or a definition to secure an understanding of the topic of the essay. But in this essay, he begins by defining what constancy is *not*.

> The law of resolution and constancy does not imply that we ought not, as much as in us lies, to decline and secure ourselves from the mischiefs and inconveniences that threaten us; nor, consequently, that we shall not fear

lest they should surprise us: on the contrary, all decent and honest ways and means of securing ourselves from harms, are not only permitted, but, moreover, commendable, and the business of constancy chiefly is, bravely to stand to, and stoutly to suffer those inconveniences which are not possibly to be avoided.

There are so many "not's" and "nor's" in that first sentence that the basic understanding is contrary. How are we supposed to be? Forward facing? Stout? Suffering? It is human nature to avoid suffering. Montaigne argues in this essay that you must fight the most human aspect of yourself—your desire to flee in the face of danger. You stand firm in the face of battle. Embrace what you do not want to do, which is run away. Negation of basic instinct is the way to win the war. I think of the humans at the end of Peter Jackson's *Two Towers* from the *Lord of the Rings* series. Even though the humans are outnumbered and will surely lose this war, they choose to fight. Bad idea. Don't do it, one shouts at the screen. But they leave the relative safety of Helm's Deep and kill as many orcs as they can on the way to their deaths. That's constancy. Not running away from certain death, Montaigne argues, that is the way to win the war.

In my essay, the war isn't against a national army. It's not even against orcs. The war is the battle with the self—the desire for sameness, the desire for change. I wonder if constancy allows for newness. On the one hand, if you're comfortable in routine, energy that would be devoted to regulating emotion, to finding an even keel, can be better used to make new ideas. On the other hand, perhaps the mind gets stuck in its grooves. There are no new thoughts in a brain that's in a rut. I go back and forth between the positives and the negatives, approaching some sort of synthesis, I hope, arguing along with Montaigne that the primary goal, in battles within and outside the self, is to try to keep it together.

10

Of Giving the Lie

BRET LOTT

All the traffic that I have in this with the public is,
that I borrow their utensils of writing, which are more easy
and most at hand; and in recompense shall, peradventure, keep a
pound of butter in the market from melting in the sun . . .

"Ne toga cordyllis, ne penula desit olivis;
Et laxas scombris saepe dabo tunicas;"
["Let not wrappers be wanting to tunny-fish, nor olives;
and I shall supply loose coverings to mackerel."
Martial, xiii. I, I.]

And though nobody should read me, have I
wasted time in entertaining myself so many idle
hours in so pleasing and useful thoughts?
MONTAIGNE, "OF GIVING THE LIE"

Here is a story:

In the fall of 2006 into the winter of 2007, my wife and I lived in Jerusalem. I was a guest professor at a university, and while we were there plenty of friends came for visits, giving us more than enough reason to see pretty much all the holy sites in Israel. But in January and nearing the end of our stay, we decided we wanted to see Petra, the ancient city carved into sandstone canyons, over in Jordan. Our friends Jeff and Hart from here in Charleston were visiting us then, and we spent one cold and sun-drenched January day hiking the bright and towering red stone ghosts of the ruins.

On our way back the next morning there came a snowstorm, and we found ourselves snowbound in a taxi at the crest of the King's Highway between Petra and Aqaba, elevation 5,000 feet, hours and hours from our home in Jerusalem.

Forty-five minutes after the driver called in our predicament, members of the Jordanian army—yes, the Jordanian army—suddenly emerged from the white all around us, having driven their emergency response truck as close as they could to us and then hiked up the highway to the cab. Jeff and I helped the soldiers push the taxi out of its snow-mired fix, then watched the driver pull away and drive off. Only then did we realize that of course he couldn't park and wait for us to climb back in because he'd get stuck in the snow again.

That left Jeff, me, and five soldiers to walk a mile or so through a blizzard back to their rescue truck. Along the way we pitched snowball fights, America versus Jordan (I actually yelled that out as I reared back to launch a snowball, and was nailed in the shoulder before I could even let go), all of us laughing, talking (they all spoke English), and trying our best not to think of the cold and this wind and all this snow. Then here was the rescue truck, emergency yellow, sharp and big with its pug-faced grill and running boards two feet above the snow-packed road. We all climbed into the warm quad-cab, the driver inside and ready for us. Eight of us jammed inside, Jeff and I in the backseat in the middle, a soldier on either side of us.

Then one of the men in the front seat pulled from the floorboard a battered Thermos, another soldier produced from somewhere a stack of four thick glass tumblers, and the one with the Thermos poured out steaming hot tea, giving Jeff and me the first two glasses.

I don't even like tea, but I cannot remember tasting anything as perfect as that sweet and strong hot tea, its steam immediately clouding my glasses.

That was when Jeff, glass in hand, turned to me and said, laughing, "This is going to be a great story."

"Yes, it will," I said.

We weren't even warmed through yet, not even reunited with our loved ones, and that cab—the story of our being saved in a snowstorm by the Jordanian army wasn't even over yet—and already we both were thinking, *We have to tell this story!*

That's how important story is.

I am writing this because I want to write it. I want to tell it. I want to share this.

But even though the fact of story is so very important, I wonder who, once I am dead, will read what I have written.

Have I wasted time in entertaining myself so many idle hours in so pleasing and useful thoughts? Have I wasted time in writing stories?

I am not writing here out of a midlife crisis. I am not. Though of course even saying such feels as though I protest too much. But it's not that. Really.

And it's not that I turned fifty-five last week. "Double nickels," I kept saying and texting and e-mailing all day long whenever the fact of what day it was came up in conversation. Double nickels, I said, because it was a silly thing to say, goofy, old-school, dumb. Stupid. Annoying.

I am like that. I will drive something into the ground to see how far I can go before someone—generally speaking, my wife—will tell me to cut it out. She tells me to cut it out a lot.

But still, I wonder who, once I'm dead, will read what I have written.

This question was never one to enter my mind when I was younger. I simply wanted to tell stories. I could do that, and I enjoyed it. I wanted to find out what happened to the people about whom I wrote, whether in fictive form or in nonfiction, those point-blank stories about me and what I wanted to understand about that middling subject.

My wife tells me I am thinking too much of the end of things now. Of retirement, of giving up writing, of simply teaching and teaching only. Of growing old. Of dying. She tells me she loves me, and I believe her, but tells me too I have other stories to tell, other things to write.

Here is another story. A longer one but one I need to tell:

Each summer I take fifteen students from the College of Charleston to our sister city, Spoleto, Italy, to live for a month, and to write, and to read, and to travel. Spoleto is in Umbria between Rome and Florence, and while there we all live in a fifteenth-century farmhouse turned into six modern apartments that look out on the Umbrian Valley toward Assisi, a beige smear on a hillside in the distance. Each year we also take a trip together into Florence, spend a day on a walking tour, then spend that late afternoon at a private wine-tasting course. All very civilized, all very Florentine: the students must dress up a bit for the occasion, and act well-mannered.

Last year the wine tasting was led by Count Niccolò Capponi, who was to present us with three different wines from his family winery, Villa Calcinaia, in Chianti. The event was held in the second-floor offices of the walking-tour company in the old city center, the room actually a salon with high wide windows and a low dais at one end, where sat the count.

He was and is what you call a character. A resident and native of Florence (as far as the family records could show, they arrived around 1200), he spoke perfect English in a broad British accent and was funny and dramatic, quite immodest and a little off-color: a blend of Terry-Thomas and Thurston Howell the Third. A professor of political science to different American programs located in Florence, and with a PhD in military history from Padua University and a fellowship spent at Yale, the count held court for an hour and a half talking about wine, about wine critics, about military history, and about writing—he had published a number of books, most recently a re-seeing of Machiavelli as not the diabolically scheming fellow most hold him to be but a bumbling political naïf who made bad choices every time.

I wasn't sure how the students would react to him, and at first the room was a little cold, what with his dramatic pauses and whispered revelations. But gradually they warmed to him, until at the end of the evening students were lined up asking him to autograph the bottles they had purchased of his wine. Attending the evening, too, was his wife Maria, a gracious and sweet and, one got the feeling, *long-suffering* woman, and their six-month-old baby boy, Vincenzo, the two of them quiet in the back of the room while the count spoke, Vincenzo in his stroller.

But right at the end of his talk, the count asked if we would care to accompany him on a little walk, for he had something he wanted to show us only a couple hundred yards from the salon. Of course we agreed, though we had no idea where he meant to take us. Later, when we all compared notes, most of us expected he would walk us to some place we'd already been shown by the tour guide earlier that day, and we'd all have to act surprised at where he'd brought us.

We left the salon and followed him. Outside, he put on his tweed jacket and lit his burled wood pipe—really—and walked down one alley and another, then crossed the Ponte Vecchio itself, a lot farther than a couple hundred yards. Once across the Arno, we turned left and followed him up the street that paralleled the river and onto another that broke obliquely away from the water.

Maybe a hundred yards up that street, along a granite block wall, we stopped. There beside us stood a huge wooden double door, twelve feet high and reinforced with iron studs. We watched as the count reached into his pocket, pulled out a set of keys, and opened the door, inviting us all in. That was when I looked back to the granite block wall and saw the plaque mounted there: *Palazzo Capponi delle Rovinate.*

This was his house.

He ushered us into the foyer, where yet another twelve-foot door needed unlocking, and then into the inner courtyard of the house, four stories high and dark and old and Renaissance Italian, with busts on pedestals high on the walls, and frescoes—frescoes!—on the walls, too. It was all difficult to process, what exactly was going on. We were suddenly inside some other world, to put it mildly, though we'd been walking around Florence all day long. But this was suddenly the real thing, a house where there lived a count and his wife and their baby boy Vincenzo, and now Maria and Vincenzo appeared from the foyer, the count and his family allowing us into their domain, their palazzo.

We stood in awe, snapping pictures of the courtyard, thinking, *This is it! This is what he wanted to show us!* But that wasn't it, there was something else he wanted to share, he said, and we followed him to a wide set of stone stairs up to the second floor, high as the third floor in a house anywhere else, and along a dark gallery with windows on the left that looked out on the courtyard, huge ancient furniture beside us, old portraits of long-dead people on the walls, and a suit of armor that seemed as natural a piece of decoration here as a lamp on an end table back home.

The count had the keys out again. He stopped at the door at the end of the gallery, opened it, and brought us all in to yet another world: his office.

I don't mean here to be writing in a manner too romantic, or purple, or simply overawed. But this was a moment when one's hairs are on end, one's antennae are up, one's faculties are fully employed: this was *happening*.

We were now in a room maybe twenty by twenty with books everywhere, paintings stacked and leaned against the walls, old silk wallpaper water-stained and hung with more paintings, and everywhere books. A huge desk in the center overflowed with papers, an old lectern stood off to the side, a stained glass window four feet tall leaned against a wall, an ancient chandelier hanging above it all. And books and books and books.

"Here's what we're after," he said, and reached up to a shelf on one wall lined floor to ceiling with white volumes thick as old library dictionaries or ancient Bibles. He pulled from the shelf a narrow flat box, opened it, and handed it to one of the students, Katie, a young woman too stunned at what was going on to say no to holding it.

"Of course it's in Latin," he said, "but it's a letter from Henry the Eighth to an ancestor of mine. That's his broad seal."

Inside the box lay a document about eighteen inches wide, maybe six inches long, affixed to the bottom of it a rather beat-up-looking piece of wax the size of an oblong coaster. We could make out some shapes and words on the wax. The first words of the document itself read "Henricus VIII."

We passed the box among us at the urging of the count, who said, "History was meant to be touched, it was meant to be fingered. It's a tactile thing."

We looked at it, awed (that perfect word again), while the count continued to bring down from the wall more of those white volumes, opening them, pulling out vellum-wrapped piles of papers: the family archives back to the thirteenth century.

And, finally, here is the point of this all, the end of the too-long path down which this story has taken me: the vellum pages that wrapped the archives were themselves pages of an illuminated manuscript, a religious text that had, at some point in history, been scrivened by a monk bent low to the page for too many hours to number, then, perhaps centuries later, deemed inconsequential enough to be used to wrap the Capponi family papers.

The count stood handing off bundles to us, the illuminated letters on the wrapping pages right there, right there. But only as meaningful to some archivist one day long ago as the wrapping on a chunk of butter, or paper around a mackerel.

The count showed us more things: a blue velvet bag brought from inside a hidden cubbyhole in the lectern that held a couple dozen florins, the coin of the realm back in the thirteenth to sixteenth centuries, which we passed around among us; that stained glass window, which he held up as best he could against the window looking out onto the inner courtyard, and for which, he told us, he still had the receipt from 1526; an initiation program from the Order of Saint James dating from the sixteenth century, inside it a passage from the Psalms written in Hebrew. "Who here can read Hebrew?" the count asked, and looked around at us. One of the students, Gabrielle, raised her hand, rather shyly, and when he handed it to her and said, "Read it aloud, if you please," she tried to beg off. But finally, after we cajoled her, she read it out to us, her Hebrew classes in preparation for her Bat Mitzvah finally paying off. We cheered her effort once she'd finished.

"What's your most prized item in this room?" I asked, and immediately he pulled down one of the volumes, unwrapped it, and brought out a folder that held ancient pages written in careful calligraphy.

"When you're doing research about a particular person," he said, "it's always best to research the person beside the person. The subject can oftentimes make himself out to be something other than what he is. The man beside him can come closest to revealing the truth."

He then read from the piece of paper in hand, translating into English the Italian. It was a memoir by an ancestor of his who had been the right-hand man ("I dined at his shoulder," the Italian read) to Giulio de' Medici, later Pope Clement VII, who would one day commission Michelangelo to paint *The Last Judgment*, the altarpiece needed to complete his Sistine Chapel. The particular passage he read to us was of a morning when Capponi came to Giulio's to find him eating breakfast and Giulio looked up to meet his eyes "in a meaningful way" and told him, "Job would not have the patience to last a day with Michelangelo."

That is, firsthand evidence that Michelangelo was a royal pain, from none other than a Medici pope. Right there on that piece of paper, penned by the man beside the man.

Then we were finished. The count thanked us all for coming and led us back into the gallery, where he suddenly decided to take the helmet off the suit of armor and place it on the head of one of our students, Chris. "Try this on, old boy," he said—he really said "old boy"—and Chris did. More pictures were taken all around before he took it off and we headed back down those stone stairs to the ground floor and the inner courtyard. And as if to give us one more thing, one more thing, he brought out his keys yet again. This time he crossed the courtyard to the side opposite where we had come in, unlocked yet another huge wooden door, and opened it to reveal the Arno right there across the street, the Uffizi straight across the river. Florence, right out his front door.

We thanked him and thanked him, as if words might be enough, and then moved across the street to take a look at where we'd been. The count leaned in the doorway a few moments, waved at us all and wished us well, then closed the door.

When we pulled our cameras out to take pictures, we all had the same problem: the Palazzo Capponi, a beautiful rose-hued stucco, was too big to get in the frame.

We'd come expecting a talk on wine from a count. What we didn't expect was the touching of Florentine history. We didn't expect word from Henry the Eighth. We didn't expect florins in our hands.

Or the tunny-fish wrapping a sacred text had become.

But this is what we found.

We stood there across the street from the Palazzo Capponi for a few long minutes, all of us looking out on the river, back at the palazzo, to the Ponte Vecchio to our left, the sun set now beyond it, light fading. Some of us tried to talk about what had just happened; others recognized words weren't enough. Then we broke up, went our ways for the evening, each of us in wonder, I am certain, at what we hadn't expected and what we'd found.

I am writing this because I want to write it. I want to tell it. I want to share this.

But I have already written fourteen books. I have already written, I fear, too much. Eight novels, three story collections, three books of essays. A number I do not know of stories in journals, same for essays. Words are with me always.

But I must be honest. I must try as hard as I am able to be the man beside the man. To be the man beside *me*, so as to come closest to revealing the truth.

I must be honest—of course I must be honest—and attest to how I tire of words.

I tire of the limits I have found inside my own writing, the way sentences and images will come out with the same words replicating the same gestures and impressions. I tire of the way I still do not know how to do this thing I have practiced so very many years of my life. I tire of the way a blank page, no matter how many I have filled, is still at its birth a blank page.

I tire of the way what I have written becomes something other than what I had intended when first I embarked. As, for instance, this essay, whose kernel appeared upon my walking through the living room toward the kitchen one evening of no particular consequence and simply glancing at the bookcases with their spans of books, dozens, hundreds of them lining the wall, and the subsequent moment of a shiver through me, small and irrelevant, when I thought, Who, if anyone, has even read everything I have already written?

It was an ordinary moment. An evening of no consequence.

There was nothing about the King's Highway and the importance of story in that moment. Nothing of the Florentine count and Michelangelo and

Henry VIII and an illuminated text used like yesterday's paper. Nothing even of Montaigne. There was only a momentary pause, there in the living room, a glance at the books lining the wall, and my thinking in the selfish way a writer thinks, the mercenary way, the egotistical and heartless way a writer looks at all things around him as possible fodder for the next foray into words, *One day I want to write about wondering if anyone has read what I have written.*

Then came the invitation from the editors of this yet-another book you hold in your hands, you reader you, to write an essay after Montaigne, and finding available to me this landmark one of his, "Of Giving the Lie," and its pondering the valor and folly of lies, the bald-faced and covert hallmarks dishonesty leaves upon the soul. The way a book one has written can end up rewriting the author in a better light than he can ever be seen. "In moulding this figure upon myself," Montaigne continues after the quote at the beginning of this essay, "I have been so often constrained to temper and compose myself in a right posture, that the copy is truly taken, and has in some sort formed itself; painting myself for others, I represent myself in a better colouring than my own natural complexion."

I'd intended to write about lies. But I am trying here to write about the truth.

I am trying to be the man beside the man.

I am whining. I know.

But I have tired of the way what I intend to write is never what I write, and what I write is never what I intend.

While the man beside me tries to write, if I will allow him, I have now turned double nickels, and wonder more than ever who, once I am dead, will read what I have written.

Another story—the last?—because my wife tells me I have other stories to tell, other things to write:

My birthday. I am late home from a charity golf tournament, though I am a golfer of no merit. I have golfed for fifteen years now, and have broken 100 only twice. I have made three birdies in my life. Still I enjoy it, being outdoors and with friends.

But I promised to be home by four or five and to make dinner, jambalaya, a favorite. When it became apparent how slowly the tournament was being played out, I texted Melanie I would be late and asked if she would go ahead and start dinner. Our two sons and their wives and our two grandchildren are coming over for the festivities, and I've apologized, told her I would be home as soon as I could.

Near six-thirty I make it in the door from the garage to the kitchen, rushed and apologizing for being so late. Zeb, our older son, and his wife Maggie are there with the grandchildren, Mikaila, age three, and Oliver, who is three months old and asleep in the black baby carrier strapped to Maggie's front. Sarah, our younger son Jacob's wife, is there too, though Jacob hasn't yet gotten off work. Melanie stands at the oven, peering in at the cherry crisp I requested for dessert, and the long casserole dish of jambalaya lies on the counter, ready and ready.

So though I am late, no one is troubled, no one concerned. I am just late.

"Happy birthday!" Melanie says, and comes to me, kisses me, and the others all wish me a happy birthday too, hugs all the way around, and I give a kiss to the top of sleeping Oliver's head, there in the baby carrier.

Lastly, there is Mikaila, who jumps up and down, clapping. "Happy birthday, Grampa! We have presents for you!" she shouts. "We have presents for you!"

I pick her up then, the girl tall as any four-year-old though she has just turned three, and settle her on my hip, her blond ringlets so much like Shirley Temple's it's a cliché even to point it out. But I am her grandfather, so this cliché is my right.

"It's my birthday!" I say to her. "Double nickels!" I say, and Mikaila says, "We have presents for you!"

That is when her father, beside us here in the kitchen and wearing a crisp plaid office shirt and gray slacks—he is an adult, he has a job, he is married, he owns a home, he is a father, he is my *son!*—pulls his hand from his pocket and, grinning at me, slaps that hand on the granite kitchen counter.

He lifts his hand to reveal two nickels, dull gray, one heads, the other tails.

"I've been waiting all day to do that," he says in a near whisper, still grinning.

I've texted him two or three times today, like everyone else, the goofy, old-school, dumb, stupid, annoying term, driving it into the ground and driving it again. And now here is my son, his daughter in my arms, turning the joke back on me. Calling me on my dim-bulb joke.

I laugh and shake my head. "That's a good one!" I say to my son, then say again, "That's a good one!" and in one more effort to pass down my penchant for the dim-bulb joke, to drive it into the ground even further, so deep it's handed on to the next generation in all its innocence and joy and blond ringlets and presents for you, I set Mikaila down, then take the two nickels and press them both to my forehead, where they stick.

I bend down to Mikaila, point at my forehead, and say, "See? Double nickels! Double nickels!"

She has no idea what is going on, what this dumb thing her grandfather is doing means. She only stands there, still with this smile on her face, looking up at my forehead, then me, then my forehead again.

Then she twists just a little, still smiling, and looks me in the eye.

She says, "Oh Grampa, so silly!"

The man is writing this because he wants to write it. He wants to tell it. He wants to share this.

And though the man is tired of words and the way they lead him down paths he hadn't intended, reveal to him things he hadn't planned to say—what he hadn't expected and what he finds—the man beside the man writes that it is in this selfsame moment of being tired that words and what they tell the man are what sustain him. The wonder of finding out what the man hadn't planned to know is what makes him write more.

While the man still wonders if he has wasted his life entertaining himself so many idle hours, and while the man still wonders who, once he's dead, will read what he has written, the man beside the man writes the truth: Oh Grampa, so silly.

The man beside the man writes that there is no posterity. There is only story. There is only a writer, and the writing of that story, and of another, of all of them, as many as he can tell, until he is dead and there will be no worry over words. Or readers.

There is no posterity. There is no one reading what he has written after he is dead. There is only living to tell the tale.

Here, the man writes. Now.

Read this.

CODA

As I tried to examine in the essay here, my initial impetus for this came one afternoon as I walked from the living room into the kitchen and glanced at the rows of books on our bookshelves. But this was long before being invited by Patrick Madden to contribute to the book you now have in your hands, and it was only after his asking that I began to think of which essay I might try to approach. What drew me to "Of Giving the Lie" was its monumental, nearly iconic quote "I have no more made my book than my book has made me." But once I got going, thinking about my own books and trying to write this essay, that line of Montaigne's was set to the side in favor of this business of wasting my life, and my words being used to wrap fish.

Back to these bookshelves: We bought the house in 2007, when I ended my time editing the *Southern Review* at LSU and moved back home to Charleston. And though we loved the place from the moment we walked in with the realtor, we just never realized there were no shelves for our books, and so we had to have these built after the fact. They take up two walls, stretch twelve feet high, line even the walls above the doorway (we need a library ladder to get to the top shelves), so walking from the living room into the kitchen is always a kind of baptism of books. Both physically and metaphysically, then, I am with books always, always reading them, always thinking about them, always shaping my own in my head, seeing the next on the horizon; I am, with both the books I am writing and those I am reading, always wondering about what will happen *next*.

That is, I seldom think about the past as regards books, especially about those books I have written (some books I've read have ended up haunting me forever, which is, to my way of thinking, a good thing, but those books are very few). On this day, though, there passed in me a thought—and I let it take harbor in me, fester actually, until I started hatching how the heck to write about what I was thinking about: who will read *my* books when I am dead? I only know story—really—and so I simply tried to enjamb three of them, one old in me (the Jordan story), one a little less old (the evening with the count), and finally, one that hadn't even yet happened when I started writing this (that whole episode with my granddaughter reminding me how silly these preoccupations with age and posterity really are).

Perhaps what I admire most about Montaigne is his apparent whimsy, the way an essay can steer one way, then another, then even another, but finally arrive by the essay's end at someplace surprising and yet seemingly ordained. That's what I was striving for in simply starting this with an old story, then bridging that one to the next with my worries about age and books and who will read me, ending with my birthday. I was trying, in writing this essay about this very thing—being the man beside me—to be the man beside me, that one who must bear witness to the truth that posterity doesn't matter, instead of pandering to these phantom worries over matters that will be out of my hands after I'm dead. I hope the offering made herewith does at least a decent job of paying homage to M. Montaigne. If not, please feel free to rip out these pages of mine and wrap your butter with them.

11

Of Friendship

VIVIAN GORNICK

One soul in two bodies
MONTAIGNE, "OF FRIENDSHIP"

In the centuries when most marriages were contracted out of economic and
social considerations, friendship was written about with the kind of emotional
extravagance that we, in our own time, have reserved for an ideal of romantic
attachment. Montaigne, for instance, writing in the sixteenth century of his
long dead, still mourned friend Étienne de La Boétie, tells us that they were
"one soul in two bodies." There was nothing his friend did, Montaigne says, not
an act performed or a word spoken, for which "I could not immediately find
the motive." Between the two young men communion had achieved perfection.
This shared soul "pulled together in such unison," each half regarding the other
with "such ardent affection," that "in this noble relationship, services and bene-
fits, on which other friendships feed," were not taken into account. So great was
the emotional benefit derived from the attachment that favors could neither be
granted nor received. Privilege, for each of the friends, resided in being allowed
to love rather than in being loved.

This is language that Montaigne does not apply to his wife or his children,
his colleagues or his patrons—all relationships that he considers inferior to a
friendship that develops not out of sensual need or worldly obligation but out
of the joy one experiences when the spirit is fed; for only then is one closer to
God than to the beasts. The essence of true friendship for Montaigne is that in
its presence "the soul grows refined."

Montaigne's friend died young, at a time when it was easy for the two men to imagine themselves lifelong intimates. What wisdom, I have often wondered, would the great essayist have given us had they lived on together into the maturity that, inevitably, would have produced divisions of taste, experience, and ambition capable of complicating not only Montaigne's perception of "soul refinement" but that of friendship itself.

I once had a friend with whom I was certain I would grow old. My friendship with Emma was not one I would have described as Montaigne describes his with La Boétie, but now that I am thinking about it I see that, in important ways, it is analogous. Ours was an attachment that, if it did not refine the soul certainly nourished the inquiring spirit so well that, for a very long time indeed, in the other's presence we each experienced our expressive selves more fully than either of us had before, or I have since.

At school Emma and I had both been prime examples of those very intelligent girls whose insecurities equip them with voices that routinely generate the kind of scorn and judgment bound to isolate one from one's fellows. In our early thirties these formidable defenses had altered sufficiently that each of us was suddenly able to see herself in the other. Self-recognition—a thrilling occurrence at this point in our lives—worked a kind of magic between us, and in no time at all we were meeting or speaking at least three times a week. The open road of friendship everlasting seemed spread out before us.

To the uninitiated eye, this vitality of connection between me and Emma might have appeared puzzling. She was a bourgeois through and through, I a radical feminist who owned nothing. She had married, become a mother, and pursued graduate work; I was twice divorced, had remained childless, and lived the marginal existence of a working freelancer. Beneath these separating realities, however, lay a single compelling influence that drew us irresistibly toward one another.

True, Emma had embraced the family, I had rejected the family; she endorsed the middle class, I loathed the middle class; she dreaded loneliness, I endured it. Yet the longer we went on meeting and talking, the more clearly we saw that to know what these "choices" meant—that is, to understand how we had come to be as we were—was for both of us the central enterprise. When we spoke together of the exhaustion of love and the anguish of work, the smell of children and the taste of solitude, we were really speaking of the search for the self and the confusion that came with the mere construction of the phrase: what *was* the self? where was it? how did one pursue it? abandon or betray it? These were the questions that concentrated our deepest concerns. Consciousness as a first value, we each discovered, was what we together were exploring.

The absorption grew in us day by month by year, fed by the excitement of abstract thought joined to the concreteness of daily life. In conversation with one another, we both felt the strength of context imposed on the quotidian. The more we explored the theoretical in service to the immediate—a chance encounter on the bus, a book just begun or just finished, a dinner party gone bad—the larger the world seemed to grow. The everyday became raw material for a developing perspective that was acquiring narrative drive: sitting in a living room, eating in a restaurant, walking in the street, we were traveling without leaving home.

We went on like this for nearly ten years. And then one day the bond between us began to unravel. I had a bad exchange with Emma's husband, and she saw it as divisive. She read a book by a writer I prized, and I was stung by her scorn. We each made a new friend whose virtues the other failed to respond to. That winter I could barely pay the rent, and Emma's preoccupation with redecorating her place got under my skin. Suddenly the adventure we had made of our differing circumstances seemed to be going sour: my cozy apartment felt sterile, her amiable husband a fool. Who *are* we? I remember thinking. What are we doing? And why are we doing it together?

Slowly but inexorably, the enterprise of mind and spirit to which our friendship had been devoted began to lose strength before the growing encroachment of the opposing sympathies out of which our lives were actually fashioned. Like an uncontrollable growth that overtakes a clearing in the forest, the differences moved in on us. The friendship that had for so long generated excitement, and exerted power, was now experienced as a need that had run its course. Overnight, it seemed, it took one long stride and moved from the urgent center to the exhausted margin. Just like sexual infatuation, I recall thinking idly one morning as I lay in bed staring at the ceiling. And then, somewhat dazedly, I realized, "That's right. That's exactly what this is like. Sexual infatuation."

In the end, my friendship with Emma did prove to bear a striking resemblance to romantic love. The passion that had flared between us now seemed an equivalent of the kind of erotic feeling that dies of its own intensity when, in the goodness of time, one begins to realize that much of oneself is not being addressed by this attraction of the senses. The irony here was that sexual love usually fails because of an insufficiency of shared sensibility, whereas sensibility was what Emma and I had had in abundance. Yet now I saw that in time, which makes fools of us all, sensibility alone could also prove insufficient.

Some twenty-five years later the phone rings in my apartment in New York. It's Marcus with a question about an editor he wants to send someone to. I answer his question, and we chat. I hear the bright hard edge of depression in his voice. I hear him struggling against it. I help by talking us into a conversation that interests us both. In ten minutes he's been pulled out of his own black hole. He's laughing now quite genuinely. Warmed by the effort and the success, I say, "Let's have dinner." "Sure," he responds, with only a flicker of hesitation. "Let's see now." He's looking at his book. "God, this is awful!" I can hear the anxiety seeping back into his voice, the panic he feels at being forced to make a date. "How about two weeks from Friday?" "Fine," I say, only a second or two off course myself.

Later in the day the phone rings again. It's Laura. "You won't believe this," she says, and proceeds to entertain us both with the story she's called to tell me. Laura is all solid contact from the moment her voice hears mine. She tells the story, we both laugh, many sentences of psychological wisdom pass between us. "Let's have dinner," I say. "Absolutely," she says. "Let's see now." She too looks at her book. "Omigod, this is ridiculous. I can't do it until late next week. Waitaminnit, waitaminnit. There's something here I can change. How about Thursday?"

There are two categories of modern friendship: those in which people are enlivened by each other and those in which people must be enlivened to be with each other. In the first category one clears the decks to be together. In the second one looks for an empty space in the schedule.

Sometimes I am Laura, sometimes Marcus. Sometimes I am both in the course of a single day. I am eager to remain Laura. She is always responsive to human contact. To be responsive is to feel expressive. I value the expressiveness above all else. Or so I say. But there are moments, even days, when any disinterested observer might justly conclude that I, like Marcus, seem awash in my own melancholy, swamped by the invading instability, suffering a failure of nerve to which I seem devoted.

New York friendship is an education in the struggle between devotion to the melancholy and attraction to the expressive. The pavements are filled with those of us who crave the latter but can't shake off the former—and so are the rooms in which we meet.

At a New Year's party Jim comes rushing toward me. Sarah nods and turns away. A year ago I was tight with one, two years ago with the other. Tonight I realize I haven't seen him in three months, her in six. A woman who lives three blocks from me appears, her eyes shimmering. "I miss you!" she breathes wistfully, as though we're lovers in wartime, separated by forces beyond our control. Yes, I nod and move on. We'll embrace happily, me and all these people: not a glance of grievance, not a syllable of reproach among us. And, indeed, there is no call for grievance. We've all simply shifted position in the pattern of intimate exchange. Many of us will meet now more often by accident than by design: in a restaurant, on the bus, at a loft wedding. Ah, but here's someone I haven't seen in years. Suddenly a flare of intensity, and we're meeting once a week for the next six months.

Never before in history has so much educated intelligence been expended on the idea of the irreplaceable self, and never before has inner flux allowed us to replace each other so easily. Our friendships are governed by an attention we pay to the most minute of psychological discomforts that makes us, ourselves, the instrument of contingent rather than essential attachment.

In the 1790s Samuel Taylor Coleridge worshipped an idea of friendship that embodied the same Aristotelian ideal to which Montaigne had subscribed two hundred years earlier. Living as he did at a time when attachment of the spirit through friendship was yearned for among persons of sensibility, its frequent failure to materialize made Coleridge suffer, but the pain did not threaten his faith; not even when he lost the friendship that defined all others.

Coleridge and Wordsworth met in 1795 when they were, respectively, twenty-three and twenty-five years old, thereby beginning a connection, one of the most famous in literary history, that is a moving demonstration of what happens when, for a crucial piece of time, two friends see themselves writ twice as large as life in the eyes of the adoring other—and then no longer do.

Wordsworth, grave and thin-skinned and self-protective, was steadied even then by an inner conviction of his own coming greatness as a poet; Coleridge, on the other hand, brilliant and explosive and self-doubting to the point of instability, was already into opium. Anyone except themselves could see that they were bound to come a cropper. In 1795, however, a new world, a new poetry, a new way of being was forming itself, and at that moment both Wordsworth and Coleridge, each feeling the newness at work in himself, saw proof of its existence reflected in the person of the other. In that reflection they saw confirmed their own best selves.

The infatuation lasted a bit more than a year and a half. At the end of that time the chaos within Coleridge doubled its dominion; the pride in Wordsworth stiffened into near immobility. The person each had been for nearly two years—the one who had basked in the unbroken delight of the other—was no more. It wasn't exactly that they were returned to the persons they had been before; it was only that never again would either feel his own best self in the presence of the other.

One's own best self. For centuries this was the key concept behind any essential definition of friendship: that one's friend is a virtuous being who speaks to the virtue in oneself. How foreign is such a concept to the children of the therapeutic culture! Today, after a century of Freud and Marx and modernism, we do not look to see, much less affirm, our best selves in one another. To the contrary, it is the openness with which we admit to our emotional incapacities—the fear, the anger, the humiliation—that excites contemporary bonds of friendship. Nothing draws us closer to one another than the degree to which we face our deepest shame openly in one another's company. Coleridge and Wordsworth dreaded such self-exposure; we adore it, because it is the great illusion of our culture that what we confess to is who we are. If only it were that easy!

When Emma and I were disintegrating, I recalled William James having once speculated that our inner lives were perpetually in transition. The transitions, he announced dramatically, were the reality; our experience, he concluded, "lives in the transitions." This is a piece of information difficult to absorb, much less accept, yet transparently persuasive. How else account for the mysterious shift in emotional sympathies that, at any hour of any ordinary day, brings connections that seemed rock-solid to a sudden startling end—or, conversely, makes a slight acquaintanceship of long standing just as suddenly blossom into full-fledged intimacy. Why do these life-changing events take place then, at that particular moment, and at no other? Why not the month before, or the year after? What is it within ourselves that has "mutated," causing attachments whose permanency we would have sworn by to change character so often with little or no warning?

The withdrawal of feeling in romantic love is a drama most of us are familiar with, and therefore feel equipped to explain. In thrall to the intensity generated by passion, we invest love with transformative power; imagine ourselves about to be made new, even whole, under its influence. When the expected transformation fails to materialize, the hopes interwoven with the infatuation do a desperate dissolve. The adventure of having felt known in the presence of the lover now bleeds out into the anxiety of feeling exposed to a stranger.

Although only rarely do friends consciously imagine themselves, as lovers regularly do, the instrument of one another's salvation, unconsciously they share the longing. In both friendship and love, the expectation that one's expressive self will flower permanently in the presence of the beloved other is key. Upon that flowering all is posited. The relationship fails, in friendship just as in love, when that expressive self ceases to feel itself served.

Of all the failures in intimacy I have suffered, the one I shared with Emma administered the shock to the nervous system from which I don't think I ever recovered. This was the relationship that fostered the greatest hope of disproving what I always suspected in the farthest recesses of my being: that the urge toward stable intimacy is inevitably threatened by the equally great, if not greater urge toward destabilization. One seeks love out of the conviction that, whether erotic or platonic, love alone has the strength to defeat the ever-present drive toward self-division. I will mourn the loss of Emma's friendship as long as I live.

CODA

Montaigne's essay on friendship—like all his essays, a kind of meander through the essayist's loosely connected associations to the subject—was particularly unforgettable for the single penetrating observation he made on the difference between the essential and the contingent in all human relations, but particularly in the one between friends. When the time came for me to think seriously about friendship myself, this insight of his became the pearl shining through a mass of inchoate thought and feeling. Over the years it has remained a kind of touchstone through all my own meanderings on the subject.

12

Of Idleness

STEVEN CHURCH

> If we do not keep [our minds] busy with some particular subject
> which can serve as bridle to reign them in, they charge ungovernably
> about, ranging to and fro over the wastelands of our thoughts. . . .
> Then, there is no madness, no raving lunacy, which such agitations
> do not bring forth.
>
> MONTAIGNE, "OF IDLENESS"

In Charles Moore's iconic black-and-white photograph, Coretta looks on stoically, lips parted, hands clasped in front, as her husband Martin Luther King has his right arm bent behind his back by a police officer in a tall hat. Someone unseen, outside the frame, places a hand on Coretta's left arm, as if to comfort or contain her. Martin pitches forward over a counter, leaning to his right, his left hand splayed out for support on the polished surface. He wears a light-colored suit and tie, a panama hat with a black band. The force of the officer's grip has nearly yanked the jacket off his right shoulder. The officer's left hand pushes against Martin's left side, bunching up his jacket, shoving him forward, bending him over the counter. Another officer stands behind Martin's right shoulder, but you can see only the top of his hat and his right arm resting casually on the counter. A hatless white officer stands behind the counter, and our perspective peers over his right shoulder into Martin's face. He doesn't look pained. Resigned perhaps, sadly familiar with this sort of treatment. The man behind the counter seems to be reaching out toward Martin with his left hand to take something or give something (a piece of paper perhaps) as his right arm blurs at the bottom edge of the frame. Martin, his eyes pulled all the way to the

PHOTOGRAPH BY CHARLES MOORE, REPRODUCED BY PERMISSION OF THE
ESTATE OF CHARLES MOORE AND BLACK STAR PUBLISHING CO., INC.

right, is either looking at the man behind the counter or at someone else we can't
see. The date is September 3, 1958, in the Montgomery, Alabama, county court-
house. Martin Luther King Jr. is there to support his longtime friend Ralph Abernathy, a Baptist minister testifying in the trial of a deranged man charged with
chasing Abernathy down the street with a hatchet. In the photo King has just
been arrested for loitering. He will spend fourteen days in jail as punishment
for his crime. The strange thing is that in Moore's photograph it is not Martin
or Coretta who looks afraid. It's the policemen who appear flustered and scared.
The photo is superficially silent. But you can still see how blurry with fear they
are of his power and presence, quivering before his radical subjectivity in that
space.

Loitering is not particularly difficult or physically demanding. It doesn't, at first
blush, appear revolutionary or criminal. Consider that "loiter" is an intransitive
verb. There is no object to it. It is all subject and subjectivity. To loiter requires

simply that you stand around or sit aimlessly, without purpose, to choose a space because it happens to be in the shade, or just happens to be there. Anywhere. The key to pure loitering—the most honest embodiment of the word's spirit—is of course to do nothing. Absolutely nothing.

But it has become bigger than that. Revolutionary. To do nothing now in the name of loitering is also to repurpose in the name of purposeless an otherwise purposed space. And we are surrounded by purposed spaces and purposed people. To loiter, then, is a kind of Zen-like appropriation, a subjective possession of objective, though often marginal space; and perhaps this is enough to make it revolutionary, enough to threaten those who are invested in the purposing or owning of such space. It worries us when someone does nothing, even when they seem to be doing nothing on a street corner, on a roadway median, in an alley or some other marginal space. We're so busy, so purposeful; in our world of increasing technological connection, we're always engaged in some activity. It's hard for us to understand the idleness of loitering. It frightens us. On some level we tend to internalize the aphorism "Idle hands are the Devil's playthings" and associate the nothingness of loitering with all manner of bad or dangerous possibilities.

One of history's greatest loiterers, Michel de Montaigne, the father of the modern essay and a man who spent a great deal of time walking around his estate and thinking about the stuff of everyday life, even recognized the danger of too much idleness. In his essay "Of Idleness" he acknowledges that he'd "retired to my estates, determined to devote myself as far as I could to spending what little life I have left quietly and privately," giving his mind the "greatest favour" of "total idleness," but instead found that "it gives birth to so many chimeras and fantastic monstrosities, one after another, without order or fitness." Montaigne uses the extended metaphor of a horse throughout the short, two-page essay to define the tendency of a purposeless mind to run wild, "ranging to and fro over the wasteland of our thoughts," and gives us perhaps a brief exploration of why we find loitering so full of dangerous potential. It gives the mind room to roam, to dabble in madness.

Part of the trouble is also that it is nearly impossible to distinguish "doing nothing" from "doing something." Even when my car's engine is idling, the car still creeps forward, still moves. People who truly loiter assume a kind of vague and amorphous but still frightening potentiality. They become idling engines in stasis. The ambiguity of their physical and moral position troubles us. After all, when is any one of us actually doing nothing in any space? Have you ever truly done *nothing*?

Montaigne was clearly able to overcome the mad pull of idleness and bridle his runaway mind enough to write and publish well over a hundred essays. Even when I putter around my yard or sit on my front porch, thinking about whatever I'm currently writing or reading, am I not still doing something, even if that something is only thinking? Essays composed and constructed often in such moments of idleness where I have the space and time to do nothing become a kind of harness as well, a way to focus my ranging mind. But as long as I'm essaying in my house, or at my desk, even in a coffee shop or a bar, I'm still using the space with an intent that seems to fit the space. I wonder how long I could loiter on my street corner, just stand around thinking about an essay I'm working on, watching people and traffic, without drawing unwanted attention to myself. I wonder if that time would be different if I lived in a wealthier, gated community on the north side of town, one of those places where they don't really have street corners. What if I stood around in the middle of a cul-de-sac and told anyone who asked that I was just thinking about some stuff? How would my idleness be perceived by others? Or if I lived in a more poverty-stricken, gang-controlled neighborhood in a different part of Fresno, would my loitering embody a different potentiality? Of course it would. I probably wouldn't have the luxury of idle rumination. The objective nothingness in my loitering would allow my subjectivity to be shaped to the expectations of the context.

Loitering, then, as an idea is as undefined, abstract, and subjective as happiness or suffering. It can be adapted and appropriated, shaped to fit the situation; and then laws or ordinances or signs that attempt to regulate loitering are the ontological equivalent of ordinances regulating or controlling happiness or suffering. They are perhaps the most common legislative manifestations of the conflict between subjective intent and attempts at objective measurement of said intent.

Sometimes I think about this when I visit the Food King market in my neighborhood, a subjectively happy place, a true neighborhood convenience store. It feels like home to me. I don't even care that it costs me nearly twenty dollars for two six-packs of beer. The brothers Mo and Najib, who own the Food King, immigrated to the United States from Yemen and are exceedingly nice to me, always calling me by name. They know *most* of their customers by name. Sometimes Najib's bespectacled son sits behind the counter working on his homework. Mo and Najib often talk about the weather, and they're usually listening to NPR on the radio. But they also have prominent No Loitering signs posted on the front of the store and a bank of video monitors that allow them to keep an eye on every part of their property. You have about as much time to linger in front of the Food King as you do in front of an airport. Pause too long and you will be hustled along.

Mo and Najib have to deal with challenges I can barely imagine. Fresno is a dangerous place filled with desperate people. Nobody really denies this reality. We just live with it. But Mo and Najib run a tight ship, more than most places. They keep their store clean and free of the crowds that loiter around elsewhere. They never hesitate to chase off the street kids and the panhandlers, the tweakers and the prostitutes; and I have to admit that I appreciate this, that it makes me feel somewhat safer as a consumer.

When I asked Mo one day about his No Loitering signs and how he enforces the rule, he told me that he just tells any loiterers to move along, and if they don't move, he might threaten to call the police.

"But would they come?" I asked.

"Yeah, sure. Maybe. But if you just mention the police, they mostly move along."

"And if they don't?"

"If they don't, I take my stick out there and I tell them, 'I'm gonna count to three and then I'm gonna hit you with this stick.'"

Mo didn't show me his stick, but I guessed it was some kind of baton. I didn't doubt his conviction. Mo meant business. To him the issue was all black and white, no gray area, no room for interpretation. This was his property, his Food King, and he was in charge of defining loitering in this subjective space. He also told me he had a gun under the counter if it came to that.

Perhaps the most extreme example of the threatening potentiality of loitering is in the context of an elementary school, an exaggeratedly purposed and morally charged public space. If you stand around outside the playground fence of a school, just stand there long enough, most likely your loitering will be seen as a threat and you will be confronted by authority figures. In Fresno all the schools are surrounded by six-foot chain-link safety fencing. If you're loitering around a school, regardless of the intent behind your idleness (maybe you're studying the architecture of schools for a class), you might be arrested or at least hassled and hustled along. There are signs posted everywhere forbidding all manner of activities, including dog walking, golfing, model airplane flying, and loitering; and as a parent of elementary school children, I'm glad to see those signs when we take our dog there for walks. I don't really care if you're flying model airplanes at my daughter's school, but I do care if you're loitering there without apparent purpose. It doesn't matter to me if you're innocently researching something for a novel or an essay, maybe snapping photos with your iPhone, I just want you to move along and take your subjectivity elsewhere. An elementary school is a place where the objective truth of the context overwhelms the subjective truth of anyone who moves through the space. Your rights are necessarily limited there, and it doesn't end at the fence. The rights-defining power of an elementary school space extends well beyond the fences, past the sidewalks, into the streets, where the rules of driving are more stringent and more morally charged, and even further beyond into surrounding neighborhoods, where legal penalties for things like narcotics trafficking are increased. In such spaces the objective meaning of the place overwrites your subjective intent.

It is also the vague undefined nature of loitering combined with the impossibility of truly knowing or measuring subjective intent that has allowed anti-loitering laws and ordinances to be used as a weapon against civil disobedience. Martin Luther King was arrested because anti-loitering laws on the books in Montgomery allowed the police, regardless of the facts of that day, to define King's presence, to shape his intent into something criminal, something they could use to control him. He was just attending a public trial. But anti-loitering laws allowed the police to arrest him for being black in a white space.

Attempts to criminalize loitering have been used more recently to try and control gang activity, drug sales, panhandling, and prostitution, as well as to control populations of homeless people and protesters in the nationwide Occupy movement. These efforts, though temporarily successful, are often doomed to failure, perhaps because of the very nature of loitering itself. Courts have recognized that anti-loitering laws can encourage racial profiling and police abuse of marginalized groups. Legislating against loitering is like legislating against nothingness.

In February 2012 New York City settled a class action lawsuit brought on behalf of thousands of citizens arrested over the years on anti-loitering charges that had been deemed unconstitutional. The city's efforts to control loitering over a span of thirty years will ultimately cost them fifteen million dollars and require them to expunge thousands of arrests and convictions. There is little evidence to suggest, however, that this will change the way anti-loitering laws and ordinances are used to control marginalized populations in this country. We are simply too purposed and possessive of our objective spaces, too frightened by the potential of loiterers.

In other communities, perhaps due to the challenges of defining and enforcing anti-loitering ordinances, business owners are turning to less obviously confrontational, more passive, subjective, and subliminal deterrence methods. They're turning to sound warfare as a way to avoid the whole messy enterprise of objectively measuring and legislating against subjective intent. Perhaps they're doing this because it protects them from images of abuse and violence and the cultural resonance created by such pictures.

The Mosquito was invented in Wales several years ago.

Moving Sound Technologies has been marketing and selling the Mosquito throughout North America. Many cities, municipalities, school districts, and parks boards use the Mosquito to combat vandalism.

The patented Mosquito is a small speaker that produces a high frequency sound much like the buzzing of the insect it's named after.

This high frequency can be heard by young people 13 to 25 years old.

The latest version of the Mosquito is called the MK4 Multi-Age. It has two different settings, one for teenagers 13–25 years and one setting for all ages. When it is set to 17KHz the Mosquito can only be heard by teenagers approximately 13 to 25 years of age.

When set to 8 KHz the Mosquito can be heard by all ages.

In case you thought Mosquito is all about annoying sound that would force the loiterers to run for cover, you would be in for a pleasant surprise!

*The Music Mosquito is a complete music system that will relay Royalty **free** Classical or Chill-out music that would keep the teenagers away to some extent. Mosquito has a strong steel body . . .*

Mosquito anti loitering device is a handy option to suppress vandalism and the issues of graffiti aggressively.

The Mosquito Device can help with Teen Loitering Problems

Mosquito has a strong steel body . . .

The Mosquito Device can help with Gang Loitering Problems

Mosquito has a strong steel body . . .

The Mosquito Device can help with Vandalism Problems

Mosquito has a strong steel body . . .

The Mosquito Device can help with Grafitti Problems

Mosquito has a strong steel body . . .

At night now in Fresno or in your city they might gather beneath the glow of a streetlamp, lurking around its penumbral cone of light. Packs of teenagers. Black kids. Brown kids. White kids. Brawny boys in baggy clothes, hats, and team jerseys; pale, inked kids wearing white wife-beaters; girls in skinny jeans, high heels, and higher hair; or a population of bearded men smiling through meth-snaggled teeth, shuffling burnouts and tweakers with face tattoos, gang bangers with bulldog paws or red lips painted permanently on their necks; or maybe it's those ubiquitous kids at a suburban mall wearing polo shirts and skinny jeans, high-top sneakers and puffy Tommy Hilfiger jackets, and they're loitering around Jamba Juice or the movie theater, around your neighborhood school, or outside your business every night. These are the loiterers, the idle enemies of consumption and purpose. These are the targets of subjective warfare.

In my hometown, the high school kids from outlying rural communities used to drive to downtown Lawrence, park their trucks backwards in the diagonal spaces along Massachusetts Street and set up lawn chairs in the beds. They watched the rest of us stroll past as if we were specimens in museums. Often we looked the part. Often things were said. Often there were fights. Often there was litter and vandalism. Several merchants installed strobe lights in the windows of their stores, leaving them on all night long as a kind of light deterrent, a passive form of loitering enforcement. It worked, too. After a while nobody wanted to park or linger in front of those shops. There were fewer fights there, less litter and vandalism. But the lights also just made the business owners seem kind of mean and intolerant.

It doesn't matter, really, what loiterers look like for the purposes of the Mosquito or for a strobe light. Such passive forms of loitering deterrence don't discriminate on the basis of color, class, caste, or clothing choice. They cannot violate rights in part because we have few clear legal protections against noise or light pollution, despite its obvious influence on subjective experiences of happiness or suffering. Noise might not violate your rights. It can't bend you over a counter and handcuff you, but it can violate your space and subjectivity. It can make it hard to think, even hard to do nothing.

What matters to the Mosquito is not the motivations of the loiterer, but simply that the subjective loitering body courses with blood and has ears with which to listen. In this way it is much like a bomb. A very smart bomb. What makes the Mosquito insidious is how it targets the age of the loiterer, his youth and the way his brain processes sound. Imagine a bomb that only wipes out people of a certain age, a bomb that targets only the young. The Mosquito doesn't care about the kinetic potential for chaos, for unpredictable behavior, inherent in their stasis. It doesn't care about anything, because the Mosquito is a machine designed to create an automatic physiological response, because its intrusion into your subjective internal space is indiscriminate and subtly violent.

The danger of loiterers at rest is that bodies will remain at rest until acted upon by an outside force. The danger is the malicious pull of idle hands toward evil deeds. And the popular imagination associates loitering—a behavior defined specifically by its purposelessness—with all sorts of bad or illicit purposes, most notably property crimes like vandalism and graffiti, as well as with gang activity and prostitution. And because there is often little else for them to do, no other place for them to gather, teenagers—the ultimate in-betweeners—are regular offenders of anti-loitering efforts and ordinances. By their very nature, teenagers embody the conflict between objective rules and expectations and subjective intent. They live perpetually in the liminal space between outside rules and their internal wills. Teenagers are all subjectivity, all solipsistic fervor; they are in essence loitering between childhood and adulthood, embodying that marginalized space with intent that is often inscrutable to those of us living outside that space.

In my neighborhood, the loitering teens move between a series of spots, these odd sort of in-between places like the island of a parking lot behind Starbucks and Bobby Salazar's Mexican restaurant, or someone's yard, perhaps the community garden, up against the brick wall of the Brass Unicorn and the Starline or in the side yard of an apartment building on Moroa Avenue. You won't find them outside the Food King, but nearby in side streets and alleyways, lounging in various liminal spaces.

Much to the chagrin of many Fresno shoppers, we also find loitering teens on the wealthy north side of town at the clay-colored strip mall called River Park, a palace to consumerism and multinational corporations that, in an effort to curb loitering, not long ago tried to ban unaccompanied teenagers from the premises. That didn't work so well. A parent or other objectively recognized adult had to be with any teenager on the premises. It wasn't clear how the mall intended to enforce this, if they planned to randomly ID anyone who looked young enough to be a teenager. Perhaps they simply should have installed Mosquito anti-loitering devices in the same places they've installed Muzak speakers and security cameras. We fear teenagers not because of their loitering itself—that gray penumbral area between right and wrong—but because the very act (or inaction) suggests the possibility for harm, for mayhem and destruction. We fear their unbridled youth and all of its sublime potentiality. We fear their marginalized status because it lives outside the boundaries of our control.

One day not long ago as I was driving home from lunch with a friend, I took a side street that parallels a major thoroughfare, a street known as a popular hangout for the Fresno street kids and the homeless. A homeowner who has been working on remodeling a large house that backs up to the street recently installed a painted wooden fence and stacked-stone planters surrounding mature pomegranate trees. He's created a lovely little oasis of landscape architecture that would appeal to nearly anyone's aesthetic; and as I drove past this oasis, I saw a loose pack of loitering teens lounging around the planters, smoking, pawing at each other, laughing, and doing nothing. All of them. Loitering. Just sitting there, doing nothing. And I felt this momentary urge to yell at them or drive them away somehow, but I wasn't sure why. Perhaps it was jealousy. Perhaps it was fear.

Unless I'm writing or reading, I have trouble sitting still for ten minutes. I can't imagine doing it for two or ten hours. I wondered if the homeowner might want to think about getting the Mosquito anti-loitering device, if he might want to agitate their space and send out high-pitched squeals of deterrent noise. I thought this might be something that I would do if I owned the house; but even as I thought it, I cringed at the idea, the invasion and violation of space, as well as the aesthetic and moral cruelty of creating an otherwise appealing place that would be simultaneously physiologically repulsive, a space whose 17 KHz of Mosquito noise would hurt the ears of young people.

These days when teenagers loiter across the street from our house, making out or smoking weed from a can or a pipe or a blunt-wrap, I mostly ignore them. Some days I want to tell them to move along or to just smoke somewhere else. Some days I want to warn them that other people aren't so understanding, that the police often patrol our street since it's so close to the high school. But the most I ever do, if I'm out front with my kids, is give the teenagers a hard stare, maybe a wave to let them know I see them, to suggest they might move along.

I've thought about calling the police, but the Fresno police frighten me more than loitering teenagers. They shoot people. Pretty regularly. I don't want these kids to get shot or even arrested. And besides, I don't really want to be *that* guy—the asshole neighbor who calls the cops on kids. The truth is they're not hurting anyone except maybe themselves. They're just hanging around because they can, because they have nowhere else to go. My friends and I did similar stuff in high school. We used to drive out into the Kansas countryside, down empty gravel roads, to find space where we could smoke or drink. These kids like to linger against the tall fence along my neighbor's side yard and sit beneath the overhanging tree on the stacked railroad ties. It's only a block from Fresno High School, away from the crush of other kids and just beyond the boundaries of school space. It seems safe enough, like a place where they can loiter in peace.

Who am I to deny them this space?

I watch them sometimes and I think about Mo and his stick, his gun under the counter. I think about the Mosquito and I wonder how I would react if the teenagers crossed the street, crossed the line and started loitering in my yard, if they even got close to my daughter and invaded my subjective space.

I'm not sure I would even count to three.

I like to think I'm a long way from those white officers in Moore's photograph, those agitated and frightened white men who pressed King against
the counter, twisting his arm behind his back, arresting him for eternity in the
objective space of that everlasting image. But I realize I'm also guilty. I've let
my own subjective fear shape the way I define loitering. I've let my imagination
carry me away, let my own context—home and family, children and dog, yard
and garden—condition the meaning of the teenagers' nothingness and I've let
it color their lingering at the periphery of my space. The street is the line, I tell
myself. It's a wide and fuzzy boundary between us. But it is a boundary.

One day a boy crossed the line. He approached the house. The kids were in
the front yard. My girlfriend met him at the driveway. I'd gone inside for a minute and came out to see her walking back toward the garage. She moved with
purpose. I followed her. The boy waited at the end of the driveway.

"What's up?" I asked.

"He wants to borrow a soccer ball," my girlfriend said with a smile as she
walked past me down the driveway and tossed him the ball. I felt my blood cool,
retreating from full boil. There was no danger, no threat. There was nothing for
me to fear.

"It's okay," she said.

The boy and his three friends, another boy and two girls, set up "goals" in
the middle of the street made of wadded-up fast-food bags and wrappers. They
played soccer on the asphalt for a while, darting out of the way when cars came.
They were out there long enough for my kids and me to drift back inside. The
boys flirted shamelessly with the girls and showed off with the ball. All of them
laughed a lot. They seemed so happy. I watched them through the windows near
the front door, listening to the sounds of their youth. They moved with ease
and grace between the curbs, lingering in the in-between spaces with such sweet
purpose.

CODA

I think what I like about this short essay from Montaigne is that its message is
somewhat unexpected. Knowing a bit about him, one might assume from the
title that the essay would be a fervent defense and celebration of idleness, of his

own choices in life, when in fact it is mostly a cautionary tale, a warning against the tendency of an unbridled mind to "charge ungovernably about." I think I also appreciate the idea of subject as a kind of bridle or rein, a constraint against the mind's natural tendency to wander or, in Montaigne's iteration, to flirt with "raving lunacy." I've written several pieces in the last few years that I think of as "constraint essays." In these pieces explorations were confined to certain subjects or words or touchstones such as "blue" and "noise," or "crown" and "shoulder," or even just the word "dither." Even this essay began as an effort to understand what it means to "loiter." For me such constraints or subjects help to corral the wild ramblings of my mind, to focus their digressive energy at least into a couple of identifiable directions. Subject in an essay thus becomes not the target so much as the sight, the lens through which you see the world.

13

Against Idleness

KRISTEN RADTKE

No pilot performs his office by standing still.
MONTAIGNE, "AGAINST IDLENESS"

The Romantics saw ruins as symbolic of the art that came before them.

Aristocrats commissioned faux-collapsing temples across their estate lawns.

The Middle Ages, assumed to be the last before Christ's second coming, watched ruin as ominous reminders of more decay ahead.

Shakespeare, certainly, set many plays among them, and aging Greco-Roman statues litter the edges of Renaissance paintings by Roberti and Bellini.

When Lord Belvedere's wife moved in with his brother, Belvedere built a ruined monastery to obstruct the view of his failed marriage.

And Wordsworth epiphanized at Tintern Abbey, abandoned nearly 300 years before.

When a boy fell through a soft patch of dirt on the Esquiline hillside at the close of the 1600s, he accidentally discovered Emperor Nero's Domus Aurea, which successors had built on top of after Nero's suicide.

Raphael and Michelangelo were among those who crawled down and carved their names into the ancient Roman walls.

CASANOVA

MARQUIS DE SADE

DOMENICO GHIRLANDAIO

FILIPPINO LIPPI

And when archeologists began to uncover what'd been preserved for centuries in the underground's dampness, they put into motion the villa's slow decay.

The house next door to my childhood home had column ruin sets in the garden, made of fiberglass and resin.

And at the bottom of my best friend's fish tank was a nearly identical model.

In 2013, Detroit housed over 70,000 abandoned properties.

DESOLATE DETROIT:
THE FORSA

NATIONAL·PO

WOULD THE LAST PERSON OUT
DETROIT TURN OUT THE LIGHT

Detroit's Beautiful, Horrible

TIME

Empty Art-Deco skyscrapers and turn-of-the-century train stations quailed on street corners before traffic lights that haven't lit in years.

We call images of Detroit "perverse" because they mirror a life we recognize.

These were a people nothing like us.

These were a people who did not have what we have now.

"Of course this place is empty now," we can think in front of Angkor Wat or the Acropolis. There are no uneasy questions of morality before Mayan temples and Roman fortresses. They drank lead, or they sacrificed each other, or they ground up poisonous flowers that brought the sun god down to them.

We forget that everything will become no longer ours.

It doesn't matter that your feet are touching the ground they're touching now.

The floors will rot, the carpet will be torn out, the cement will crack and shift and be pulled from the earth, the dirt will be tilled and changed and rained away, and someday there will be nothing left that you have touched.

War comes, or quakes or wind or water, industry leaves.

Who knows which pieces will matter when we have gone and the aliens land, or a new brand of human mutates from organisms in some forgotten cave, or when the world is underwater or when there is no water. Who knows what will be significant when we have all died and moved on to whatever is waiting or not waiting.

You will have touched nothing on the earth.

So tell me then what is so vulgar in these empty high-rises.

In these calcifying rust-belt American cities.

Tell me what in these rotting hallways.

Tell me what in these bedrooms that look too much like your own.

CODA

The essay is a form for the restless, and curious, and maybe confused, and often its practitioners have to quell and nurture their impulses while they sit and sit and try to pull something out of themselves they didn't know they held inside. In "Against Idleness" Montaigne explores the roles of rulers in and out of action, declaring that no king should claim ownership of his army's victory if he did not fight on the field himself. Citing Seneca, Montaigne writes that "the ancient Romans kept their youth always standing, and taught them nothing that they were to learn sitting." Like any essayist, I've spent a lot of time studying and pondering and chasing an obsession—in this case a personal and cultural fascination with ruins. The fact that ruins are often born in the wake of dormancy is easy enough to sense. Idleness, the very state in which we must often keep our bodies in order to translate our ideas to the page, leads to decay and rot: what remains stationary begins to crumble. "The most extreme degree of courageously treating death, and the most natural," Montaigne begins the essay's final paragraph, "is to look upon it not only without astonishment but without care." Could the same not be said of ruins?

14

Of the Affection of Fathers for Their Children

ROBIN HEMLEY

> To this, such as it is, what I give it I give absolutely and
> irrevocably, as men do to their bodily children.
> MONTAIGNE, "OF THE AFFECTION OF FATHERS FOR THEIR CHILDREN"

Our children haunt us until we die, and then it is our turn to haunt them. When people are troubled, we say they have "demons," but they're not demons, only the ordinary sadness and regret that makes life so melancholy if we survive past the age of forty or so. Anyone who doesn't have regrets is most likely lying or himself a demon. We don't always feel the same about our pasts—sometimes a simple memory or an old photograph of our children, the eldest at five, dressed as Little Red Riding Hood, the other at three, dressed as the Big Bad Wolf, facing us from a distance of nearly twenty years, gives us simple joy. Other times, we contemplate what it means to see them now after so long, though they can't see us. Unlike in a stranger's photograph, we have all the context we need, too much context, which floods upon us and threatens to tear us from our fragile mooring in the present. Was this taken before or after the divorce? We wish we could reach inside and bring them to us just once more as children. Costumed now in adulthood, they can't be carried around the way they once were. We can't swing them through our legs. We can barely sit with them in a restaurant without someone thinking or us *believing* that someone thinks we're cradle robbers, the kind of man so afraid of his own mortality that he has to be with women young enough to be his daughter, but not. Some of us *are* that kind of man, or partly that man—afraid, yes, but please, we're with our daughters, not our girl-friends. And we want to hear everything about their lives, to still be included, in some way a part of them, and that's why we lean forward, barely touch our food, find their most banal comment utterly fascinating. Perhaps we're not even really listening to them, but looking for a glimpse of Red Riding Hood or the Big Bad Wolf. Who are these people seated across from us? Please, if you're holding our child, if you've devoured her whole, can you tell us at least if she's okay, if she's being well treated, if there's anything we can do for her to make this captivity more tolerable?

Some of us have married more than once, and this creates a kind of unthink-able dilemma. Should we have stuck it out with our first wife? But then, the other children we love so much would never have been born. Should we never have married the first time? But then our first children whom we love so much would never have been born. And we never would have missed them, never would have thought of them once, their oblivion only heartbreaking because now it's the last thing in the world we would wish for. And what of those poten-tial children, the children we could have yet with our wife? One more, maybe two. It's not too late, but we don't want to be one of those men whose sons and daughters are young enough to be their grandchildren. We don't want to go to the parent-teacher meetings and the talent shows and sit among the other parents young enough to be our children. And we don't want to die before our children really know us. To start haunting them so young seems cruel. Some of us whose parents died young already know this pain. We wouldn't admit this to our wives, but there are times when we can imagine ourselves the man in the restaurant sitting across from the woman young enough to be our daughter, but who isn't. Our wives are not stupid. They know this full well, though there's a tacit agreement that our glances should be brief and circumspect. It's not all about sex, about the biological imperative. Yes, we want more babies. There are more babies to be born, ever more babies, and some of them could still be ours. They're lurking in the wings. We know their potential and they, we suspect, know ours. Maybe we have always wanted a girl. Or a boy. They're remarkable, these invisible children. We care nothing for them now, but give us a good year and we won't be able to live our lives without them. We will hardly be able to imagine a time before they were born, hardly be able to bear the thought of their deaths.

But there are times we have resented them. Times when they were for Raymond Carver "a heavy and baleful presence." That's too strong, too harsh. Never baleful. He didn't feel that way, not really. He loved his two children and never should have committed those words to paper. But male writers who are also fathers, when they're feeling self-pity, that no one loves them enough, are bound to lash out, themselves heavy and baleful presences upon the world. And then they drink or smoke or practice baby-making. Was there anything ever more self-defeating if what we wanted, after all, was affection?

These children wanted nothing but our affection, and our affection was always split between them and our other children, the incorporeal ones, the ones who made us cruel, who made William Faulkner tell his daughter, Jill, "No one remembers Shakespeare's children." It's a commonplace to say that no man on his deathbed ever wished he'd spent more time at work. But men on their deathbeds have regretted what was still locked away inside them, what they suspected still lurked in the wings. The poet Lucan died reciting his own verses, as Montaigne has it: "a tender and paternal leave of his children, in imitation of the valedictions and embraces, wherewith we part from ours, when we come to die." If his corporeal children were with him at the time, Lucan might well have preferred to embrace them. But these other children he could summon to his side in his need, and they would fly to him. Our embodied children we cannot be so sure of, as King Lear learned too late.

We don't remember Lucan's daughter, alas, if he had one, but we honor Faulkner's poor daughter, who only wanted him to stop drinking, who only wanted a radio by her bed, and Faulkner wouldn't allow her even that, because this would distract him from the children he wanted to survive. We do remember Carver's children, who forgave him for what he wrote in a fit of bitterness. We do remember Montaigne's daughter, Léonor, about whom he wrote so lovingly, and how could he not, when all his other four daughters "died at nurse." No wonder he and his wife could never raise a hand against her, could not bear to correct her until she had reached upwards of five years of age, and "then words only, and those very gentle." Another reason to love Montaigne, such a good father—this is what loss will do—who never spanked Léonor, because he knew that a child's fear is not a good substitute for a child's love and respect.

Our children don't simply spring from our biological yearnings or our pens, but from our wills, our obligations, and our losses, and to these last we sometimes show the most kindness. When Faulkner's brother died in a plane crash, Faulkner adopted his brother's daughter and gave her away at her wedding. In the last five years of Montaigne's life, he adopted a young woman who felt that in his essays she had at last found a kindred spirit. She had lost her own father at a young age, and Montaigne filled this long-vacant role, their relationship as father and daughter one of the most important of his life, one that Léonor, though she had every right to resent, apparently didn't. She and Marie le Jars de Gournay became as sisters, though this new daughter was old enough to be Montaigne's mistress and apparently was not. Perhaps her acceptance of this new fully-formed sibling stemmed from her own father's kindness toward her, and her trust in him was a gift repaid.

René Descartes's daughter Francine died at the age of five of scarlet fever, but many years later, when he was summoned by the queen of Sweden to tutor her, he took passage on a ship and claimed, so the story goes, that he was traveling in the company of his daughter, Francine. The sailors had never seen Francine, and one day they decided to search for her. They found his quarters empty, but on their way out they opened a chest. Inside was a girl, or something like a girl. A mechanical doll that moved. The captain, fearing black magic, ordered the doll thrown overboard. And so Francine died a second death, and Descartes followed not long after of pneumonia. Whether the story is true can only be the subject of speculation now, but it's been told many times since his death. When it comes to our children, even the father of reason, it seems, was as helpless as the rest of us poor fathers.

This is what we want to say to our children. This is what we must say, the fathers of two kinds of children: the ones we should have loved better, or the ones who were taken away too soon. *We love you. We love you dearly. We are so thankful you have walked with us upon this earth. But we cannot always be with you. We cannot even always be with ourselves.*

CODA

I tell my students that the thing they are most afraid of writing is often what they should be writing, and it was this way for me with this assignment. It is a particularly difficult time for me because I have moved to Singapore for a new job, while my family remains in Iowa for the year. So, for the most part, I'm alone in a way that daily phone conversations do not fill.

When I started writing this essay, it was inevitable that my melancholy over being separated from my four daughters would be a large part of it. Still, I didn't want the essay to be a whiny exploration of my own situation, so I opted to take on the voice of all absent fathers, especially those who are writers. Montaigne's original essay speaks directly to the notion of a writer's works as his children, and so it seemed natural for me to go this route too, though somewhat differently. Montaigne chooses in his essay to elucidate and justify the ways in which writers consider their imagined children and perhaps prefer them to their real ones. I decided to look at this from a slightly different angle.

Several years ago, Stuart Dybek mentioned Carver's famous essay "Fires" and suggested Carver never should have written it. In the biography of Carver by Carol Sklenicka, she too wonders why Carver chose to write such a resentful essay just when his career was coming together for him. His children, it seems, forgave him for what he wrote, and Sklenicka tries to understand it in the much larger context of Carver's obvious love for his kids. Faulkner likewise was a complex writer dad, and I've long been fascinated with the cruel statement he made to his daughter, Jill. There's no doubt he was a bit of a bastard. Once, to give himself more privacy, he remodeled his home while his wife and daughter were away; when his wife returned, she was so angry she wanted to divorce him. But he was kind, too, to his late brother's daughter, and hopefully kinder at times to Jill and his wife than the above anecdote makes out. Finally, I'm fascinated by the story of Descartes's daughter. It's such an odd story, and it's impossible to know whether there's truth to it, but it encapsulates so much of what being a father means to me, to carry the loss or potential loss of our children with us at all times.

15

Of Wearing My Red Dress

[after "Of the Custom of Wearing Clothes"]

BARRIE JEAN BORICH

Someone asked a beggar, whom he saw in his shirt in the
depth of winter, as brisk and frolic as he who goes muffled up to
the ears in furs, how he was able to endure to go so? "Why Sir,"
he answered, "you go with your face bare: I am all face."

MONTAIGNE, "OF THE CUSTOM OF WEARING CLOTHES"

The red wrap dress has a copper paisley pattern and a low-cut front, décolletage framing, a little too sexy to wear to the office even though the hem falls to my knees. I wear the dress with tall boots, tights, and a good underwire bra. Men on the street, and some hard-eyed women—cops, firefighters, truck drivers—turn and look at this dress. Yes, I say the dress, not me; I phrase intentionally here, because I know what the lookers don't. I know that some days they look and other days not so much. I know the woman they see in this dress is made of a design, a bra, a posture, a stance, a mood, an attitude, and more story than body. Long-married-me wants to text my beloved to tell her I'm all dolled up, wearing the red dress, so where is she taking me to dinner? Middle-aged-diva-femme-me wants to belt out a show tune, one of those Sondheim half-bitter, half-fuck-you-I'm-still-here numbers, to acknowledge that I'm not dead yet, that the bra, the posture, the stance, the mood holding up that dress is still possible. Feminist-me wants to motion them over, those lookers with their cutting, dangerous gazes, and whisper in their ears what I assume they don't want to hear from a blond woman in a low-cut red dress. I want to tell them that they're watching a pantomime, a container for some girlie in their head, not me, and furthermore that I'm cognizant of the whole thing, both their looking and my own hyper-awareness of their slamming, starving, arousing stares. Our back and forth is a funhouse of gaze and avoidance I don't exactly invite, yet a story I have come to expect when I put on the dress.

In high school I made a list of my clothes.

One long blue floral corduroy wrap skirt that I made at a weekend sewing class, the first and last skirt I sewed myself. This was freshman year, soon after my family moved to a new school district, the autumn I tried and rejected making new friends by rejoining the Girl Scouts, a high-school-level troop I'd heard got away with not wearing the ugly green uniform. Even in their street clothes the Scouts turned out to be too much the good girls for me, but I did walk away with a cute new skirt.

One scoop-neck knit top, stretchy and pale yellow, not typical for me then. Breasts weren't in style quite the way they are now, those being the pre-implant, pre-prime-time-porn-star days. I wasn't thinking how the shirt fit my form. Rather I was drawn to the feel of the rough, clingy fabric and the contrast of subtle yellow against my olive skin and how the shirt would look while I sat at my desk, at school, in English class.

One button-front gauzy cotton shirt, red with white pinstripes. In those days the rare female newspaper reporter on television dramas wore wide-legged jeans, a loose blazer, and a pinstriped shirt unbuttoned just above the bra line. I wasn't sure I wanted to grow up to write for newspapers, these being the days when we assumed there would always be newspapers, but aside from those passive Masterpiece Theatre letter writers in corsets and poofy buns, female journalists were pretty much the only image available of women writing on TV. My red-and-white pinstriped shirt made me feel reportorial.

One turquoise concert tee with the YES band logo brought back to Chicago from that Florida airbrush shop, just off the beach. I'd watched the surfer kid working the counter apply the band logo to the T-shirt I chose off the rack, carefully positioning the image, then using a pressing machine that looked like a giant waffle iron to make the match permanent. The shirt was my consolation. This was the day after I watched my arty and art-rock-loving best girlfriend, who'd come to

Florida with me and my family at my invitation, break our music-taste pact by falling in love with a guy we met at a late-night bonfire, a southern-rock-loving party boy who immediately wanted to marry her. She said yes to the boy; I said yes back to the girls we'd planned to be.

Two pairs of broken-in jeans, because jeans, as I was never able to explain to my mother, were more necessary than shoes, and *one pair of denim overalls*, because old-fashioned painter's overalls, worn with one strap unlatched, were in style among my new friends, a small circle of brainy stoner girls from my English class. The look wasn't sexy so much as committed to relaxation and resistance to buttons, and had lots of pockets, in case we were holding.

Two bandanas, red and silver-gray, for wearing knotted around my neck when I wore the overalls and red shirt—but not the YES T-shirt, which resisted accessories. The bandanas were a useful tool, I'd find out later, when I found myself an arty and art-rock-loving boyfriend and needed to cover up my hickeys.

I don't recall listing socks and shoes and underwear in my inventory, but otherwise my apparel list was meant to be comprehensive, including sub-lists of what was missing—*one billowing circle skirt with pockets*, and *one sweater with tiny buttons*, and one more *reporter shirt in green or gold*—items I wanted but might never possess.

This accounting was meant for school, the public realm of my life as a lanky outsider teenage girl who loved reading and late-night Chicago art-rock radio and hated football and flirting and had plenty of boyfriends but just one I really liked, and couldn't figure out how to make conversation with the popular girls. I never really used the wardrobe list, or at least never went so far as to work out a formal rotation or even a laundry schedule. Rather, I applied the list by making the list. Listing was my private project, my attempt to solve my body, pages scratched out on lined paper while listening to what were then the freaky pre-electronic rock sounds of late-night Chicago FM radio, sitting on the floor surrounded by walls I'd gotten my dad to let me paint a moody pinky purple shade, making my bedroom feel like the interior of a lava lamp, my notebooks a methodology of parsing out difference and wanting, perhaps even my first attempts at writing desire, by which I mean acknowledging that what I longed for had something to do with not just selfhood but wanting to make a self who would be wanted.

As a teenager I felt my natural self had too much face—all nose and cheeks and chin, an uncomfortable balloon of me-ness, only the parts I hated showing, never the interesting stuff, the hidden stuff. By too much face I did not mean that I put myself all out, that I was fully toughened to the world. I was the opposite, too self-conscious, too often exiled from my own body—swimming an exception, training as a synchronized swimmer a rare point of synthesis, but most of the rest of the time my big bare mug smacking against high school, all that exposed nose and cheek and forehead more obstacle then revelation. The rest of my body, in contrast, felt to me a shapeless and unappreciated weight, dragging behind that blown-up face.

My school was a typical midwestern sprawl of industrial cinderblock, parking lot, and football field in the first ring of Southside suburbs, an interracial lower-middle-class mix of kids whose families were either still working in the failing steel mills or not admitting they were only a generation away from the blast furnaces. I wanted to be sharply and hotly desired in this place that had made me, my first sexual preference anyone who wanted me. The right clothing choices would give me that want-able definition, would free me from my facial frontload, would protect me from the elements, by which I mean not Chicago winters so much as the seasons of teenage discontent.

High school society broke down in the usual ways—the team kids, the arts kids, the stoner kids, the student council kids, the nobodies, all of us either clamoring toward, combining, or rejecting some membership. I never wanted to be one of the cheerleaders who wore their uniforms to class on game days, didn't envy their long middle-parted, ruler-straight hair, pleated gold miniskirts, and shined-up saddle shoes, though thinking back on those girls now, I wonder if they were not so much snotty as standoffishly self-protected. They must have guessed their perch, the skittish status that comes of not playing but watching the game, would not last much past high school. But even assuming, as we all tend to do as teenagers, that the lucky kids would stay lucky forever, I did not want what the cheerleaders had. What I wanted, like everyone, was to be pretty, to attract, but more than that I wanted to be fast and sharp and confident, my repartee smart, my sarcasm cutting, the lady reporter, fast on her feet, first on the scene, special enough to flabbergast admirers, stunning them hard, like a good punch in the nose.

My real and imagined apparel lists were a magic zone I inhabited where I was that formed and dressed-right girl, an internal country where I drifted in and out of elaborate fantasies of wearing my clothes in surprising combinations, an inner chess game of garment moves leading to even better verbal moves, reconfiguring that formlessness—which was also speechlessness. I believed my self-consciousness would vanish by means of this imagined perfect wardrobe, my big face dissolving into Chicago nights yellow-lit by the sound of the rock bands YES or King Crimson or Renaissance, all piano and flute and tarot card mystical, that self I wanted to be constantly emerging, slant-symphonic, wise, dressed.

I didn't realize then that the clothes on my list were themselves little stories— the gauzy shirt my ambitions as a writer, the corduroy wrap skirt the rejection of the Girl Scout laws, the YES T-shirt the defense against girls who would keep leaving our perfect dreams for imperfect boys. The wardrobe list was a narrative as well, but of something larger, even when the actual clothes didn't work out, no matter how well I wore them. The clothes were never just clothes, but also the story of clothes, the longing represented by clothes.

Most of us look and feel better in some clothes than others, but the problem of living has never really come down to what we're wearing. The problem has always been the body, and the ways we match up the story of our bodies and the story of what we do with our bodies. These stories are why I have a hard time pulling myself away from TV shows about clothes—clothing design shows, personal shopper shows, wardrobe makeover shows, drag competition shows. I watch some of these programs with the same passion the neighbors I see through the courtyard windows of my Chicago apartment bring to football and hockey, jumping from my chair at pinnacle moments—a last-minute hem save or that miraculously repaired seam—shouting out when I see a dress I really love, holding my hand against my heart and shaking my head when a designer makes an irreparable mistake. What was he thinking when he made that un-walkable dress with the silk organza layering that looks suffocating even on the million-dollar model's body? I keep score as if I believe any of these shows are merely about the clothes. I remind myself here of that old *Saturday Night Live* bit about Elvis Presley's Coat, where the king is long dead but his gold lamé jacket continues touring without him, shimmering from a coliseum stage while fans scream. If the coat is the star, what do we need of the body?

But even I have to admit, despite my claims for the red dress, that clothes have no stories without the body, and without the human lives that clothes both project and protect. The rich suburbanite reality TV Housewife waves her hand in front of her swaddled cleavage exclaiming that she can't cover up the girls, as the designer-garbed shoppers she's hired roll their eyes because they're just trying (they tell the audience later, via private camera) to yank this lady's taste level up a notch or two. *You look so good* the shoppers croon while their client stands in front of the mirror shaking her head because she can't find her story from within this beautiful, alien dress—pretty, but too much like the Elvis coat, shimmering only in spite of her.

A slender and simply dressed friend of mine advised me recently about ways to edit my wardrobe before my spouse Linnea and I moved from a roomy house in one city to a small apartment in another. She told me: *Just get rid of any item that doesn't make you feel amazing.* I found this is a hard rule to follow, because so many clothes carry not just stories but expectations, the first narrative threads of what I imagine could be amazing if I just took the opportunity to weave them forward. My off-white knit shirt with the shimmery surface and brown skirt with the foldover waistband I bought for work but have never once worn out the door because of the ten pounds I need to lose to make the clingy fabric work on my body; or those cotton jersey floral shirts I bought on sale because on the hanger I thought they looked chill and retro but when I wore them they were the wrong kind of way-back machine, sinking me into my old dissociative too-much-face feeling. *I hate how my body feels in this shirt* is how the scenario goes, *so I will jettison the body, release my physique into the ether, a spent fuel tank, become all face and empty shirt, until at least I can come up with an excuse to change my clothes.*

But what of jettisoning our clothes? When Linnea and I were in our mid-forties we both lost quite a bit of weight. This was weight we'd gained over nearly two decades of living together, sitting in side-by-side recliners, dressed in baggy sweats, eating Linnea's cooking and watching movies or cable TV series—my favorite was all that baked ziti we devoured while bingeing on *The Sopranos*—and first happily and then unhappily immobile together. When we first set up house, this was how we inhabited love, but looking back I have to say, we should have noticed the negative signs—the weight gain, the low energy, the slow loss of the urge to try anything new. Beware, I say now, of any enterprise that does not require changing your clothes.

Then one sodden winter we decided to return to the moving world, take on diet and exercise, lose the weight. A year later and sixty pounds lighter, I had to replace all the clothes that no longer fit me. I have tax-record photographs of all we gave away, snapshots of our fat clothes spread across the guest room bed of the house where we luxuriantly gained all that weight, image after image of the opposite of the Elvis coat, shells lacking life, detritus of a once happy time abandoned for the sake of a future still able to catch and hold the light.

I expected all that trimming away of the body to be a strip down as well, a reveal of some surprise I'd been hiding under all those big clothes, all that body. What I found instead was another story, the fable of the female body I wish I'd finished reckoning with in my twenties. After the weight loss I had new energy, longer and blonder hair, new clothes I couldn't afford when I was young and single and skinny and shopping only in thrift stores, and so immersed in my local boho lesbian coupling and uncoupling world that I was largely unaware of the relationship between wardrobes and heterosexual dating customs, inexperienced in being the recipient of the eviscerating, breast-grazing, woman-categorizing male gaze. The lesbian world may have changed in this regard since my youth, the lesbian gaze yet another story, but the way we dressed and arranged our bodies in the time Linnea and I fell in love was to me more liberatory than fraught. I was known as the lesbian with the arty haircuts and loud vintage dresses. Linnea was known as a standard attractive butch. From our first date we looked like a couple who had dressed to belong together.

A gay male friend I chatted with about this told me he thought men's sexuality is more visual than women's, which is why the gay men's world is so much more looks-oppressive than the lesbian world, which might be why I was so attracted to women at a time of life when I might have gone either way. With women I came to reject conventional definitions of beauty, embracing the body democracy of the 1980s lesbian world, rejecting my no longer supportable longing to pull my body from formlessness to some socially recognizable form. If only simple rejection were enough to solve the body for good.

Years later, by the time Linnea and I had lost all that weight, the ways we lived in the world had changed. We no longer inhabited a remote lesbian nation; we had a house in a city neighborhood with all manner of neighbors and jobs and colleagues. When my body shrank—from a size 18 to a size 8—I moved as well from the margins to the center of clothing stores. Clothes that hadn't fit me for the past decade, becoming exotic in their unreachability, were possible now: low-slung jeans, tight boatneck tees, red wrap dresses with low necklines that revealed a bit of cleavage. All these new choices. I didn't actually start making lists the way I had in high school, except in my head where I was listing all the time, wanting this shirt or those pants or that dress. I bought those clothes, this time more than I could afford, going into debt to get the next item on my always-regenerating mental list. (I'd made the high school lists, luckily, in the days before teens could get credit cards.) My face and my ass finally felt in conventional proportion to one another, and I was giddy with body.

What I didn't expect was that as my body shrank, old wantings reproduced, in forms grittier than when I was a teen. I knew now about sex, about body triggers, about what I liked. Yet I was not prepared to represent as that woman I'd never learned to be, that woman that men who didn't know me assumed me to be, a blond babe in a red, or a green-patterned, or a purple-print dress. I was stunned when the same guys I'd shared a campus with for years didn't recognize me, assumed I was new blood, heterosexual, dressing for them. Then they were everywhere, leaning toward me, sidling up to me, welcoming me to the campus. When I caught these men staring at me during meetings, they'd often try to get me to meet their gaze as they went out of their way to pass me the cookies (ironically, as I no longer ate the cookies). When I caught on, I always looked away, but that made things worse, as I then appeared demure, acting out a story without having read the script.

More than once one or another of these men made a point to walk with me out of a meeting, only to abruptly step away as their wives pulled up in minivans, with kids. I was pissed off each time I realized our conversation had not really been about the learning outcomes and teaching loads and the students I'd thought we'd been discussing, yet was intrigued at the ways my story and these men's stories of me did not cohere. This was a *thing*, I was beginning to see, that women had to *deal with*, and here I was, too old to have never learned how.

So why—and this question seems obvious, was obvious to me even then— did I continue to dress in a way straight men assumed was meant for them, when the last thing I needed was men in my life? The first answer is that I cannot now, and could not then, allow the vague pressures of a cookie-passing panopticon dictate what I wear, especially when what I'm wearing to work is just wrap dresses, Diane von Fürstenberg–style professional wear, brighter than a business suit but not in the least what the *What Not to Wear* TV pundits called hoochie-mama clothes, and in an academic workplace where the men are as likely as not to wear sloppy shirts and jeans. And too, I love color and arrangement, my dressing as much art play as necessity. And Linnea loves how I look in these dresses, the boots, my hair bright against my neckline, and even loves when men love the way I look. "But you're with me" is what she says still, smiling and slipping her arm around my waist. Show me a woman out there who doesn't like it when her spouse finds her sexy, and I'll show you a woman who doesn't much like her spouse. I dress for my own gaze but also for the gaze of my marriage.

My reasons foreshadowed what my closet-cleaning friend would say to me later about when to, and when not to, purge my clothes. I didn't and still haven't let go of my wrap dresses, because of how they make me feel—sexy, yes, but also synthesized and solved, the woman I'd wanted to be when listing my clothes in high school, the good end of a long story (or so I let myself believe) I'd begun writing at fifteen.

At the same time, I admit, I'd become fascinated by the whole business; what had started as accident became my surreptitious feminist experiment. I began to take note of these men, too aware of me, watching as I walked into faculty meetings and then pretending they hadn't seen me when I said hello, running after me at the close of meetings to tell me some very important unimportant nothing (all these guys middle-aged married men themselves, I'll add, lest anyone feel bad for them) especially if they didn't remember sitting in the same meeting with me sixty pounds earlier.

I would not have minded so much if they'd just told me they liked the way I looked, inviting a laugh, a slug on the shoulder, and some honest banter about all the ways middle age mirrors adolescence, all the ways we wish for what doesn't exist. A couple of times I tried to just say what I saw, but my words never led to frank conversation. These men weren't the communicative lesbians I was accustomed to, and I'd landed in a game, I saw soon enough, that was to be played only indirectly. So I learned not to comment, only observe, as these guys softened their voices when they spoke to me, their speech turning singsong and teasing, too personal, but not in ways that inquired about my life, leaving me too few professionally appropriate openings to mention that I have a longtime husband and she happens to be a woman.

I eventually found ways to come out, early and often, even if awkwardly, then made myself more accurately visible with queerifying tattoos my clothes couldn't cover, then changed jobs and moved to another city altogether. But those first months, in all my new clothes, I just watched, silently recording all the ways so many straight men of my generation don't see women until we shrink into their acceptable-dress-size frame, and then what they see is so much less than who we are.

But here's where my reasoning becomes confused. As time passed, I came to hate-love or love-hate this male attention, sometimes becoming enraged, even after Linnea said, "Oh, forget it. They're guys; they can't help it." Worse, I began to occasionally, perversely, invoke this attention, just so I could hate it harder. I was thinking by now of a story I'd once heard about Marilyn Monroe, not comparing myself to her cinematic starriness—I've always been more the smart bespectacled sidekick than the bombshell lead—but remembering how she'd talked about turning "Marilyn" on and off at will. If "Marilyn" was turned off, she'd told a friend, Norma Jean could walk down the street in Manhattan without anyone noticing her, but once she switched her famous persona on, the fans would *see Marilyn*, recognize her, mob her, prevent her from walking further, her power made of a dress, a dye job, a very good bra, and an inner light switch she'd learned to flip on or off at will.

It's true I never wanted to be that high school cheerleader queen, but that doesn't mean I didn't want her privileges, which is partly why I started wearing my favorite red, green, and purple dresses to campus meetings a little bit on purpose. I tried out the Marilyn principle, enjoyed flipping on and off my own lights, played around with what my fancy paternal grandmother with the politician boyfriends had called female wiles, fleetingly enjoying a profoundly phony straight-girl-style agency that at least made the otherwise dull academic meetings more dramatic.

All this may be defensible until I also admit that, for a few months around the time I turned fifty, I found I couldn't always control the game. Power corrupts and a well-placed neckline corrupts absolutely? It's just a dress, I'd say to myself. It's just hair, just a hint of boob. But something had shifted, inviting a dissatisfactory chill. Those men all knew I was a queer by now, which in some cases just made matters worse. Though aging myself, I'd been cast as the stock not-wife, some last-chance bohemian dream girl, a receptacle for their own once-youthful rebellions that got away. Though I still don't know what—had I been that imagined woman—could or should have come next, what did happen was that sooner or later these guys' unrequited interest turned to anger, dismissal, my body seen but talked through. Clearly my experiment had run its course. Plus I'd become weary of colleagues offering me cookies but never asking about my work.

Since then I haven't changed my wardrobe much. Most of my dresses are solid work clothes, tasteful, flattering, look nice with my tattoos, daytime dressy, and I wear them still, though more often now, at work, with scarves and sweaters. I did, however, in the months before leaving that job, stop flipping on those stage lights when I wasn't actually on stage, my show going dark as suddenly as it had started. The Elvis Coat has left the building.

Before that happens, one balmy April afternoon, I'm walking down the street in the Village in New York City, on my way to read on a public panel about women in publishing, wearing those tall boots and that red wrap dress with, okay, I'll admit, a somewhat plunging neckline—an ensemble I've worn before when giving readings but never to work meetings, a dress my spouse, who will attend this panel, still loves me to wear—and all my lights are on because they have to be, because I'm about to be the artist, to speak to an audience, to perform, when a man on the sidewalk, a classic New York Italian-American type some would call a Guido, not unlike some of Linnea's Jersey cousins, stops cold, blocking my way, staring at me. As I move around him, he nods and croons, "Niiiiiiice."

What surprises me most is not what's happening here. Such things are happening all the time lately. What takes me aback is that I don't knock his block off, as I might have a year or so earlier. I don't even frown. Rather I slow down and laugh. I plain like the attention. I like that I've figured out how to take what I need, forget about what I can't change. And then I walk on. Clothes are a custom we use to protect, project, and write stories on the body. The story of this moment is I am fifty going on fifteen, and fuck it, I'm just happy my red dress still fits.

CODA

I chose to write from "Of the Custom of Wearing Clothes" expecting to dash off a somewhat light piece both confessing my lifelong preoccupation with my wardrobe and attempting to argue for a relationship between clothing, aethetics, and joy. But oh the essay—the form once again tricked me into writing what I didn't know I knew. After rereading the original Montaigne piece a few times over, what kept sticking with me was the relationship between clothing and protection. Most of Montaigne's anecdotes refer to protection against environmental elements, but I immediately found myself writing about social elements and all the ways what we wear does and does not protect us. Once I followed the instinct to move a particular wardrobe item to the opening of the essay, I knew I was writing into intimate realms having to do with a complex synthesis of clothing, the body, and looking—all hinging upon my experiences with a certain red dress.

16

Of the Power of the Imagination

DESIRAE MATHERLY

> I have undertaken to talk about only what I know how to talk about,
> fitting the subject-matter to my capacities. Were I to choose a subject
> where I had to be led, my capacities might prove inadequate to it.
>
> MONTAIGNE, "ON THE POWER OF THE IMAGINATION"

In my childhood, my mother encouraged my belief in the supernatural, much to my fascination and horror. At dusk she called me in from play, threatening that vampires were waking up. Though I grew out of my fears, I am someone for whom the imagination is sometimes a dangerous predilection, especially when in the company of others too much like me: prone to flights of fancy and self-deceit. I need little encouragement to believe the worst and best, and like a sickness, fantasy is catching in my consciousness; so much so, I have lost my grasp of reason with the barest of provocations from others. Delusion in someone else becomes my own affliction as if spread by contagion.

My empathy for others is sometimes so strong that I'd rather be socializing with strangers than in close quarters with a miserable friend. Others' problems become my own, giving voice to my inner demons. I do not find it at all unusual that giving rein to the dark thoughts that dwell within us can sometimes bring illness, both mental and physical.

When I have, despite my better judgment, put myself into an obligatory visit with someone ill, by the end of the evening he or she may claim to feel much better even as I feel worse. Surely I am not alone in recognizing the ways others can drain the lightness right out of us while they heal themselves. I am reminded of the vampires in my childhood, though now they are of the type that drain happiness and warmth from my spirit and give nothing in return. It is a hazard of sanity, to become host to the afflictions of others, simply by caring too much. Somewhere there is a balance that allows giving to others freely without bloodletting one's own vigor. But who can know when and where the line is drawn? The best of doctors are sometimes ill themselves, as if they have made a livelihood of redistributing wellness.

Perhaps this is why I dabbled with psychology without studying it in practice. Not having consulted therapists often myself, surely the blade cuts both ways. It has been my experience that a study of malaise can bring more malady on.

The imagination is enough, in most cases, to make us feel well or poorly. Permitting my obsessions to run is like loosing a windhound, that unfortunate dog that outpaces its own memory of where it has been. I will lose track of days if given over to longing overly much for what is gone; my attachments overrule my good sense when linked to people, objects, or happiness I can't seem to recover. I may squander a set of days completely heartsick, until my very dreams are filled with visits and encounters that leave me weak in the morning. Even when I've shaken the hold nostalgia has over me, my imagination encounters it again in sleep, sweaty and real-seeming in the fevered dreams that the unconscious makes for me against my will. I talk in my sleep and, when younger, was a somnambulist. When I was married, my husband claimed that I sometimes came to his bedroom in my sleep and we made love. These unremembered compulsions were no doubt at play when I was a small child and claimed to transform into a horse at midnight and gallop the halls. Surely in my dreaming I was what I imagined myself to be when awake. Gratefully, we can disassociate ourselves from the fools we are when asleep, and become blameless victims of the imagination.

Once I knew of a woman who identified herself as a witch. The last time she worked magic against someone, she regretted it, and warned of trying too hard to bend the wills of others. It was black magic, she said, that worked in the spell she cast on an ex-boyfriend who had rejected her. For months after, she believed, she paid a price, as he began to stalk her and wanted her back again with a violence that was terrifying. This is not the only story I've heard about unchecked desire leading nowhere good. Fairy tales are rife with wanting that becomes a sickness, a hoping to possess this or that object or person so badly that one falls into a fever that does not abate. Sometimes even getting what one wants is not the cure, but rather an extension of the pain. In my own case, praying to God for wisdom as a young girl has led to a melancholy I can't shake. Fortunately, my prayers to be a man instead of a woman were not heard, though it was an earnest child that wished it so.

Friends used to joke that my penis envy was more than philosophical. Partly I spoke my desires aloud to get a laugh at parties, but really, there was so much loathing attached to my body, and to being a woman in my twenties, that I did sometimes imagine that I'd be happier as a man. Perhaps the men in my philosophy classes would take my ideas more seriously, or I could finally appreciate the pleasures of women from another end instead of my own. A failed lesbian after a six-month relationship at nineteen, I blamed biology. It didn't matter to me then that I only desired women from the perspective of an imagined maleness; now I see that I was projecting my own overwhelming heterosexuality onto other women, wanting to be the man that I wished would be there for me. This struck me after a memorable conversation with a friend whose wife had transitioned from being a man to being a woman, and a lesbian at that. In her case, she always believed herself to be a woman, and brought her imagined self into reality after a long process requiring several years of therapy and a surgery that split and folded her member back upon itself to make a vagina. Marveling over how this was done, I pondered aloud my old desire to have a penis, and my friend described how a muscle in the forearm is used to construct it. But then she told me about the pain her wife experiences during sex, so much so that they avoid it. My friend sought male lovers to make up for what she could not enjoy in her marriage with her transsexual wife. My mind swarming with the complications of bisexual polyamory and the human engineering of sex parts, I realized that I'd never really wanted a penis enough to give up sex completely. But for some who make the transition, the sacrifice is made without regret.

Thinking back to my friend's taking of lovers outside her marriage for the fulfillment of her sexual needs, I sometimes wonder about the sacrifices that we make on behalf of those we love, such as allowing them to have other affairs, or remaining faithful when we'd rather not. Recently I was in a relationship that seemed ideal for the first six months, until my boyfriend expressed a desire for ours to be a polyamorous relationship. At first I tried to live inside the dream he imagined for us, but I couldn't overcome my shock. Part of the problem was my own Baptist upbringing; I suppose I've spent most of my life measuring love by sacrifice, and understanding salvation as a matter of belief. Though I have never seen or studied the miraculous wounds of saints, I've known people who have loved so hard that their reason appeared to have left them, as they sacrificed their own needs for those of another. I wonder whether, if I'd grown up in another way of thinking—perhaps with yogi parents, believing that my own inner consciousness had infinite potential for growth and expansion—my outlook on human relationships would be any different. If instead of bleeding saints punished for holiness, I'd learned about the Tiger Swami who could fight Bengal tigers barehanded or, better, the Perfume Saint, Gandha Baba, who had learned his secrets from a Tibetan master said to have lived past the age of a thousand. Gandha Baba, according to Paramahansa Yogananda's account of their first meeting, could make scentless things smell like specific flowers, and could even manifest them at will. Even though Yogananda dismissed Gandha Baba's gift as "spiritually useless," beyond the purpose of entertainment, it would make for such a better world to learn about God apart from the miseries of crucifixion.

My inner skeptic coughs "imagination" into her fist while smiling at the possibility of trading one potentially solipsistic patriarchal system for another, as if any ontology could tell me about the ways human beings *actually* experience love. And, truth be told, my belief lags behind that of earnest seekers who fervently believe in the miracles they read or hear tell about. I've met too many Christians more afraid of Hell than in love with the most beautiful aspects of their faith, such as unconditional love, forgiveness, and charity. And I've met a number of the professedly devout from other traditions who seem more involved with their own search for wealth, knowledge, power, or self-perfection than spiritual advancement. I confess that I have selfishly desired these things too, at the expense of any true and loving relation with any god. If so many people cannot believe in or worship something, anything, greater than themselves, how can they love anyone at all? Anxiety and fear can push us away from loving in an infinite number of ways, justifiable only to ourselves. The same magical thinking that presupposes Hell for nonbelievers can push people away from their potential to love and be loved in ways they find natural and fulfilling. For instance, I know a woman so well, she could be mistaken for my twin, who, after hearing her mother and grandmother relate stories of abuse and infidelity in their marriages, developed a mistrust of men that ran so deep, she feared she'd never be able to love with a full heart. After one unhappy marriage ended, she felt fated to be alone for the rest of her life. And yet she found her cure within her own ailment. In public, she confessed her fears so openly and frequently, and with such humor, that over time her affliction lay lighter upon her, and men found her resignation charming. She relaxed into the potential for relationships to go either way—toward happiness or its opposite, depending on the pendulum's swing—and thus became open to the idea that accepting one's fate was a sure means of averting its power. No one is incapable of love or of being loved, so long as they have experienced it once.

The misadventures of romance are so bound to our immoderate desires that I think us to be better off in lukewarm relations with our lovers than hot ones. I know one woman who finds it easier to maintain sexual relations with her ex-husband than to seek out new partners. Growing older, she finds herself drawn less to new dalliances that could result in unpredictable pains than to this passion with a ceiling: a familiar love that is already delimited and mapped.

Returning to the idea that our immoderate desires compel us to fail romantically more than not, it's been the case in my own life that arming my imagination with some kind of ritual has been handy in exorcising many a soured relationship. But let me explain.

My most recent affair with the polyamorous gentleman evolved from the night of our first meeting, when he gave me a red piece of blown glass in the shape of a flattened ring. He called it a "token," and though we had only corresponded for a month, and had only been in each other's presence for just a few hours, I felt on the precipice of a great love. I was getting over someone else at the time, and I carried that glass amulet around on a string in my pocket and touched it hopefully whenever I wanted reassurance. I venerated the glass ring until it became a symbol of my growing affection and trust in him, and for half a year I carried the ring in my backpack, which went with me everywhere. When he began to date other people, I broke up with him and placed the ring in an envelope, tucked among books in my bookshelf. In some ways, my over-affectionate investment in the object was a metaphor for the relationship so casually and confusedly ended. We resumed our relationship twice, before the final break came months later. Because I can become a slave to my own imagination, I sometimes need a symbolic experience to free me, to make sense of what is real. For this reason, and no other, I took the glass ring to the grave of my cat, a loyal friend of seventeen years, and placed it under the heavy stone slab marking her tomb. I was able to leave the ring there, though I haven't stopped thinking about how we attach meaning to beings and objects and must let go of these meanings when we finally let go of their anchors.

It is precisely these foolish tricks I play on myself from time to time that make my way of getting through trials a little more eccentric than that of other people. It is not my way to follow people home from work or call their voicemail obsessively. But I'll burn letters and tie knots in rope and bury the gifts they've given me. In some way, then, my ex-lover gave me the very means for removing him from my heart when the time came. Most people offer us our goodbyes in advance, if we stop to notice.

I was led to such an absurd practice by a helpless anger and confusion that I had no name for anymore. It was more than heartbreak, and I'm normally opposed to working such spells on my consciousness when a relationship ends with a natural snap. I dislike this folly of mine, even though it serves a noble purpose. The way of it speaks to weakness, even if the intent was to strengthen my resolve.

Zora Neale Hurston, in writing *Mules and Men*, her collection of African American folktales and her account of the voodoo rituals she observed as an undercover practitioner, once boiled a cat alive and passed all of the bones through her mouth in order to find the one that would render her invisible. It always seemed ironic to me that she died in obscurity, which is a type of invisibility, and I actually believe she must have found that magical bone from the cruelly treated cat's corpse. I shiver to recall her commitment to her search for truth. Most of us would prefer ignorance to knowledge, if the path leads through subterranean labyrinths with unrecognizable outlets and ends.

Our hearts are mazes we enter, though we cannot see the conclusion of them. Men and women are wrong to give impressions of love too quickly, to gesture toward affection that can be revoked or changed with the slightest whim. It would be better if we all approached one another with the immediate understanding that love is a fleeting emotion, whereas true partnership, or honest friendship, exists as another mode entirely. It is a bad start to a relationship when two people say "I love you" too quickly, involve their every weekend plan with each other, and perhaps even their children too, on the assumption that they're building something longer-lasting than a sexual affair. In hindsight, my lover and I might have enjoyed a briefer time together had we never allowed ourselves to believe concurrently in separate visions of happiness. At least by talking about it earlier, we could have averted a massive misunderstanding. We might have remained friends instead of cultivating the long silence that's grown around us. The human heart cannot help whom it loves, as my grandmother was wont to say, but we can decide how to invest our time, given that some relationships, such as those with children and aging parents, are of far greater importance and longer lived. This is the thread of Ariadne's we follow back to the beginning, when hopes collapse into yet another ruin of the imagination.

Married people may begin to take their love for granted, but what a secure relation; to know that both parties are in agreement that the relationship they have cemented with legalities does not come apart so easily. It's a good discipline, to study commitment, and to see our choices written into every aspect of our compliance. Though we intend for a marriage to outlast us, there is time, at least, to ponder what a marriage means, before it comes undone. The things we bury then are far more precious than a blown glass ring.

What an organ, this mysterious heart, that loves and then ceases to love whether or not we want it to, without any trace of rhyme, reason, or consent. Yet if I were to be asked to write a defense of it for some court in a faraway land where things like hearts could be tried for treason, I'd be inclined to say that it has been unfairly brought to trial, given the involvement of those other parts of us so equally invested in loving and unloving pleasures—the sexual organs, for instance, and the pheromones that appear to conduct the orchestra of our passions. Our noses and eyes and ears that love the smell of our lover's hair, the sight of his muscled body newly emerged from the shower, the sound of her laughter when in the throes of delight. And in what way does the imagination pull all of these parts of us together at once, when we remember the pleasures of our hands that go all of the places hands go, with or without our consciousness in them, or the gasps and moans that erupt from us when we aren't thinking about music at all? Our tastes, our desires, both long-standing and fleeting, dress in the clothes of our hearts and go walking, committing crimes in that shameless visage, and dredging up alibis when taken in for questioning. We might as well interrogate the stomach too, so tied to appetites beyond our control, and wonder what it does with the evidence of our past pleasures. Every organ is an accomplice to love, if we see the whole body, even its digestion, as a greater actor than its metonymic parts. When jilted, we may accuse our ex-lover of being an "asshole," but what we really mean is that we feel passed through someone else, as routine as a morning expulsion and scrutinized with far less attention.

Six months into my last relationship, I knew something was changing when I saw a copy of *Sex at Dawn* in the bathroom. My ex-boyfriend did most of his reading on the toilet, so it was no surprise when he began to mention the book in our conversations, and wanted to talk about the unnaturalness of monogamy for human relationships. I ended up reading the book, which was a *New York Times* best seller, though the authors' scientific interpretations were shaky and far-fetched. By the end of the book, readers are to accept two things above all: that monogamy in humans is unnatural and the result of cultural indoctrination by patriarchal institutions such as the Church and the State and, secondly, that all women are sluts who unconsciously desire multiple partners and orgiastic sexual encounters. I was willing to consider some of what the book argued, but my lover bought into it completely. It didn't matter that I accused the authors of cherry-picking and wrote long e-mail diatribes to my boyfriend citing criticisms of the book's science; he had finally found a text that told him a story he already believed about human relationships, that he'd taken on faith of his own experience. I'm suddenly delighted by Montaigne's mention of a man "who could arrange to fart in tune with verses recited to him," and I carry this perfect non sequitur to the conclusion that human beings are awkward animals, caught as we are between a ridiculous mortality and divine artfulness.

Still, we blame the heart when it leads us onto pathways that destroy us and make us weep, because we have no means of harnessing its power once it has taken hold of our imaginations. Does it not make us love most inconveniently? Do we not give ourselves away to people who will never appreciate our nobler attributes? May it please the court to consider that the heart of one is subject to another, to the words and actions of the one we love, who easily becomes our reason for loving at all. And yet we blame our own hearts for failing us, though led there by someone else. By this we see the cruelty in blaming ourselves for loving when it is not returned; by this we see the joke played on us by Nature—none of us falls in love unaided. Nature has endowed us with a divided comprehension of our only immortal achievement. Whatever immortality we can pretend to as human beings may come to us in that moment when we feel completed by another, loved by a separate body, for more than the moment it takes to discharge our ecstasy. For although Socrates attributed divinity to our generative function, and considered Love the immortal *Daemon*, the mode of divine activity that brings us to procreate, he also speculated we were once whole in Love and then split apart, until we remember the one who became for us the Half that made every other redundant.

By virtue of the imagination, we leave one coast of pain and return on a different ship bearing an entire cargo of suffering. When I finally realized that I'd been

OF THE POWER OF THE IMAGINATION

divorced over the same ten-year period my polyamorous lover had been married, I knew that our passages were marked by bad timing and black sails. The metamorphic elixir for both of us lay in loving, however transitory the affair. Sometimes it is enough to brush up against what we have lacked for so long, to know that we will never be satisfied without it. Freedom for one, and bondage for another. Imagination plants the seed of healing in the agonies of loss.

I am reminded of how every hike in the woods for me has been laden with a fear of snakes, and how, the day I broke up with my lover for the second time, we sat on a rock overlooking a man-made lake. He commented that it must have been beautiful as a river before it was dammed. I returned that rivers are too changeable, lacking the depth and predictability that makes a lake useful. Suddenly his dog yelped, and I knew what had happened. As we clambered back over the rocks, a copperhead recoiled from where the stunned dog shivered. Betrayal strikes us similarly, as secretly, quickly, and as remote-seeming as a serpent. That afternoon, while the snakebit dog was at the vet's office, I lay on the couch with my boyfriend's other dog, a consoling arm around him. Days later I scratched a dozen flea bites on my torso and reflected on my grandmother's sage advice: "You lie down with dogs, you get fleas." My love had been ridden with illusions all along. It took three breakups to separate from what could never have been more than it was, and still I tried.

In elementary school I contracted lice from a young friend who had spent the night at my home. My thick, curly hair was a torment, since even the thought of a bloodsucking tick on my head could send me into a running panic. When my polyamorous boyfriend's son ended up with lice, I was again reminded of my paranoia, and frantically checked my scalp and my own son's for the next fortnight. My boyfriend seemed to neglect little problems until they emerged as hydras, just as he favored impractical, self-serving scenarios that asked too much of me. I worried that we would never be compatible. How then polyamory, especially at the point when he decided in favor of promiscuity? Could I assume that he'd wear a condom or that it wouldn't fail? Sixteen years earlier, within a month of marriage, I had acquired crabs while napping with my husband in the infested bed of his friend, an indiscriminate bachelor. We were checking up on his apartment while he was out of town, and though my husband had nary a louse on him, this was the explanation we settled on. Oddly, the relief came when we finally figured out the reason for my discomfort, and my husband plucked every pest from me while I cried. No such relief could ever come from discovering a venereal disease, the invisible ailments that I imagined would crowd my life should I continue in a relationship with my polyamorous lover. He swore that he hadn't been intimate with anyone else, but by that point my trust was gone. After the relationship ended, I asked my doctor for every blood test available, and breathed easier when they came back clean.

My mother is fond of Einstein's remark "Imagination is more important than knowledge. For knowledge is limited, whereas imagination embraces the entire world, stimulating progress, giving birth to evolution." Taken literally, it would seem that our imagination and our creativity form the root of our progress as human beings. I recall times in my life when fantasy kept me aloft and helped me escape from moments that seemed interminable, when my stepfather and mother fought, or when I felt alienated from my teenaged peers. For this reason, it appears that imagination can bring us levity when we are most in need of it. My aunt insists that Alzheimer's is at least a peaceful way of going for the patient; so long as he or she is cared for and protected, attachments and regrets fall away, and the imagination takes over. The darker side of the imagination reveals itself in latter days, when my elderly great-uncle with Alzheimer's goes missing one winter night and we wonder if he thinks he's on the beaches of Normandy again. (He was in his barn, disoriented but uninjured.) Or, recognition sets in, that an imagined happiness usually conceals a harsher reality. At thirty-eight I was contemplating whether my fears of catching a disease were enough to prompt a third and final goodbye, and I decided that they were.

Even animals register attachment that some humans cannot feel. As easy as it is to claim naturalness at the base of our sexual desires, beasts sometimes mourn and grieve, or dream as vividly as any man or woman. How different are we, then, from creatures who transcend their limited sentience by demonstrating behavior that resembles loyalty and love?

Perhaps we continue to find evidence of the heart's distribution throughout bodies, when sense can speak for sensibility, and simple affections appear as mirages of attachment. The beliefs of one person can infect another, just as surely as the germ migrates. One man's imagined happiness of multiple lovers is possible, provided that the foulness of jealousy can be put aside. Some cultures have provisions for mating that preclude attachment—rituals that allow or promote group intimacies that might seem barbaric to our Western Romanticism. Consider alternatives enough, while pondering separation from someone you love, and it all seems possible. One can contract a fantasy as easily as the plague when faced with what seems far worse. Loneliness is the evil eye of adulthood; once one is cursed, all energies turn to revoking what seems at the time to be a permanent brand. Rather that someone is there in the bed, whether or not faithfulness is a part of it.

There must be some kind of preternatural maturity in someone who is able to love and keep on loving without the assurance of being the only Beloved. Still, I count such a person a poor authority on human love as it has evolved so far, given that the persistent toil of compromise seems intrinsic to what most people believe about it. It's more plausible that polyamory is a cover for sexual gratification, and therefore devoid of courage, depth, and empathy. Those who would disagree may hold commitments with lovers they consider primary, but I would not know this ethical relation from personal experience. The argument against jealousy is easy enough to understand. No one should be a possession, and love should be freely given without promise of permanence. Whether it is in our natures to share what we love with perfect strangers is another matter. My cat—alarmingly territorial—once chased three large dogs out of what she understood to be her yard. In her imagination, she may have been three feet high at the shoulder, and the fleeing dogs must have sensed this about her. Had I not witnessed it myself, I would not believe it. Paramahansa Yogananda writes of a similar victory of the imagination over the greater reality when he tells of not one but two kites that he managed to obtain as a child, simply by praying to the goddess Kali to make them fall from the sky.

Or so he claims. Whatever examples I use from others I trust to be as true as the stories I tell about myself; I put my faith in people who have nothing to gain by relating their personal histories. There is no shortage of tales, and it does not matter how famous or unknown the storyteller is, so long as his or her experiences fall within what is possible to imagine. It may not be an exact science by which I ply my art, but my entire being depends on speaking the truth whenever I can, and making sense of the reality I observe through the facts of my own experiences and the assumed facts of others. Inexhaustible variety sweetens the fruits.

Generally, how can we ever know if someone tells the truth? Writers and thinkers of every sort line their books with anecdotes taken secondhand. Not a one would stand before a judge and swear to absolute enduring fact about someone else's experience, just as no one can remember conversations from ten years ago with any accuracy.

I have always found it safer to write about the truths of my own experience as opposed to someone else's. Some people have urged me to write fiction instead of essays, claiming that my imagination is enough to recommend me to that craft, given that it seems to exist in such greater proportion than reason in my consciousness. Fame, lucrative movie deals, and bulging book contracts belong to writers of popular novels, not essayists, and really, my practice is built on the rewards of reflective digression. I go overly long, I ramble, without coming to fit conclusions. I have an immature sense of knowing when to stop, when I've said too much. But I still choose to write only about what I know, and the greenest thoughts, the freshest wounds direct me. If I had to write in any other way, I doubt I'd put a word to paper. The same who say I'd do better to write fiction would not think it so if I took even greater license in my work, when what I do now at least pretends to be careful when involving others. I do not know if reading about one person's mistakes can make the burden lighter for someone else, though that's the hope.

A story told about someone's life is safely sealed with a single name, unlike a work of fiction, whose cast becomes all of existence dancing toward cataclysm or illumination indefinitely.

CODA

I've spent the last three years working to build a manuscript based on Bach's *Art of Fugue*, converting his measures into prose, so it seemed natural that a "cover" essay in some way match the original in terms of measures and scoring. For each of Montaigne's paragraphs translated by M. A. Screech, I wrote an equivalent paragraph of my own, trying to work with the cadence of the song as it was written, while imparting my own style.

17

That Our Mind Hinders Itself

JOSÉ ORDUÑA

> Whoever shall presuppose a packthread equally strong
> throughout, it is utterly impossible it should break; for,
> where will you have the breaking to begin?
>
> MONTAIGNE, "THAT OUR MIND HINDERS ITSELF"

The anatomical model of a neuron looks like Malou Airaudo in a pale pink slip, her shock of hair cresting back and forth as she agonizes during a performance of *Café Müller*, in which the stage is densely littered with black chairs that she impacts with her body as she moves about like a somnambulist. This is before the man in the black suit emerges, trying frantically to predict her trajectories in order to keep her from slamming into the chairs. I'm daydreaming about this when the end-of-period bell rings, so I quickly scribble *axon* in the blank space next to the threadlike part of the neuron that transmits electrical information to and from the soma.

It was fall, eleventh grade, and usually I'd have a sinking feeling walking through the science wing, away from the biology lab where I'd just barely finished another of Ms. G's pop quizzes. But on that day I remember feeling unmoored, like whatever tethered me to the world had been snipped and I'd floated far enough away to lose any visual marker to orient my tumbling. That morning, studying, I'd remembered the structure of the neuron because the diagram reminded me of the beginning of Almodóvar's *Hable con Ella*, when two men watch a performance of *Café Müller* and one of them weeps. The memory of this scene had for some reason evoked an image of my grandmother Estela lying next to her oldest son Victor after she'd been sent home from the hospital where a brain tumor that had grown back was removed for the second and final time.

By the eleventh grade Estela had already passed away, and I hardly ever thought of her, because she stayed in Mexico when my parents and I immigrated to the United States in the late '80s. But the image of her buzzed head covered in a white mesh that held a surgical dressing in place, both eyes blackened and her face so swollen it looked as though she wore a mask, started to present it-self more frequently those autumn days. I was twelve years old when she had her first surgery, and my mom and I went to Fortín a few weeks before it was scheduled so that she could spend some time with me, should the worst hap-pen. I didn't realize this until the eleventh grade when those images of her kept creeping in: that she'd probably held an image of me, repeating our last words in her mind for as long as she could, while strangers in masks rolled her into the operating room; that I had been part of an unspoken ritual of departure, a final goodbye. But she didn't die then.

Remembering her that fall compelled me to look for things that she had touched. My parents kept a box of objects from their lives in Mexico, and among them were a pair of blue baby gloves she'd knit for me with impossibly small fingers so that I wouldn't scratch my face. Reading through old papers, I pieced together her thwarted attempts to come to the United States. I remem-ber coming to the realization that although I'd never been able to feel much for her, she'd lived wounded by both of her sons' departures, and by all of the joy my absence denied her. It caused a tightness in my chest and that same feeling of vertigo I'd felt in the science wing after the first time her image had come to mind. The pain I hadn't felt when she died—a pain that, if I'd known her as my grandmother, would have been acute, visceral, logical—bounced between my lack of love and her surplus of pain. It cycled and renewed itself, and never seemed to diminish, because it wasn't tied to the person that she had been. Looking across my lunchroom table at the brown faces of high school friends, I wondered how common this erasure was, wondered if any of them found them-selves in the same feedback loop of dislocation.

Something ruptured that year; it was as if I'd crossed a threshold and had myself handed to me with the backdrop of an intractable world. A couple of years earlier I'd been confirmed, which is supposed to be a rite of passage into maturity, but it had been too soon, and it was lost on me because my family's liv-ing room when I was growing up looked like the sunny corner of a communist bookstore. If the rite had retained some of its pre–Vatican II tenor—the imagery of a soldier Christ battling in a world of sin, the slap across the face from the clergyman as he bestowed peace upon me—I might have realized what I was being prepared for. My passage had been gradual, devoid of ritual, like water evaporating from an abandoned glass, but in the eleventh grade it tipped over and emptied when two young men who'd been my friends abruptly died.

When I heard about L, an old neighborhood kid I'd lost touch with, I wasn't surprised. In fact, I wasn't surprised whenever I heard that any one of the kids I grew up with had been killed, because that's what I'd been trained to expect, that's what everyone expected us to do, die violently on the street, or slowly be effaced by a cage. L's life had proved unlivable for him, and at first his death was unmournable for me. Just another brown body gone cold—so what else is new? He was shot on the corner of McLean and Leavitt, right in front of the old school, just blocks from where he lived. It wasn't until B died, a prep school friend from an affluent family, that L started visiting my thoughts. When I heard about B's hiking accident, I was unsettled to the degree that we all should be when a young person we know dies suddenly. His family announced his passing over the intercom at school in an appropriately somber and dignified way, and they told us that grief counselors would be available for whoever needed or wanted to speak to one.

When B died I dreamed of L. Several nights in a row he appeared, nothing special, just him in the distance standing in the park where we used to play twenty-one before they tore down the basketball hoops, his broad back facing me in the dusk, the grape and skunk smell of ditch-weed blunts in the air because the older kids had come to the courts and pushed the runts off except for the best two or three players. In the mornings I'd wake up wondering whether L had seen it coming. I hoped he hadn't. And I hoped that if he had been alone when he was shot, at least someone who knew him was there watching when the cops drew the sheet over his face.

One memory drew another like gas pulling itself through a siphoning hose. During this same period we were confronted with questions of Being in theology class, and their confluence with actual death had the effect of deepening some bottom I had inside. The concepts we were treating in advanced biology— apoptosis, the mitochondria, cellular division—only complicated things, and our upcoming dissection of a fetal pig seemed like some brutal cosmic joke. This period feels like the hinge where childhood turned over into something else.

As a six-year-old I assimilated everything. When a young man sitting on our building's front steps was shot in the throat, I went to school the next day without batting an eye. Many years later, well into my twenties, I learned the details of the incident, because it took that long for me to become curious and ask. He'd been drinking a beer in a paper bag, and a car drove by and opened fire, hitting him in the throat. I didn't see any of it happening, because we lived on the third story of the apartment building, but I do remember hearing the crack of the shots, the gurgled screams as he called for his mother, and the flashing of the blue and red lights on the ceiling of our living room once the cops showed up to take away the body. I don't remember ever thinking about it, and at the time it didn't seem to jar anything inside me. There were many shootings after that one, and those too were just experienced and absorbed and lived through. I wasn't even scared to play on the basketball court where most of the shootings took place; in fact, I played on it every day. It wasn't until I showed an elementary school friend a spent bullet casing I kept in my pencil case that I started to understand that these kinds of incidents were not part of the course of everyday life for most kids. And it seems like the trauma was housed there, not necessarily in the events themselves, but in the friction that happened in reviving them, and thinking about them. It was almost as if they'd needed my capacity to experience them to expand so that they could unfold themselves fully and really blanket my mind.

In biology Ms. G led us through a lesson in which we learned about the structure of eukaryotic cells. She walked us through a slideshow in which she broke them down into their constituent parts, but I had trouble focusing because my thoughts kept drifting to B and L. At some point in the movement between mitochondria and two dead teenagers I started to wonder what it meant to be alive, and more specifically how life in general differed from the life of a human being. Looking at the diagram of a cell, it was incomprehensible how the sentience of B or L emerged from a collection of inhuman parts that functioned mechanochemically. How could cells coalesce to make a mind, to make a person with an identity who had the capacity to suffer?

As we learned about the science of life, I grew increasingly unnerved thinking about the materiality of the body. I knew very little about the experiences my grandmother Estela had, only that she lived a life in which everyone she loved left her, some for reasons like the impossibility of living in the emptying cookie jar of geopolitics, and some for reasons as common as men abandoning women who'd borne them children. And then, when she was in her sixties, she was told that her recurring headaches were caused by a brain tumor.

A human body is the result of cellular division, and somehow human sentience emerges from there. Ms. G had been a nun, but wasn't anymore, and that fact always drew me to her. She was in her mid-fifties, and struggled to move about the room when she lectured because she was so overweight. She wore the same shoes every other nun wore, black leather penny loafers with a square front, and when she stood on her tippy toes to write toward the top of the dry-erase board, her ankles revealed a dense network of thin purple veins that snaked in every direction. I'm not sure how I heard about her situation, or if it was really true, but I found it supremely interesting, and imagined some complicated lattice of circumstances both immanent and abstract for which she'd left the cloth. I wanted badly to ask her about it, but I never dared; instead I tried to listen for inklings of her in the way she taught biology.

Leading up to the lesson on the role of cellular division in human development, I'd anticipated that Ms. G would try to draw an impossible line that marked the beginning of a human life because of what I thought I knew about her. A previous incident, in which a history teacher placed "pro-life" posters—brutal close-up photographs of aborted fetuses—in his classroom, had revived my disgust with proselytizing. I'd always been resistant to people who held beliefs so fervently they'd presume to know something I didn't and, rather than trying to make me understand, would simply tell me what I should feel. The history teacher's move went several steps further than this, because he shared his classroom with a teacher who was seven months pregnant. It had been an occasion for me to reflect on just how ugly certitude can become in some people, and another example of a white man claiming the right to control other people's bodies and minds. So when Ms. G started the lesson on cellular division, I listened intently for what I thought was coming, but it never did. She explained that when two gametes, which in the case of human beings are the ovum and the spermatozoid, fuse, it is called fertilization, or conception, and that each gamete has distinct DNA. When they fuse, she explained, they fuse DNA to form a distinct third cell called a zygote. She made it a point to explain that this third cell was not just a combination of the two gametes, but a whole new entity altogether. The zygote, she said, contains all the genetic information necessary to render a human being; all it has to do is divide and divide and divide.

When an injured cell speeds up the normal process of division, and its growth is unmitigated by programmed cellular death, it can form a tumor with its own blood vessels, or colonize an organ or bone. The same process of division that creates human life also blots it out. When I first learned about Estela's tumor, I asked Victor, my uncle who'd gone to but never finished medical school, what was happening. Her body, he said, had made a mistake. After they brought her home from the hospital, and she lay sedated in her own bed, I remember feeling repelled by her body; I avoided her, and couldn't even approach the room in which she lay. I was old enough to understand the seriousness of cancer, it was often the one-word answer to why so many loved ones had died, and so I understood that she too would die because of it. What I didn't understand was what it meant to die; I only knew the obvious: that once a person dies, you don't see them anymore except when they visit in dreams, and memories, and these visitations are really only with ourselves. The notion that her body had made a mistake, and that these mistakes are fatal, was the first time I thought about death enough to feel like I had come up against a limit in my mind, like a man who crashes into a wall in his own home. It was disorienting and unfamiliar to come to a place of complete lack, a frightening tabula rasa onto which language could never be applied. It felt like I lacked even the material with which I could attempt to understand, and this feeling was accompanied by the uncanny notion that my body was not mine in the way I had always assumed it was. Two decades have passed, and any progress in understanding is in understanding the inability to apprehend this through language, in understanding that metonym fails to carry meaning in relation to that word. Estela seemed so alien to me on the bed, her swollen face and shaved head rendering her unrecognizable, and for weeks I lay on the couch in the living room adjacent to her room thinking about the impossibility of opening someone and peering into the networks of meat and electricity that allow us to live the way we do, wondering where *she* was among that biomass, and about how distant our own bodies seem to be from *us*. To look at my toes curling over the end of the armrest felt like I was watching parts of an object move within a logic that was inaccessible to me.

When a cell kills itself, sometimes it's fulfilling a function that was meant to be. In the body this death often ensures the health of the organism, but if there's too much cellular suicide, the body atrophies and begins to disappear. When L started visiting me in my dreams, he was always facing away or rounding a corner. I can't remember what he looked like, what the movements of his features across his face amounted to, only that he was thick and square, and that his skin was light, his eyes even lighter: a pale gray, almost white, with ripples that made them resemble marble Atlas stones. Once he started, he visited me incessantly, and the more he did, the more disgusted I felt about my reaction to the news of his passing, about the readiness of my acceptance, as if his life was always moving toward this and his actual death was a kind of redundancy. It was as if the bullet that crossed his heart simply delivered him to the ghost that always had him, and there was never anything to be done.

It may be that one of the only practices that crosses all cultures and spans all periods of history is our progression toward death, but when I heard that B had been killed while hiking with his brother, I was far from feeling this kind of resignation. Like any other public good, or public bad, the ability to remain alive into old age is inequitably distributed, and in direct proportion to that is our amount and quality of mourning. No one I spoke to about L's death called it a tragedy, and the burden he'd been made to live under exacted its final blow by robbing him of this word. Today Chicago is called Chiraq, which is an apt nickname, not only for the sheer force of violence that makes certain areas look and feel war-torn, but because only some deaths count.

The second time Marco weeps in *Hable con Ella*, he stands in the courtyard of a Spanish villa surrounded by a silent crowd. They listen to Caetano Veloso sing "Cucurrucucú Paloma," a song about the wailing of a man who's been confronted with one of the most vital discontinuities life has to offer: love. The man dies as a result of love lost, and people begin to see a dove that they swear is the soul of the wailing man. He continues to wail after death, except now his wails take the form of a dove's coos. When I watched this scene I'd already started receiving visitors in my dreams, and it made me wonder whether B or L ever had the opportunity to be devastated by love before their passing. I wondered how many decades had gone by without Estela feeling the particular kind of sustenance only offered by an intimate—whether or not she died longing for it. Before, I'd never noticed that the song is sung in the third person, and when I did, something that had never occurred to me emerged. The song had seemed to focus on this man who was devastated by love, but the presence of the pronoun "they" seemed important for the first time—they say, they say, they swear. *They* are the witnesses to this man's pain, and even after his suffering has ended, they remain haunted by its memory. To them, even the coos of a dove sound like the wailing of the man.

I don't recall precisely how long these visitations lasted, but one day I noticed that they had stopped. I don't think I believe in ghosts, but these apparitions seemed outside my control, and my will. They were persistent, like there was something I hadn't done for them, something that needed to occur, and perhaps at some point I managed to do it, but I'm not sure.

CODA

"That Our Mind Hinders Itself" has always acted as a sharp edge that ruptures. Rather than offer solace, it has always reminded me of the intractable condition that underlies life, a condition that renders it an unknowable and sublime mess. Whenever I read it, it grafts itself onto whatever present circumstances swirl around in my mind and offers an occasion to wade in the indeterminacy of a situation. It is all too easy to calcify into a state of resignation, to lazily wield cynicism as a mode of unthinking. The challenge that Montaigne offers is essentially what I consider the mark of adulthood, which is to accept this intractable condition and somehow continue to live a life in which meanings are tentatively forged, pulverized, and forged again. In my essay I've attempted to home in on a period during which I felt myself entering adulthood, which has meant discarding a singular way in which to read experience, and struggling with the binds that I have been born into as well as the ones that I have created for myself.

18

Of Books and Huecos

JUDITH ORTIZ COFER

> I seek, in the reading of books, only to please myself by
> an honest diversion; or, if I study, 'tis for no other science
> than what treats of the knowledge of myself,
> and instructs me how to die and how to live well.
>
> MONTAIGNE, "OF BOOKS"

After her death I begin the customary cleaning and disposing of my mother's personal effects. I volunteered for this task when I saw her husband Ángel wandering around the house looking forlornly at her *cosas*, all the objects she had collected and displayed to represent her life. Rather, her two lives: one before my father died and one after, when she moved back to Puerto Rico and eventually met and married Ángel. Two different lives.

I begin with an inventory of her books, many of which I had sent to her by Amazon.com. We liked shopping long-distance. I would call her while browsing on the Libros en Español website and read out titles. We compromised between her areas of interest and mine. She liked the mind candy of Nora Roberts and Danielle Steele. The books I wanted her to read ranged from Gabriel García Márquez ("One talkative hombre," she would say) to Isabel Allende ("Talks a lot too, but she has great female characters. What a storyteller!") to the contemporary writers whose stories I hoped she'd find familiar: Amy Tan, Julia Alvarez, Sandra Cisneros. She would often tease me by claiming that her favorite Latina writer was Isabel Allende. My part was to act offended so she could say, "I don't think of you as a Latina writer, *hija*. You are my daughter, the *Puerto Rican* writer." I loved her takes on the stories she read. She admired the strong female characters, but only if they showed *respeto* for their parents and did not reject their ethnic heritage. She enjoyed Amy Tan but did not like what Tan said about her mother, mainly about the broken English she spoke. That my mother had been judged less than intelligent when people heard her speak her imperfect English remained an abiding source of resentment for her. My mother's deeply personal interpretations of the books I often taught kept me going back to them for the human experience she extracted from her reading, a counterbalance to the more detached literary criticism of academia. I run my finger over her signature, carefully inscribed inside the front cover of every book: she was a lending library to her relatives and friends, and she wanted her books returned.

She bragged that she received more boxes by UPS that any of her neighbors. I found one final unopened Amazon box on her little desk—one of my choices, a Steinbeck novel, *La Uvas de la Ira*, *The Grapes of Wrath*. To give her all the books she ever wanted was a privilege I relished. When we lived in Paterson, New Jersey, in my childhood, I had been the one who bought her 25-cent romances at Schwarz's drugstore, who saw her happiness when she received the rare packages from her father of *Reader's Digest* in Spanish and the women's magazines collected by her sisters. I had been the one who brought her the few books in Spanish I could find in the university libraries in the seventies and saw how she plowed through Unamuno's dense philosophical works (*Ave Maria, que pesado*—heavy and pessimistic), and how she delighted in Lorca's poems. *Verde que te quiero, verde*. She needed to read *palabras*, in Spanish. They were her soul food.

Romance, Mystery, Travel, Philosophy. I pack the boxes in categories and put them in the hallway. My aunts, who will be coming to help me sort her things in the afternoon, will divide them among the family. I'm glad that I helped to feed my mother's hungry mind, for she had fed my imagination. Why was she so crucial to my work? Over the years, I've decided that she represented a sort of convex mirror, in which I saw an alternate life for myself, one I might have led if I had not taken turns away from the culture and language that defined her. The emptiness I feel at losing her is indicative of something stronger than the usual mother-daughter emotional bonds. I go looking for my mother's animus—the source of her undaunted spirit—among her earthly possessions.

On to the hundreds of photos in albums and boxes.

Photos do not reveal the empty places in our lives. Their original purpose is to record the days we thought worth remembering. Sometimes they reveal more, but by accident. Here are my brother and I posing with our mother in one of our living rooms in Paterson. The room is uncluttered, and the view from the window—that white shade was almost always down, so the photographer (my father?) must have needed more light—is of a gray building and rooftops beyond. It became a family joke that the dismal city view almost always triggered one of my mother's dramatic sighs, usually followed by "Si tuviera alas." If only I had wings.

She stands very straight, chin up, attentive to my father's directions, but she is not smiling. Photo after photo taken in those days shows a sort of detachment in her eyes. She is not there; she seems to be always looking beyond the present moment. To me, she looks like a woman waiting for life to happen, but I don't think she would have agreed with my assumptions. She did not intellectualize; she endured, and her philosophy was basic. *Así es la vida*, that's the way life is, was her almost automatic response to complaints about things that must be accepted. She usually brushed aside my questions about her loneliness during those years, but recently I had asked her again how it was to live so far from her family. She said, "Me sentía defraudada." She had felt defrauded? Cheated? Of what? Her right to pursue her happiness in her own way? Going home to her mother's casa was my mother's singular goal, but soon after her arrival on the Island, my mother began to prepare herself for an independent life. She had felt stifled by maternal vigilance. Her mother was an old-fashioned woman who believed in *luto* forever and disapproved of my widowed mother's new set of wings. "She waits for me on the porch when I go out," my mother told me, "and later complains that she is not getting enough sleep because of my gallivanting."

My mother's "gallivanting" mostly involved church-sponsored events, political rallies, and dancing with friends—but one night, she excitedly told me, she and a woman friend had stopped to use the restroom at a nightclub, a place called El Otro Mundo, and The Other World turned out to be a gay club! She enjoyed this excursion, and perhaps even more so because her mother would have been outraged. Even though I worried for my mother as she tried out those nascent wings, I saw that she was going through a belated adolescent rebellion. She had married so young that she had missed the opportunity to face off with her possessive mother, and vice versa. Although I loved and admired my strong-willed grandmother, the woman who taught me the power of storytelling and whose strength of character I have often written about, I understood that for my mother to survive in the country she had left as a very young wife and mother, she was going to have to learn to fly. Our weekly phone calls in those days, when

I was trying to get through graduate school with a toddler at home and only John's income to support us, were two-way therapy sessions, she encouraging me not to give up on my dreams of teaching and writing, I coaching her on becoming a liberated woman. It must have felt both like a victory and a betrayal when she finally rented a little house in the middle of town, under the shadow of the church on its hill. "I can hear the padre say mass from my porch! I can also hear the jukebox from the café down the street." *Hay vida.* There is life to be lived and savored. Mamá would still send her hot plates of food daily via one of the grandchildren, and my mother visited her every day, which was a tribute my *abuela* exacted from her children until she died. She was the center of our family, and she remained on her throne until the end. She had not needed wings: her kingdom was her casa, and we all arrived there, and returned there, like homing pigeons.

A car pulls up. The aunts are here to collect my mother's things, take what they want, and donate the rest to her church. Ángel calls me to the dining room. He points to what he calls her altar, a credenza covered with *miniaturas* and religious objects, pictures of all of us and souvenirs, and he whispers, "Por favor, no quiero huecos"—I do not want holes. At first I don't quite understand what he is saying—that is, until he points to the objects and to the picture-covered walls. He doesn't want empty spaces in the house. He wants the things she so lovingly collected for their home to remain as she left them. The empty spots would hurt him. "Por favor," he says again, "no huecos." Do not leave me with more holes to fill.

"Está bien." I promise him that I will not give away anything other than what was in her closet and in her dresser drawers. I show him the boxes and the clothes on the bed. I ask him if I can have the photo albums of my brother's family and mine.

While my relatives and I carry boxes and bags to cars, Ángel sits at the table, occupying himself by trying to fix a wall clock that stopped sometime during the week before she died. I read that it was once the custom to stop the clocks at the time of a person's death, and also to draw the curtains and drape the mirrors with dark cloths so the spirit of the deceased wouldn't get trapped in the looking glass; a black wreath would be placed at the door to announce that the house was in *luto.*

But all we must do is give away what we can no longer bear to keep, and hold on to the things we need. After everyone leaves, I sit down with the bulging photo albums, which tell her story and our family's in no particular sequence. I look for the points of intersection and departure in these images. I see her as younger and sadder, then older and happier. I grieve for the lonely girl in exile, and feel pity for the orphan, me, before I was an orphan. How old can you be and call yourself an orphan? I am parentless. And the strongest tie I will ever have to the country of my birth is gone. Without my mother, I am no longer at home in my native land, no longer at home in my mother tongue.

In these old albums and scrapbooks she valued so much, I look for myself before the fork in the road, before duality became my main mode of being; I experience what is sometimes called marginality as a vortex of living in the past and present at once. My past is intrinsically connected to her, and now there is a *hueco*, an empty space like the ones Ángel does not want to face. In trying to find a sequence and a timeline for her life, I start to see why my mother became whole as I became divided. She knew who she was and where she belonged from the beginning. No matter where she found herself, no matter how much the journey may have seemed like a detour, she was always heading back to that place of belonging. She kept an idea of home alive in her imagination—an instinct, a dream map. And she would reinvent the place, if she could not find it where she had left it so long ago.

I have no dream of home that can compare to hers. Home to me is where the people I love are at any given time. I go on filling the *huecos* in my life, as I always have, with words.

CODA

Montaigne's library tower lined with books would have been an ideal place for my mother to spend her afternoons. Montaigne and my mother both reveled in their reading, and their appetite for all manner of reading material was more than eclectic; it was joyfully random.

Montaigne claimed, "I do not bite my nails about the difficulties I meet with in my reading; after a charge or two, I give them over." Neither did my mother. She bounced from book to book, looking for surprises, amusement, and a little knowledge. Montaigne allowed himself the pleasure of moving from topic to topic, happily following the divagations of his curiosity. Montaigne read Boccaccio and Rabelais for pleasure, and made no bones about the fact that Ovid and Plato bored him. My mother, no overwrought literary critic, called some of the canonical "greatest minds" *pesados*—humorless pedants—but read them anyway. She made connections between the lives she read about and her own in an unforced, natural way.

Montaigne said the best poetry (all good writing) is without affectation, that poems should, like the dancer, "represent their ordinary grace and presence." He liked to extract practical knowledge from his readings and sought out authors who "treat of manners and rules of our life." He deplored inflated writing and, as he says of Cicero, works where "I find nothing but wind." Montaigne found such effects a waste of time, "For me, who only desire to become more wise, not more learned or eloquent." Such a statement could have been carved on my mother's headstone. She read for pleasure and a little wisdom. She disliked writing that sermonized and expounded elevated philosophies. As I read Montaigne's essay, and I write about my mother's love of books, I am reminded that one of the greatest pleasures of reading is the shock of recognition, of discovering oneself in the (no matter how unlikely) other.

19

Of Diversion

SHANNON LAKANEN

> Some painful idea gets hold of me; . . . If I cannot fight it,
> I flee it; and by my flight I make a diversion and use craft; by
> changing place, occupation and company I escape from it
> into the crowd of other pastimes and cogitations, in which it
> loses all track of me and cannot find me.
>
> MONTAIGNE, "OF DIVERSION"

I am sometimes intensely aware that escape is always an option, that there is invariably a way, legal or not, to pull together airfare or gas money, that I am capable of packing up the most basic of necessities, emptying the contents of my house onto the curb within an afternoon, and hitting the road for good with my son, leaving behind every unpaid bill, unanswered e-mail, and unreturned phone call. I hold on to this knowledge some days as if it were the only safety rope left unfrayed by the cataclysmic or mundane, depending on the season, events of daily life. Ropes weaken, after all, just as often by an accumulation of minor frictions as they do by severe blows. But regardless of its condition, losing my grip means free-falling onto a thick-mossed ledge of stability and the short-lived relief of a firm landing on a square meter or so of solid rock jutting from a cliff face until I realize what limited room I have to navigate, what little hope there is of making my way up or down from there. I have been stuck this way too many times—financially, emotionally, professionally—for it to ever happen again. So these days, should the rope snap, should my hands slip, I'm more likely to kick myself as far from the bluff as possible, with every intention of propelling my body all the way down to its base.

While I've resisted, in the most recent third of my life, taking to the road so dramatically, I have traveled across my own or other countries every year of the last twenty. I've wandered enough to know that, in the end, it isn't the destinations that attract me but my passage between them: the slow rocking of the train between Belgrade and Podgorica, the bob and swerve of buses headed from Dubrovnik to Sarajevo, the jerking progress of songthaews down two-lane roads in central Thailand. A conference in Hamburg becomes a train ride to Berlin, a cheap flight to see family in Helsinki, another stretch of rail to Nakkila, and a side trip to Amsterdam before returning home. A short-term teaching position in Seoul stretches into backpacking through Southeast Asia for the rest of the summer.

It's the person I become in transit that lures me out, the winnowing of concerns to finding only shelter, sustenance, and transportation from one place to the next. It's being responsible for only my passport, backpack, and, when he's not back home, my son. I'm a cheap traveler, staying most often in hostels and eating street food, preferring trains over planes and subways over taxis. Movement itself becomes addictive, the sometimes hardscrabble struggle to get from place to place seducing me: the heat pounding up from urban sidewalks and curbsides in summer or, better yet, the crumble of roadside pavement; the negotiations of floor space on overcrowded trains; the sudden, startling luxuriousness of cold showers or icy beers sipped on one-footed benches under trees; the uncertainty that any route will lead where I'd hoped; and the flexibility that makes sleeping in an Ayutthaya station as reasonable an option as my own couch in Columbus, Ohio.

In between these journeys, I have lived for the past decade what many would see as a fairly stable life: I have a tenured position at a respected university, a house in the suburbs, two dogs, and a son, all of which I sustain, at least in part, with the knowledge that I am choosing in each moment not to follow another path. I renew our passports long before they expire, prioritize in our budget owning a vehicle I can reasonably rely on to get us to any edge of the United States. As I pull off the highway at the Ackerman Road exit nearly every single evening, I know that I *could* in fact keep driving south to Interstate 71, or pick up 670 to the airport, or loop back north on the Columbus bypass. I am a runner at heart. I ran away from home for the first time when I was in fourth grade, though I made it only as far as the back of my father's pickup truck. I broke leases more often than I fulfilled them during my undergrad years, mastering the art of breaking down secondhand furniture by hand and hammer until it fit into Dumpsters. My son and I trekked all summer from Ohio to Florida to Colorado to Michigan and back in the aftermath of my split from his father, who was so ravaged by addiction that we barely recognized him. After his first incarceration two years later, I packed up our lives to move to Montenegro for a temporary teaching position, and we returned to the rails so often during those six months that our apartment in Podgorica at no point felt like a second or even a third home.

But diversion is anything but easy. The truth is, despite all of this running, there are few things in this world more frightening to me than never finding my way back. "Wilful self-deception" is how M. A. Screech describes Montaigne's working definition of "diversion." Another take, perhaps, on Didion's stories "we tell ourselves in order to live." And my fear churns in the possibility of buying into those stories wholesale, of no longer distinguishing between them and the realities recognized by those surrounding me: holding faith in the power of love long after it's stopped sustaining us and has started instead to destroy us, in our own ability to navigate the world long after we've lost our way.

As much as I'm seduced by the interims when I've left home more times than I came back, coming home is what I eventually do. And no matter how much I have longed for the people I return to, the homecoming has always felt like accepting the short end of a compromise. The small-by-U.S.-standards rooms of my house feel more spacious after weeks spent in hostel rooms and train cars, my own bed more comforting, grocery stores more decadent, the streets wider, the cash larger, my vision clearer—but after a handful of days, no matter how I try to fight it, I feel myself fall into the rhythms of a life that I can only describe as deadening: the crosstown treks to campus, the monotonous passion of colleagues' e-mails about the latest administrative upset, the coordination of carpool duties with parents of my son's teammates.

In those first weeks back, I fight to hold on to the distance between these concerns and how it felt to wake up to the calls to prayer in Istanbul each morning, to breathe in the aromas of Seoul's streets at dusk, to pass entire weeks or months without a working cell phone, to stuff all I needed deeply into my jeans pockets, but the disconnect eventually fades. And when it does, I can't help but mourn the shift of perception, the loss of diversion, the greatest and inevitable price of traveling.

The last time I came in from the rails, my response to that loss was to start dating again for the first time in years. I began a relationship with a color-blind cartoonist under the e-mail subject line "Distract me." After a couple of weeks of correspondence through an online dating site, I suppose one would still call our first meeting at a blues festival twenty miles away from the city where we both lived a blind date. Though I'd seen a photo of him and he of me, I fretted over whether or not I'd recognize him in person. Several times that morning, it crossed my mind to text him with a description of what I was wearing so we could both avoid awkward introductions to strangers who weren't expecting us. But every description I came up with began in color . . . gray shirt, faded jeans, purple Doc Martens. How, I wondered, could gray or faded denim possibly help him find me?

He told me that first afternoon that his visual world wasn't in fact as limited as I'd imagined. He has trouble with all shades of yellow and some reds, which didn't seem so bad to me until I realized it covered two-thirds of the primary colors. He draws comics in black and white and then sets himself loose on a variety of grays, relying on another artist to add color afterwards.

He wasn't a traveler, had never left the country and, as far as I could tell, had been out of Ohio less than a handful of times, but one night he showed me the stack of pages that comprised his latest book before sending it off to another friend for lettering. He explained the narrative as I perused each black-and-white panel, and these were the journeys that connected us: how he could unravel the worlds that existed only on his pages, or fabricate absurd significances for statues in parks, spin fantastical histories for the flocks of wild turkeys we encountered on hikes through the woods. How freely he could weave any fiction into the experiences we shared.

A couple of months later I ran across a link to an online color perception test. Completing it was a tedious process of arranging several series of slightly different-hued squares into spectrums from mustard yellow to pale pink, from a nearly pastel green to what I want to call azure until I realize that it looks nothing like the dark blue I always imagine it to be. (I am equally alarmed by how tinged with red indigo really is.) I didn't trust the results of the test once I finished it. The site told me that my color perception was seventy-eight percent accurate, which seems to be about average for women my age, but I'd grown weary of the task less than halfway through. By the time I was arranging the final rows of boxes, I found myself speeding up, moving on to the next even when I spotted my own missteps while scanning the nearly finished spectrums, too uninterested in the drudgery of fixing them. Not so different from the way I responded to the end of my relationship with the cartoonist after he reluctantly tried to explain that it had been the idea of me, rather than the reality of us, that he'd fallen for.

Color blindness, of course, is a difference in perception, a translation of the world into a wider array of grays, perhaps, than a color-perceptive person can distinguish, though none of us can ever be entirely sure. And the cartoonist wooed me, in part, with that vision, though I'd led him to believe, eventually led myself to believe, it was his charm that won me over. On more than one morning, I'd wake to photos on my phone of his work from the night before: half-shaded line drawings, penciled sketches, series of panels not yet connected. Though he'd published several collections, he shared only these works-in-progress with me, and I'd never asked to see any of his finished products. When we split, I was left with the realization that I'd been looking so closely not at what his work was but at the point of its refraction, the surface on which his draft and my interpretation of his intentions met. What I'd in fact fallen into was only my perception of what he might have created; I'd been filling in the blanks, coloring the panels myself all along.

Astigmatism is an abnormal curvature of the cornea, blurring the refraction of light rays onto the retina. It's evidently one of the most common vision defects, and I've had a mild, ever-evolving form of it all my life. For the past ten years, my optometrist has told me that glasses are helpful but optional most of the time and more necessary for driving at night. I've sometimes gone the better part of the year between appointments without wearing them at all, but when I do put them back on, the most noticeable difference I perceive is feeling slightly taller than I had without them. With each passing week this summer, however, I stretched my arms a little further to make out transit line numbers when reading maps of Tokyo, Seoul, Bangkok, and Shanghai. Part of the tedium of my homecoming, a couple of weeks before meeting the cartoonist, was an eye appointment at which Dr. Beals told me that while my astigmatism had corrected itself altogether, I was in desperate need of reading glasses because it was now, of course, the objects closest to me that I had the most difficulty seeing clearly.

I write this essay in the initial weeks of my second sabbatical. I spent my first teaching in Montenegro, so back then, as soon as final grades were submitted, I had suitcases to pack, last-minute hotel reservations to make, arrangements to coordinate for spending six months abroad with my son. And then it was a whirlwind of travel and teaching until days before the next term started at my

home university. This time, however, I simply walked out of my final class meeting early on a Monday afternoon, a few students acknowledging the beginning
of my eight months of freedom in a hallway conversation after the others had
dispersed. And then I stood alone on the ground floor of the building that held
my office and most of the classrooms in which I teach, keenly feeling the hefty
absence of exhilaration, of identity, of perspective.

When I got to my car, I wept without understanding why. Instantly, the
music I'd been listening to since summer, dozens of tracks mixed specifically
for road trips and train rides and airport layovers, was intolerable. Instead of
making my way toward the highway that would lead me to that ever-optional
Ackerman Road exit, I headed north on State Route 3, and then onto Old State
Route 3, and then onto nameless-to-me two-lane roads, at first telling myself
that I was seeking out a restaurant a friend had recommended, and then finding
the restaurant and not stopping, driving on out of Galena, farther north and
east without knowing why. No longer crying but more deeply sorrowful than I
had been in the faculty parking lot, I filled up my gas tank, bought a bottle of
water at a convenience store, and kept driving in silence, kept twisting my way
along rural roads until I realized I had looped back west and found myself at I-71
again, faced with the option to head south, back toward the life I had in those
moments so much difficulty recognizing, or north toward further wanderings.
The clock on my dash caught my eye, and I turned south to punctually fulfill, I
told myself then, my carpool duties. But the hardest truth of that moment was
that I wasn't as thoroughly disconnected as I at once yearned to be and have
always been terrified of becoming. And for better or worse, I don't think I ever
will be.

Once I'd made it to my son's high school, I stepped out of the car, walked
across the parking lot, and waited with one foot propped against the fence surrounding the football field behind me. I watched a series of suvs and minivans
pull in, my hands stuffed deep into my pockets, fingers wrapped tightly around
the ring holding only my car and house keys, realizing again that for all my
trekking toward the ideas of destinations at which I cannot arrive, I've never
managed to outrun anything I've left behind.

CODA

I began this essay in agreement with the quotation from Montaigne that serves as its starting point, pulling out several more passages that left me nodding my head at his take on diversion. And then I sat down to write, his words pinned above my desk as reminders of where I was headed: a contemporary version set on complementing his praise of diversion, distraction, willful self-deception. I was thinking about how the essay itself thrives on its digressions, and how a life dedicated to the freedom of meandering may be the life best lived.

But, as is often the case, I eventually realized that my take was not as simple as that, and I'm not sure that Montaigne's is either. At several points in his essay, he leaves readers little choice but to argue against him. I realized along the way that I was both in love with and terrified of the potential for escape that traveling holds. In the end, I think that meandering may be productive or useful only when it ends in the simultaneously rewarding and difficult return to that from which one initially sought diversion. I hope that the essay performs this idea as much as it explains it.

20

Of Sex, Embarrassment, and the Miseries of Old Age

[after "On Some Verses of Virgil"]

ROBERT ATWAN

> I have absolutely no other passion but love to keep me going. . . .
> it would restore me to vigilance, sober behavior, graceful
> manners and care about my person; love would give new strength
> to my features so that the distortions of old age, pitiful and
> misshapen, should not come and disfigure them.
>
> MONTAIGNE'S "ON SOME VERSES OF VIRGIL"

Personal essayists continually test the boundaries of shame and embarrassment. They can't hide behind fictional or dramatic characters, or lyric detachment. Their bitter humiliations, defects, ignorance, vices, and blemishes all insist on escaping concealment. They demand to be expressed, exposed. The size of his penis embarrasses Montaigne, and he freely admits it in the long, late, and at times challengingly obscure essay "On Some Verses of Virgil"; after all, he began the *Essais* as an attempt to portray himself exactly as he is, so why shouldn't the portrait include every part of him?

The diminutiveness of his member is not his only cause of embarrassment; now an old man, he must acknowledge that, limp, flaccid, and soft, it hardly works any longer. "Nature," he complains, "should have beene pleased to have made this age miserable, without making it also ridiculous. I hate to see one for an inch of wretched vigor, which enflames him but thrice a week, take-on and swagger as fiercely, as if he hath some great and lawfull dayes-worke in his belly."[1]

His farewell to sex ["Je prens l'extreme congé des jeux du monde"], "On Some Verses of Virgil" is the most erotically charged chapter in the *Essais*. Never shy about the topic, Montaigne writes about sexual matters throughout his essays, but never with an equivalent concentration. The essay has justly been called by James Grantham Turner "perhaps the most profound meditation on sexuality in the Renaissance."

After a few pages on the physical and mental miseries of old age, Montaigne—who was then only in his early fifties—states his topic unequivocally: "the genital activities [*l'action genitale*] of mankind." These are "so natural, so necessary and so right" that Montaigne wonders: "what have they done to make us never dare to mention them without embarrassment [*sans vergnone*] and to exclude them from serious orderly conversation? We are not afraid to utter the words *kill, thieve* or *betray*, but those others we only dare to mutter through our teeth. Does that mean that the less we breathe a word about sex the more right we have to allow it to fill our thoughts?"

The essay—so wide-ranging it truly resists summary or colligation—then moves suddenly, though strategically, from reflections on our verbal inhibitions to a consideration of love in ancient poetry. Montaigne wonders why in his day poetry has lost contact with the god of Love (L'Amour). Though he has "been struck off the roll of Cupid's attendants," he acknowledges that his memory is "still imbued with [the god's] powers and his values," and that there still remain "traces of heat and emotion after the fever. . . . All gross and dried up as I am, I can still feel some lukewarm remains from that bygone ardour." We know from other essays that Montaigne experienced sex so early he's unable to remember when he lost his virginity; that he visited prostitutes and twice came down with transmitted diseases; and that unruly sexual passions ruled his youth.

Here are the lines from Virgil that excite him so:

> She [Venus] spoke and here and there with her snowy upper arms the goddess
> warmed the hesitating [Vulcan] in a soft embrace. He suddenly
> knew the familiar flame, and its known heat entered
> his marrow, and ran through his shaken bones:
> not unlike what sometimes happens when torn by trembling thunder
> a vibrating fiery beam tears through the clouds with light.
> His spouse felt it, happy in her wiles and conscious of her beauty. . . .
> Having spoken these words

> he gave her longed for embraces and sought peaceful
> sleep in her limbs, falling into his wife's breast.
> (*Aeneid* VIII, ll, 387–92, 404–6; Montaigne's ellipsis)

These lines occur in a narrative context that Montaigne pays no attention to in the essay. Concerned with the fate of her mortal son Aeneas, who—with his remnant of defeated Trojan warriors—has landed on the coast of Italy and must prepare for war, the goddess Venus attempts to persuade her oft-cuckolded husband Vulcan to help arm Aeneas for battle. Her seduction succeeds, and Vulcan's crew of Cyclopes crafts the helmet, sword, armor, spear, and magnificent shield that will, in Virgil's version of history, lead to Aeneas's triumph and the founding of Rome.

Montaigne's interest in the lines (he will return to them later in the essay) is wholly sexual, but in an unexpected way. He cites them not to offer a titillating moment that indicates he is still capable of arousal but to show that "the powers and values of that god [L'Amour] are found more alive and animated in poetry than in their proper essence." The lines demonstrate that "Poetry can show us love with an air more loving than Love itself. Venus is never as beautiful stark naked, quick and panting, as she is here in Virgil." In other words, for Montaigne, erotic poetry can be as sexual as sex itself. It's the verbal expression of sexuality and the power it has over the imagination that occupies his always restless mind throughout this essay.

On Some Verses of Mine

One of the many embarrassments of old age in men comes from their entertaining—despite all evidence to the contrary—the illusion that they still remain attractive to younger women. This not uncommon delusion can appear akin to dementia when the geezer comes on persistently and perhaps crudely to someone who could very well be his daughter, or even granddaughter. Mistaking a young woman's natural politeness for interest, his fantasies aflame, he moves into full pursuit, unaware of how ridiculous he appears. Elderly women, of course, are not immune to delusions, but theirs may take the form of an exaggerated self-esteem coupled with the positivity that so often governs their thoughts and behavior (the old man rarely meets an old woman who isn't more *upbeat* than he is). But the mature woman, in public view at least, rarely engages in the aggressive and unseemly flirtatious conduct we often see in that stock figure of comedy the *senex amans*, the lecherous old man.

When my father turned forty, I thought he was old. When I turned forty, I would never have applied that adjective to myself, though apparently Dante thought old age began at forty-five. I didn't consider myself old at fifty, as Thomas Aquinas and Montaigne did. Nor did I even think I was old at sixty, the age at which the ancient Romans defined *senectūs*. But certifiably old now, some twenty years older than Montaigne when he wrote his essay on sexuality, I've certainly experienced my share of pathetic and embarrassing moments, spurred on by delusional romantic fantasies bordering on dementia, though they may not have always been public. My only solace is that I am aware of my improprieties and, perhaps more important, can still recall them. Now and then, usually on my way to sleep, I will involuntarily play back a ridiculous moment that makes me cringe.

Only a few years ago after a literary event, I convinced myself that an attractive young woman had signaled me to join her:

AT THE RECEPTION AFTER THE READING

She looks across the crowded room
and I think she's looking at me,
old as I am, fit for a tomb,
yet eager, and reckless, and free.

She smiles and waves a blurry hand—
I'd taken my bifocals off.
It's tenth grade as I slowly stand
And—summoning a nervous cough—

push my way unsteadily through
the young things at the reception
until I see I've bumped into
the object of her attention.

No one around me realized my pathetic error, and yet I felt embarrassed by my self-delusion.[2] As the great sociologist Erving Goffman notes, embarrassment does not require the observing presence of others. Nor was I embarrassed to write this little poem, though I confess I find it embarrassing to share it in print.

Not just because I portray myself in a foolish, vulnerable position but also because by doing so I display my inadequacy as a poet.

I am no poet, but I like to write poetry. I have even published a handful of poems, though I compose many that I don't submit and many that I never intend for publication. I have a large cabinet drawer full of unsubmitted poetry. One good thing about unsubmitted poetry is that it has never been rejected. We place a great deal of importance on publication, prestige, prizes, but there's little attention to the private enjoyment people feel in composing a poem that expresses a tiny portion of what they think and feel. (Too many amateur poets make the mistake of revealing their work to others instead of simply concealing it for their own secret gratification.) Once we become adults, many of us live embarrassed by a lack of proficiency and cannot enjoy activities if we cannot perform them skillfully. I'm happy with many of my poems, though they might not please or impress anyone with genuine poetic gifts. And as Montaigne says of his own early dabbling in Latin verse, they "clearly revealed the poet I had last been reading." In my case it is usually Stevens and Frost and especially, having grown up in Paterson, New Jersey, William Carlos Williams.

When my thirty-year marriage ended in 2008, I felt the need to write about the experience: of finding myself suddenly alone, dejected, and presumably undesirable, with few nearby friends, in a large, empty, and rapidly deteriorating house at the advanced age of sixty-seven. In the first few months I did what I imagine other men might do in a similar situation: I bought a new, high-performance sporty car; I had my hair colored; I joined a gym; I spent some money on cosmetic dental work; I visited a few bars where the women were most often young and uninterested; I drank more than usual in the evenings at home; I spent hours watching sports on TV; I felt sorry for myself. It's a boring, embarrassing story that I soon abandoned trying to essay.

The coloring proved to be an embarrassment when one day I noticed my once whitish gray hair didn't look the mature salt and pepper the hair stylist had promised, but had taken on some weird artificial shade of red, as though my hair now blushed for me. The new car, however, proved to be liberating. My daughter was now attending college, and my old station wagon was too unreliable for the nearly twelve-hour round-trip visits to her campus. The new car had its rejuvenating effect: it was quick, powerful, perfectly balanced, and fun to corner at high speed while shifting into fifth. But the long drive could still be tedious, and without company I needed something to pass the time. I soon grew tired of my favorite music, I dislike talk radio, I can't focus on an audio book, I don't like idly chatting on the cell phone. As a result, I often drove without stopping and in complete silence.

Then one bright October afternoon a few years later, unmindful of the lush foliage and nearing my last exit on the Massachusetts Turnpike, I began composing poetry in my head. The autobiographical essay that I'd contemplated shortly after the marriage ended had somehow begun to take shape as poetry. Since I was behind the wheel, I needed to write in my head something I could remember when I reached my destination. I'd been revisiting the gems of seventeenth-century British poetry (one of my cherished eras) and lines from Andrew Marvell's "To His Coy Mistress" seduced my thoughts. Soon I was thinking in octosyllabic rhythms. I don't know which came first, the meter or the memory, but on the New York Thruway, while passing through Albany, I began versifying a recent experience at a bookstore reception where I foolishly imagined a lovely young woman had enthusiastically beckoned me.

Montaigne says in "On Some Verses of Virgil" that his best thoughts came to him when he was least able to write them down, often while on horseback. I decided the only way to compose in my head while driving was to rely on a poetic meter and form that would stick in my memory. Old people are advised to do crossword puzzles or other mental exercises to keep their brains from atrophying, so I could see the poetry as therapeutic in more ways than one. My poem, of course, didn't come together at once. As I drove, I would start and restart, fumble, forget, and begin all over, reaching for rhymes and weighing words of appropriate syllables. The three stanzas finished, I realized with delight and some dismay that I had traveled from Schenectady to Syracuse with no idea how I'd done it. There seemed nothing in between. The miles and time had flown by, and here I was, close to my destination. I might have been out on anesthesia. Still, I had passed the time and had a little something to show for it as well as a satisfying mental workout. In my motel room, I quickly jotted it down in a notebook so I wouldn't forget. In three weeks I'd be seventy.

"Had we but world enough and time . . ." That famous line got me started. Time was on my mind. I had spent the past few years stagnant, and when you reach seventy you realize that time may be running out and you don't have a lot of it to waste. The time in Marvell's wonderful poem is inseparably tied into seduction and sexual frustration; a fellow is trying to persuade his girl to get with it, to succumb to his advances without all the stalling. Sure, if we had endless time, "This coyness Lady were no crime." But the clock is ticking. The word "world" troubled me. Saying it both silently and then aloud as I drove, it felt like two syllables—*wur-uld*—but for the eight-beat line it needed to be pronounced as one. The word "world" itself altered time, stretched it out just for a delicious split second.

I felt I had found an inviting and enticing lyric form. The three stanzas of four octosyllabic lines with alternate rhyme could express both the forlornness and farce that I was beginning to associate with old age. I enjoyed the requirement for autobiographical concision and the occasional struggle for an unusual rhyme. The scheme seemed perfect for encapsulating both the heartfelt vignettes of nostalgia and the sheer comic dilemma of trying to recover romance in old age while managing to retain just a shred of dignity.

By then I had been living alone for nearly three years and my early expectations that I would inevitably enter into another intimate relationship had all but vanished. When young you're in some promising social mix nearly all of the time; I didn't realize how different it would be when you reach old age. I see now that I should have taken Montaigne's advice about dating: "If anyone asked me what is the first quality needed in love I would reply: knowing how to seize an opportunity. It is the second and third as well." But the hard part of coping with rejection is that it makes you even more sensitive to the possibility of rejection, and—given the law of self-fulfilling prophecy—you start to become assured that to be rejected is your destiny, and thus you grow more hesitant in making any advances or submissions that might invite further rejection. Montaigne himself admits his sensitivity to both rejecting and being rejected and regrets he didn't take his own advice, having missed many opportunities.

So, of course, like many disconsolate seniors, I entered the safer world of online dating sites, which would prove a source of both annoyance and amusement. Most contacts I made there never materialized into actual dates, but some supplied material for satiric verse:

TO HIS COY BRIGHTEYES167

Two months of guarded messages—
always three days between replies—
so despite those famed "Passages"
the teenage Rulebook still supplies

the official code of conduct
for all old ladies, even those
who still imagine being fucked.
So Brighteyes dallies 'cause she knows

her "life has only just begun."
And here on pause well past our prime
we might have snatched a bit of fun
had we but world enough and time.

More enjoyable than any date I may have had with the dawdling Brighteyes—as some readers may appreciate—was finding a near-perfect rhyme for
"conduct." When an actual date resulted, it often ended badly—usually, it
seemed, because I acted "inappropriately," as in this next "driving poem" that
recounts what occurred one night when I boldly attempted to take Montaigne's
advice to "seize an opportunity."

THE RAKE'S PROGRESS

Our first date, Thai food near her place—
she took my arm crossing the street—
I pictured next a warm embrace
but knew a hug would be discreet

and also more "appropriate."
Second date: a cute French bistro,
but perhaps I may have rushed it
when suddenly I lost control

and gently kissed her stiffened lips.
Wasn't I more than just a friend?
We all read from conflicting scripts:
Next day she e-mailed: "this should end."

A Stream of Chatter

What's so erotic about the lines of Virgil? Actually, late in the essay, Montaigne
acknowledges that they are "reserved" and "discreet" in their depiction of sexual
pleasure. Throughout the essay he cites many explicitly erotic lines from Juve-

nal, Martial, and Catullus, which make the Virgil passage seem linguistically tame in contrast: for example, he refers to the Roman empress Messalina who in an oft-repeated anecdote reputedly engaged with twenty-five partners on one evening until "at last she retired, inflamed by a cunt stiffened by tense erections, exhausted by men but not yet satisfied" (Juvenal, *Satires* VI, 128–29).

But he prefers, he tells us, the lines of Virgil precisely because they are more indirect than those of the others: "Let Martial, as he does, pull up Venus' skirts: he does not succeed in revealing her all that completely," he says, and "some things are hidden in order to reveal them more." Although he at one point claims that love is simply a discharging of our vessels, he has nonetheless suggested all through the essay that sex is largely a function of the imagination. Virgil's lines are sexier than sex itself.

For all his talk of candor and of his daring challenges to propriety, Montaigne often pays respect—as he notes in his short preface "To the Reader"—to the social conventions. How much of oneself can be revealed?[3] "On Some Verses of Virgil" is characterized by a steady clash of opposites: youth/age, art/nature, ancients/moderns, male/female, prose/poetry, but the chief dichotomy may be found in the dynamic tension he maintains throughout between revelation and concealment. Images of secrets, omissions, and hidden things figure throughout the work.

More aroused by the modesty of Virgil (and Lucretius, whose lines on Venus he subsequently introduces) than by the more graphic verses found in Martial and Catullus, Montaigne adds: "There are revelations in that sort of modesty; especially when, as they do, they half-open such a beautiful highway for our imagination." He then proceeds to again equate sexual activity with its depiction and makes a startling observation—one that will drive the essay to its conclusion: "Both that act and its portrayal should savour of theft [*le larrecin*]."

In "A Consideration upon Cicero," Montaigne offered readers a hint on how to read him, especially his often decontextualized quotations from ancient literature:

> Neither these stories nor my quotations serve always simply for example, authority, or ornament. I do not esteem them solely for the use I derive from them. They often bear, outside of my subject, the seeds of a richer and bolder material, and sound obliquely a subtler note, both for myself, who do not wish to express anything more, and for those who get my drift.

As Charles Rosen aptly puts it, this is an "open invitation to read between the lines." In many of his essays, I feel, Montaigne seems to be saying: the more I reveal of myself, the more I conceal. Who's to say that we are more ourselves naked than fully clothed?

I cannot think of a more subtle, intricate, and oblique quotation in all of Montaigne than the one that concludes the Virgil essay. It is from a short poem by Catullus in which the poet finally delivers on a promise to send a friend, a famed orator, his translation of another poet. The delay, he explains, was caused by the death of his beloved brother, and he has only now been able to fulfill his promise. He doesn't want his friend to think his request was overlooked:

> Lest you think that your words have slipped out [*effluxisse*] from my mind,
> Vainly trusted to the wandering winds
> Just as an apple sent as the secret gift of a lover
> Rushes out from a girl's chaste bosom
> Which, tucked under the soft gown of the poor forgetful one,
> Is shaken loose when she jumps up at the approach of her mother,
> And it rushes quickly in a downward descent;
> A conscious blush trickles onto her sad face.
> (Catullus LXV, 19–24)

Surprisingly, Montaigne introduces this odd extended simile of a young woman caught in an embarrassing moment to describe his own writing. Now that he has reached his conclusion, he casually dismisses the literary value of his essay, saying that it "has escaped from me in a stream of chatter [*un flux de caquet*], a stream impetuous and at times injurious" (translation mine). It has escaped from him, in other words, like the apple tumbling out of the blushing girl's gown.

As James Grantham Turner points out, Montaigne's term for his essay, "un flux de caquet," has a gendered connotation with a significant consequence in an essay so focused on sexuality and gender.[4] For Montaigne, the phrase would have suggested a flow of *female* chatter in particular, an important connotation lost in translation. His essay, as opposed to the "virile" forceful style of the Latin poets he has praised, can be viewed instead as mere chatter or babble, presumably trivial, and issuing from a woman's voice.

The simile of the hidden apple tumbling out of a gown is surprising enough in the Catullus poem; it is even more surprising when repurposed by Montaigne to portray his essayist style. Clearly, the poet's word *effluxisse* triggered Montaigne's *un flux*, and the girl's embarrassed reaction can be seen as analogous to the essayist's response to his own self-exposure. Can Montaigne's invitation to read him "between the lines" be applied to this enigmatic simile? If so, what is being concealed? Does he expect his readers to know Catullus's whole poem and fill in the context? Is the poet's much beloved dead brother a sad reminder of the essayist's beloved dead friend Étienne de La Boétie, his spiritual brother? In "On Affectionate Relationships" he writes: "The name of brother is truly a fair one and full of love; that is why La Boétie and I made a brotherhood of our alliance." Montaigne freely admits that he began his life of licentiousness as a way to divert himself from a profound and engulfing grief.

Consolations of the Imagination

Like Montaigne, I considered the loss of sexual vitality one of the chief vexations of old age, and like him, too, I thought it especially unkind of Nature that sexual desire doesn't conveniently disappear once we are unable to perform adequately. Too ashamed to face a woman in the morning after making a poor impression, Montaigne eventually throws in the towel, consigns sex to youth alone, and takes comfort in erotic poetry and fond memories of a former vigor.

I too found consolation in poetry and memories, except that the memories were often those I transformed into autobiographical verse. If they could be transferred to a screen, my most vivid memories and sensory impressions, creatively edited and sequenced, could probably yield a three-hour erotic autobiography, beginning with prepuberty and ending with the present day. These wouldn't be pornographic and prolonged images of actual sex but flashes, clips, and snippets from all kinds of visual experiences over a lifetime.

THE MIND'S EYE: LORETTA

A half century later, you
can still see them in your mind's eye—
the broads you knew you'd never screw,
girls who fell for the other guy

never the likes of you: skinny,
too young to drive and scared to swig,
but still a sucker for floozy
types—like Loretta with her big

boobs, nail polish, and skin-tight skirt;
Ron bragged he banged her in the back
seat of his Dad's Bel Air. "Hey, squirt,"
she'd tease while you pondered that rack.

As the Old Man Poems (as I began calling them to myself) accumulated, I started to shape them into a collection, one that I continually added to and fiddled with, but which I knew would never be made public. In a way they were my "stream of chatter," impetuous and potentially injurious. I shared a few with one close friend, and when he died young, suddenly and mysteriously, I assumed the more obscene poems were safely hidden away in files that would never be opened. My good friend was an accomplished poet and I'm not sure what he thought of my forays into erotic, even pornographic, poetry. He was probably amused by my versifying, perhaps even embarrassed by my self-disclosures. I'll never know.

ALMOST A POET

I could always measure and rhyme
and might have made a fine Poet,
except for the mere fact that I'm
lacking the penetrative Wit

that takes one beyond sound and sense
by piercing the dark tangled core
where images grow deep and dense,
and Truth resides in Metaphor.

Without that creative coupling
what remains is celibate verse;
there's no genuine song to sing
and my obsessions make things worse.

There are many more Old Man Poems, but the majority are not suitable for print, so I will here conclude. I have embarrassed myself enough.

CODA

Although I had read scattered essays of Montaigne here and there, starting in college, it wasn't until 1985, just as I was formulating *The Best American Essays* series, that I sat down with the Donald Frame translation and read him cover to cover. That's when I discovered "On Some Verses of Virgil." I still have that edition with my marginal notes. At the time I was in my mid-forties, happily married (or so I thought), the father of a bright and cheerful two-year-old (who would one day prepare the Latin translations cited in this essay). On that first reading, I found it amusing that Montaigne considered himself old and impotent in his early fifties. From my notes I can see that my approach to the essay was largely aesthetic and academic. But I never forgot the Virgil essay, and when I was invited to contribute to this collection, it came immediately to mind. I wanted to test what my response would be after nearly thirty years, a broken marriage, a sudden solitude, and a dwindling libido. This time I read with a much greater sense of identification and emotional reaction. I too now found myself overwhelmed by fond erotic memories and felt foolish whenever I pursued intimacy and romance, overly sensitive perhaps to my age and infirmities. Montaigne, acknowledging he's no poet (though he clearly shows his "poet-envy"), saturates the essay with quotations, mostly sexual and decontextualized, from classical verse. I identified here too, and though not a poet either, I had been entertaining myself by transforming my sexual memories and experiences into erotic verse. In rethinking the Virgil essay, I found it might provide an occasion to print a few of the more printable poems, and so, braving embarrassment, I seized the opportunity.

21

Of Sleep

JERALD WALKER

The knowledge we have of the greatness of this man's courage by
the rest of his life, may warrant us certainly to judge that his
indifference proceeded from a soul so much elevated above such
accidents, that he disdained to let it take any more hold of his
fancy than any ordinary incident.

MONTAIGNE, "OF SLEEP"

It is 3:16 A.M., and my wife rejuvenates her brain while I lie next to her wasting mine. I am thinking about the papers I have not graded, the debt I have accrued, the careless mason who built our porch, our tenant's complaint about his un-level toilet, and then, as usual, about my two pubescent sons, wondering if they are not simply shy but rather slow or autistic or maybe just unkind in their reluctance to respond when strangers say hello. Over and over I replay an argument I had with a belligerent colleague before imagining it escalating into a tussle, and while the fantasy of shoving his face into a chalkboard is satisfying, it accelerates my heart rate, and now I am thinking about my blood pressure, which my doctor said should not get much higher or I could have a stroke. He recommended that I get more sleep.

"Six hours a night," I told him, "is plenty." It is actually more like four, but my doctor practices his trade aggressively, so it is better to downplay my symptoms than to leave his office with a pocketful of prescriptions and an appointment with a specialist. Every time I go for my annual checkup, I spend thirty minutes being poked and prodded for evidence of a rare disease. Finding no good leads the last time, he settled on my near-hypertension and future stroke being caused by a chronic lack of sleep.

"You need seven to nine hours," he said, "in order for your body to function properly."

I assured him that the functions of my body were very proper.

"There's no need to be defensive," he responded. "Insomnia is actually quite common."

He rattled off some statistics, but he was preaching to the choir. I decided to flaunt my knowledge of the subject with a bit of trivia, gathered over the course of my three-decades-long affliction. "You know, Margaret Thatcher slept for only five hours a night," I said, and then I quoted her line that "sleep is for wimps," the kind of observation one would expect from a person whose nickname includes a hard metal.

"Sleep is for life," he countered. "You do, I presume, want to continue yours?"

Now I am thinking about how much I would like to continue my life, so maybe I should keep the appointment he made for me with Dr. Patrick D'Souza, a somnologist. At the very least I should consider filling my prescriptions for Ambien and Halcion, which would put me in the company of the 10 million average Americans who take sleeping pills. But when I think of taking sleeping pills, I think of not waking from them, and that would put me in the finer company of Jimi Hendrix, Marilyn Monroe, Judy Garland, and Elvis Presley.

I would much rather be in the company of Charles Dickens, Alexandre Dumas, and Abraham Lincoln; they treated their insomnia with long walks through their cities' dark streets. Or maybe, like the actress Tallulah Bankhead, I could hire a gay man to hold my hand. I could treat my unwanted wakefulness like Marlene Dietrich by eating sardines, or by drinking a glass of milk and cognac like Theodore Roosevelt, or I could lie beneath an umbrella being splashed with water from a hose in the manner of W. C. Fields. What I would most like to do, however, is to make good use of this extra time in the way Groucho Marx made good use of his: with prank phone calls.

I am thinking of the prank phone call I would like to make to my doctor. I would say I am Patrick D'Souza, the somnologist. I have poked and prodded your patient and, as you might have guessed, I found a rare disease. It is called Fatal Familial Insomnia, caused by a mutation of the PrP^c protein that inhibits the brain from reaching a state of unconsciousness. There is no cure for this disease. The life expectancy of its victims is eighteen months. During that time, your patient will suffer from paranoia, hallucinations, panic attacks, severe weight loss, and dementia before succumbing to what Proverbs tell us is the sweetest sleep of all. He will leave behind a mentally rejuvenated wife, two shy but probably normal sons, ungraded papers, unpaid bills, a crooked porch, a slanted toilet, and a belligerent colleague with a disfigured nose.

CODA

When I was in my early twenties, my first undergraduate creative writing teacher introduced me to Montaigne. I do not recall what the particular essay was that I read, but I do know that I found it confusing, meandering, and dense. And that was only the first paragraph. I promptly returned my attention to fiction, which I aspired to write at the time, vowing never to read Montaigne again. Subsequent creative writing teachers had other plans for me, however, and I am grateful to have been spoon-fed bites of the master's *Complete Essays* until I first acquired a taste for his style, and then came to understand that confusion, meander, and density can be a profound and elegant thing.

So, too, can concision, the ability to get at the heart of a thing in a matter of a few hundred words, and here Montaigne excels as well. One of my favorites of his shorter pieces is "Of Sleep," as I've always been fascinated by his account of people who can sleep in the face of monumental events. These people, he assures us, must be in the possession of elevated souls. Perhaps that's true. But it may also be true that elevated souls reside at the other end of the spectrum. We insomniacs, after all, put in a lot of overtime thinking, and it is thinking—not dreaming—that requires courage. So my aim was to rebut Montaigne by paying tribute to those of us who find sleeping difficult, not only in the face of monumental events (forget it) but also, at least in my case, in the face of trivia.

22

Of the Inconvenience of Greatness

AMY LEE SCOTT

> The strange lustre that surrounds him conceals and shrouds him
> from us; our sight is there broken and dissipated.
> MONTAIGNE, "OF THE INCONVENIENCE OF GREATNESS"

Once, when I was a child, my brother chased my sister around with an axe while I cowered under a desk with our two youngest siblings, my arms gripping their small bodies so close that I could not distinguish one racing heartbeat from another.

The sun threw itself across the carpet and landed in disjointed shards. From beneath the desk I could see two sets of feet circling and circling. Their shadows jerked behind them. There was panting, shrieking.

We huddled under the desk trying to make ourselves as small as possible. I heard a cough that sounded like a smothered laugh, and then the shadows stopped.

I could see my sister trembling beside the couch, her mascara dripping in leaden streaks down her cheeks. Her sodden eyes.

I could see dust motes suspended in light and my brother's feet stepping toward the desk. One striped athletic sock in front of the other. The soft, trained stalk of a hunter.

My baby brother and sister burrowed deep against me and tried to suffocate their sobs. I could see the fine down of their arms, so white against their summer skin.

There was the axe.

Its familiar splintered handle, its shining steel blade. This was the axe my father used each winter to chop dead branches into logs that would fuel our fireplace night after night.

The axe hung from my brother's right hand. It swayed as he crept toward us.

I remembered watching my father teach my brother how to chop wood. The slish-slishing of blade against whetstone. The dull thwack of blade against oak. The thin, private smile that slithered across my brother's face with every blow.

My brother's striped feet padded closer and closer. They stopped a foot away from the desk. We did not breathe. We did not exist.

He tugged his sagging jeans higher on his hips and crouched down to our level. He smiled. He had beautiful teeth. White and even, like rows of Chiclets gum. They were the teeth of a movie star.

Which explained everything: we were in a movie. There was no other explanation. Somehow, behind my back, our family room had transformed into a soundstage, strung with bright lights and mic booms. A camera kept watch somewhere, whirring through reels of film.

This was not real.

It could not be real. My brother was just another actor, pretending. Soon the scene would end. Everyone would shake hands and retreat to their dressing rooms. They would make dinner plans. And we would loosen our cramped limbs, crawl out from beneath the desk, and carry on like before: Build forts. Pilfer cookies. Quarrel. Just like other children, like other families.

My brother's teeth shone like porcelain. He balanced the axe on one of his bent knees. His charcoal hair was parted down the center of his head. The severe line exposed his scalp's white skin. Such a vulnerable, uninhabited expanse.

I could imagine him fresh from the shower with a towel wrapped around his waist. I could see him, as I saw him every other day, running the tip of a fine-toothed comb across his head. I could see him plastering each hair into place with aloe-scented gel.

This was my brother: pressed T-shirts and bleached socks. Heavy-handed cologne. Meticulous nails. Gleaming teeth.

I tried to ignore my body, which kept urging me to flee. I could not leave the two children huddled by my side. I could not take them with me. We stayed put.

I stared at my brother's mouth. Its smile twisted like putty.

I knew that sneer. It was the same one he had used earlier that summer when he dunked me in our pool and held me down just long enough for my lungs to fill with water. I had heard our father shouting something from the deck and felt my brother's grip release. I broke through the surface, hacking, sputtering, desperate for air.

"We were just horsing around," my brother explained, all smiles. He looked at me. I could see the dagger beneath his grin.

My brother said nothing as he peered beneath the desk. The air thickened with his silence. He bided his time, allowing fear to pull storms into our atmosphere. I was glad to find that the two bodies by my side were nothing but shells. I pressed my hands against their spines and willed them to disappear.

Though my eyes were shut tight, I could still see him. I could see the smooth skin of his face, its olive glow. His inquisitive eyes and sharp jawbone. His Adam's apple that wobbled when he cried. These were as familiar to me as sleep.

This was the brother who spent hours mending things. Whose fastidiousness was both mocked and envied in our chaotic home. Who sat and coached me through flash cards and fractions.

My brother's abusive personality could remain hidden for weeks at a time, or even months. During a lull he would make pancakes, play Marco Polo, mow the lawn. Like all the other guys in our neighborhood, he would listen to rap and BMX on weekends. Clean his diamond studs.

He could be so normal, even kind. And then I would catch him throttling the cat or setting things on fire or punching holes in walls.

It took me years to understand that beneath all of my brother's swagger was the soul of a coward.

My brother peered at us beneath the desk, his lips drawn into a grotesque facsimile of a smile. He made a soft sound in his throat. It was the same cooing I made to soothe our dog during a thunderstorm.

I watched the axe on his knee. How lightly it rested.

He would not use it. It was enough to see us hunched in a corner, shaking. Such was his power: he could eradicate what made us exist in the world, reduce us to a pile of rubble, all without saying a single word.

My brother stood. He stretched his legs and walked away, the axe swaying back and forth with every step, his striped socks receding until they finally disappeared around a corner.

Perhaps my brother felt a thrill when he hurt things. Perhaps he mistook the burning in his chest, the electricity brewing in his spine, for courage.

Perhaps he did not know—not really—that it takes a small man to inflict such great and pointless wrath.

Because only a coward would corner three small children beneath a desk and feel strong.

Only a coward would chase his sister with an axe just to hear her scream.

CODA

"Of the Inconvenience of Greatness" begins with a deliciously layered thesis: "Since we cannot attain unto [greatness], let us revenge ourselves by railing at it; and yet it is not absolutely railing against anything to proclaim its defects, because they are in all things to be found." This sentence contains everything I love about Montaigne's writing: wit, poetry, and empathy. But what I love most is its reflection of his acrobatic mind. To me, Montaigne's greatest strength is his ability to take a theme and gnaw on it from every angle. His keen observations jump from era to era and then manage to land somewhere unexpected.

For this piece, I wanted to nudge a single memory from different vantage points—my experience as a child and my adult hindsight—while riffing on the dark side of greatness. Montaigne seems to both admire and distrust greatness

because of its "easiness and mean facility of making all things bow under you."
As a child, I viewed my brother with the same kind of wariness. He was great in
every sense of the word: kind, awful, powerful, and cowardly. To paint him by
solely showing his defects would be wrong; to delete them would be far worse.
I cannot deny that my brother did these things, but I can complicate his profile
by laying out the details that make him so uniquely himself. He is, as we all are,
human. And what a thing that is.

23

Of Solitude

CHRIS ARTHUR

When the time comes to lose them . . .
MONTAIGNE, "OF SOLITUDE"

When I was growing up in Northern Ireland, speedometers were regarded as unnecessary and dangerous accessories on a bike. I was forbidden to have one and envied boys who did. But even though it rankled, I could see the sense of this parental prohibition. Cycling down the road pell-mell, eyes glued to the dial, willing that red indicator needle to edge ever further up the scale, legs pounding the pedals furiously, crouching close to the handlebars to minimize wind resistance—such rapt attention to speed meant a perilous disregard for traffic and pedestrians. In such circumstances, accidents were inevitable. Fortunately, none of my contemporaries suffered anything more than minor mishaps, despite a few close shaves. They were unrepentant, reckoning, in the foolhardy arithmetic of boys, that some trophy cuts and bruises were a small price to pay for being able to boast—improbably—that they'd reached thirty miles per hour.

Mileometers, by comparison, were considered safe, so my parents raised no objections when I got one. Mine was called a "cyclometer" (we never used the more technical-sounding "odometer"). It consisted of two parts: a little spur designed to register each turn of the wheel, and the counter, a gray metal barrel about an inch and a half long containing four rings of numerals set side by side, visible through a rectangular window. The counter was mounted on a bracket on the front wheel-shaft, and the spur was affixed to one of the spokes. Each time the wheel went round, the spur clicked against the counter's mechanism, turning the numbers. I don't know what portion of a mile is represented by one full revolution of a bicycle's wheel, but these were the increments by which, click by click, this slowly burgeoning measurement swelled.

The accumulating evidence of distance covered was a compelling novelty at first. But apart from this brief initial phase, when I glanced down frequently to see how far I'd gone, I soon forgot the mileometer was there. The only other times it called attention to itself, in the distracting manner of a speedometer, were on those odd occasions when I happened to notice transitions between readings that seemed epochal in their own small way (from 99 to 100, for example), or if for some reason I wanted an exact measure of the distance between a journey's start and end.

I can still remember the pleasure of taking the virgin cyclometer out of its box, its four unsullied zeros lined up behind the pristine glass of the counter's tiny pane. I had a sense of achievement in gradually notching up those first few miles, and then a sporadic feeling of surprise mixed with satisfaction whenever I noticed how far I'd traveled. All those little bike rides that were so much a part of daily life back then—to friends' houses, to the shops, a race across the fields, going bird-watching, cycling from home to school and back—seemed to amount to something when they were put together and considered as a single measurement.

I can't remember now what my final tally amounted to, or what happened to the cyclometer, but I'm sure that all four rings of numbers were in use before I dismissed such a gadget as too childish an accessory to warrant transfer to the racing bike I bought when I was sixteen.

We all start with the corporeal equivalent of the cyclometer's virgin zeros. Then time ratchets up the hours and days, inexorably turning the wheel of our passage. Whether we look at it or not, the numbers on our life-counter are always turning, always moving toward that moment when they'll stop. Calibrated in years, a few of us call three numerals into play by the time we're done. But for most, two numbers are enough to mark the total distance traveled. Tragically, for many, a single figure suffices to record the brief duration of their lives. Of Michel de Montaigne's six children, only one survived beyond infancy, his beloved daughter Léonor.

No doubt these repeated infant bereavements, the death of his close friend

Étienne de La Boétie, his own near-fatal riding accident, and the warfare, sectarian killing, famine, and plague that beset France at this time (nearly half the population of Bordeaux succumbed to the Black Death in 1585) all contributed to Montaigne's intense sense of mortality. But I suspect there was also something in his individual cast of mind that made him vulnerable to having his awareness of life's brevity, its susceptibility to accident, honed to such a particular edge by his experiences—experiences that were by no means unusual for someone living in sixteenth-century Europe. At that time, according to Saul Frampton in his appealingly titled *When I Am Playing with My Cat, How Do I Know She Is Not Playing with Me? Montaigne and Being in Touch with Life*, close to half the children born required only a single numeral to record their span of years. Average life-expectancy wasn't much over thirty. As Terence Cave points out in *How to Read Montaigne*, "the precariousness of life was no abstraction." Montaigne's writing is indelibly imbued with a sense of this precariousness. He was ever mindful of the numbers on his life's mileometer, aware of their uncertain continuance, unknown total, and inevitable end. Reading Montaigne, I sometimes feel like I am on a bike whose clicking cyclometer is a constant refrain. Here is prose laced with a vivid realization of life's flow and transience. "I do not portray being," Montaigne says, "I portray passing" ("Of Repentance").

Such passing means change, not fixity. Montaigne recognizes his own "unstable posture" and suggests that "anyone who observes carefully" will "hardly find himself twice in the same state." His careful introspection finds him by turns: "Bashful, insolent; chaste, lascivious; talkative, taciturn; tough, delicate; clever, stupid; surly, affable; lying, truthful, learned, ignorant; liberal, miserly, and prodigal." His essays explore the "gyration and discord" of this flux of impermanent states ("Of the Inconsistency of Our Actions"). Montaigne's patient soundings provide navigation charts that are sufficiently accurate still to be of use today to anyone seeking to understand the varied currents of the self. His life exemplifies the fact that, as Lydia Fakundiny puts it in *The Art of the Essay*, "You are what you do with your time." Whatever he did, however his time was filled, it was done with a lucid awareness of time's passing and an unfailing interest in the experiences it contained. Kenneth Clark once described Leonardo da Vinci as "the most relentlessly curious man in history." Montaigne would surely have run him a close second.

One of the reasons I'm drawn to Montaigne is because there's an almost Buddhist feel to his outlook. His is a sensibility attuned to what followers of this great tradition refer to as *anicca*, impermanence, something so fundamental to our experience that it's regarded as one of the three "marks of existence." The other two, *dukkha* and *anatta* (roughly speaking, suffering and the fact that the self succumbs to change), also find echoes in Montaigne. Taken alone, this could easily give the mistaken impression of a somber, if not morose, "sick soul" (to use William James's designation), someone preoccupied with the fleeting nature of our being, the unavoidability of pain, and the imminence of extinction. Yes, Montaigne is acutely aware of our finitude—he never loses sight of the turning numerals on life's cyclometer—but the impression that comes across is of a man of warmth and good humor, a genial conversationalist with endless curiosity about the world and an irrepressible zest for living, however hard the circumstances that attend it may be. "The surest sign of wisdom," writes Montaigne, "is constant cheerfulness" ("Of the Education of Children"). I find the Buddhist elements in the *Essays* attractive not because of their emphasis on impermanence, suffering, and death, but because of the way in which Montaigne looks at these inevitabilities with an unclouded eye and takes them in his stride. His manner not infrequently recalls the robust, good-humored serenity of Buddhism at its best.

Buddhism and Montaigne might seem an improbable, eccentric linkage built only on the shaky foundation of my personal idiosyncrasies—the fact that I happen to be an essayist who's been influenced by Buddhist thought. I find it reassuring, therefore, that one of the most perceptive modern commentators on Montaigne, Sarah Bakewell, also reaches for a Buddhist touchstone. In *How to Live: A Life of Montaigne in One Question and Twenty Attempts at an Answer* she points to the way Montaigne seems sometimes to have achieved "an almost Zen-like discipline; an ability just to be." One of the reasons the *Essays* have exerted such an appeal over the centuries is that they record the outlook of a man who's able just to be, yet without shutting his eyes to uncomfortable truths. Rather than wearing the usual blinkers of custom and routine and drifting through life without thinking much about it, as so many of us do, Montaigne proceeds with a clear-sighted deliberation that's impressive. His was a life lived in pretty much continuous awareness of death—the kind of awareness that Philip Larkin expresses with magisterial, if chilling, fluency in his poem "Aubade." Montaigne's realization of time passing, his ability to "see what's really always there," namely that our lives are rushing to their end, is integral to the watermark of his personality; it pervades what he writes. For me, much of the appeal of Montaigne lies in the way in which, as you turn the pages of the essays, you can hear the incessant click-click of life's cyclometer. Yet instead of being paralyzed or disheartened by this deathwatch beetle in his timbers, far from reaching for some convenient set of blinkers or distractions, Montaigne surveys our doomed human vessel with a kind of dispassionate compassion that's slow to judge, quick to smile and question, determined to inquire. Instead of taking time's passing clicks merely as a countdown to disaster, Montaigne is fascinated by the cargoes that they carry. Reading his essays is like hearing the pounding of our mortal metronome parsed into meaningful rhythms.

When the numbers on Montaigne's mortal cyclometer clicked round to September 13, 1592, his course was run. He died on that date, of quinsy and complications relating to that horrible affliction. Nearly four centuries later, Graham Good's *The Observing Self* was published, a book subtitled "Rediscovering the Essay." Appropriately, the opening chapter is devoted to Montaigne. According to Good, "Anyone who can look attentively, think freely, and write clearly can be an essayist; no other qualifications are needed." These are deceptively simple qualities to ask for. But I need only reflect on how often my looking is inattentive, my thinking chained to some dull presupposition or other, my writing muddled, to recognize the difficulty of the criteria Good lays down. And it becomes instantly apparent on reading Montaigne that he possessed these elusive attributes in abundant measure. (As an aside, I find it interesting that Good, one of the key modern authorities on the genre, is himself a Zen Buddhist and that he's recently explored the question "Could there be an affinity between Buddhism and the Essay?")

Sometimes I think of Montaigne as standing within a kind of impregnable palisade that, moment by moment, draws more tightly round him. Like every individual, he's encircled by time's stockade. Our little fortresses of hours and days, the capsules of duration in which we draw our every breath of being, bear us through—define—our existence, but garrote us in the end. Time's cord loops round us, at once umbilical and lethal. Its lifeline-noose lays down iron laws and imperatives common to us all—but there's sufficient variation in its weave and texture, in how it falls upon us, how we wear it, to nurture the rich spectrum of diversity that enriches our humanity. One of its laws is that we are each alone; one of its imperatives that we seek companionship. It is the creative tension of solitude seeking company that powers one of our strongest drives: the urge to communicate. This is a powerful motive behind Montaigne's writing. "No plea-sure," he says, "has any savor for me without communication" ("Of Vanity").

In part, I think Montaigne's personality was cut into its particular shape by a kind of constant abrasion. His heightened awareness of the wash of time against him, the way he was always conscious of the click-click of life's cyclometer, acted like water or wind or sand on stone, smoothing and wearing the intimate landscape of his person into the unique features it displayed. Of course we all undergo such erosion—the impact of the world around us, how family, friends, and strangers lay the touch of their influence upon our lives, the way our own biology hardwires us. I'm not sure what mesh of factors sets the level at which we're self-aware, or aware of time's passing, the extent to which we feel solitude and a desire to reach beyond it, but if Montaigne is anything to go by, these key indices are all closely interlinked.

I've come to picture Montaigne consulting his life's cyclometer with the same frequency and intensity as my boyhood friends looked at their speedometers. But whereas their preoccupation with going as fast as possible made them blind to what was going on around them, Montaigne's preoccupation with life's pass-ing led to more acute perception and, far from inculcating any kind of disregard for others, enhanced his interest in them. It's these qualities that give Mon-taigne's prose its enduring appeal. They combine to form a kind of key that lets him unlock and throw open the shutters we usually close across sights we find unnerving, distasteful, commonplace, or embarrassing. Whatever he looks at— sadness, friendship, sleep, smells, vanity, "the unruly liberty" of his penis ("Of the Power of the Imagination")—Montaigne's honesty is engaging. Throughout the essays, his readiness to lay things open on the page, his unflinching exam-ination of idiocies, atrocities, and intimacies, his preparedness to subject himself to the same scrutiny he brings to bear on others, is disarming. It creates an affec-tionate bond between reader and writer. Montaigne's is a voice that invites us to trust it. The humanity of its timbre makes light of the centuries that separate us.

My old cyclometer was calibrated on a simple scale, readily comprehended. Its four rings of numbers measured out distances it's easy to imagine. Even their maximum reading—9,999 miles—gives a figure that the mind can encompass: the distance between France and Australia (or, to put it in terms more appropriate to a sixteenth-century perspective, close to twenty times the length of the river Loire). A similar cyclometer geared to measure time would likewise give a manageable tally, graspable in straightforward examples. Click the numbers round to just a little over 400, and that's the stretch of years lying between Montaigne and us. Bring all four rings of numbers into play, set them to their maximum, and it takes us back only ten thousand years. Such measures don't challenge the comprehension, or stymie imagination's ability to generate pictures of what's meant.

Of course time's passing and life's fleetingness characterize our experience just as much as they did Montaigne's. But the cyclometers we have to face today throw our transience into even starker relief because of the scale we now know they're set to. We know, for example, that the Earth is around 4,600 million years old, that the first living cells appeared on it about 1,500 million years later. We know that the universe, of which our planet is so infinitesimal a part, came into being somewhere between 10 and 15 billion years ago. We know that, threaded through the immensities of space, there are hundreds of billions of galaxies. And when we turn to the stupendous array of microcosms surrounding us, innumerable cells, innumerable atoms lie beneath the simple visual structures we can see and touch. We also have a much more accurate picture of where we stand within the human swarm. Worldometers (www.worldometers.info)—a kind of global cyclometer website, its electronic counters clicking round continually—assesses current world population as over seven billion. The number of births and deaths on any given day is shown, likewise births and deaths per year. But what I find most arresting in the daunting array of numbers provided by Worldometers is the facility to estimate an individual's place in terms of where they fall in the long line of people who have lived since humanity began. When I was born I was the 76,136,299,830th representative of *Homo sapiens* to appear.

It's easy to be unnerved by such multitudes, to feel any sense of individual significance swept away as we recognize how minutely fractional a part of the species we are—the proverbial dust speck or sand grain or whatever other icon of irrelevance appeals. In this blizzard of other lives, each of us stakes out our tiny claim of time and space, pirouettes within it for an instant, obedient to our desires and fears, affections and regrets. And then we vanish—we have to bid goodbye to whatever relationships we forged, whatever achievements we accomplished, whatever possessions we accumulated, "when the time comes" (as it will come) "to lose them." Surrounded by inconceivable numbers of others, we are yet each of us alone, sequestered in the solitude of individual existence.

Click, and at any moment we can take readings from the cyclometers that are whirring all around us. We can look at the numbers that show our age, the temporal distance that we've traveled. Spin the counter and we're gone; our time is past. Spin it in the other direction and we've yet to be. Montaigne was right, surely, to insist that "it is as foolish to lament that we shall not be alive a hundred years from now as it is to lament that we were not alive a hundred years ago" ("That to Philosophize Is to Learn to Die"). From any personal perspective, the vastness of time is almost entirely characterized by our absence. Lament may be foolish, but wonder is not. Stand back and spin the cyclometer so that individual history blurs and species-calibration comes into play. We're soon back to when humanity had yet to hatch from its prehominid precursors, and beyond that to when life was no more than unicellular. Or switch to a geological scale and spin the massive numbers that it bears: go back a million years, ten million, a billion, or go forward by the same. These dizzying readings are hard to grasp beyond a vague apprehension of annihilating extent and duration. Our tiny mark is easily overlooked, so vast is the canvas on which it's painted.

If, after leaving Montaigne's chateau, you head toward Ménésterol and Mussidan, then drive east along the busy A69/E70 for nearly sixty miles, turning off for Montignac, you'll soon come to one of Europe's most famous Stone Age sites, Lascaux. It's a drive of about an hour and a half through the beautiful Dordogne countryside. I like the fact that as he sat in the round tower of his library, this cave of treasures lay waiting to be discovered only eighty-five miles away. The magnificent Paleolithic art at Lascaux is thought to be more than 17,000 years old. There are almost two thousand painted forms in the caves, showing animals (by far the largest group), one human figure, and various abstract marks, mostly dots and squares. Lascaux was discovered accidentally in September 1940 by eighteen-year-old Marcel Ravidat and three friends. An unpromising hole they stumbled on turned out to lead into another world—an interlinked series of caverns, the walls and ceilings of which were resplendent with images that are now so much a part of our common cultural heritage that they more or less define what we understand by prehistoric art (though the caves themselves have been closed to the public since 1963 to avoid visitors' breath further damaging the colored pigments).

It's been suggested that the paintings may have served some kind of astronomical function—that they show the moon's phases and provide rudimentary star charts, attempts to plot and orientate our position, to map where we are in relation to the heavenly bodies above us. Whatever their stellar significance, it's certain that these magnificent artworks represent a reaching out, an attempt to find navigable meanings, touchstones to help us plot a course through life. That's a property they share with the essays that would be written millennia later less than a hundred miles away.

Montaigne extended hospitality to anyone who called at his chateau. With some temporal sleight of hand, it's easy to imagine him inviting the ancient Lascaux artists to sit down and talk with him over a glass of wine. He'd have been interested in surmounting the communication barrier that lack of a common language would have interposed between them, interested in asking about their art and what it meant, interested in their mode of dress, their diet, customs, beliefs, sex life, body odor. Montaigne would have relished trying to understand them—as he tried to understand cannibals, cripples, thumbs, cruelty, drunkenness, sleep, ancient customs, liars, and a host of other topics. In each case he would further understand himself in the process. He was ever obedient to one of the educational principles he laid down: that we should "rub and polish our brains by contact with those of others" ("Of the Education of Children").

When the Lascaux paintings were done, it's unlikely the world's population was much over a million. Our swarm has grown enormously since then: 100 million by 3000 BC; 250 million by the time of Christ; around 450 million during Montaigne's lifetime; the stupendous current total. Each of these millions lived as we do now, sheathed in their solitude, shaped by experience, garnering memories as local and particular as those of my boyhood cyclometer. We each reach out to others, strive and falter. All of us perish. Whatever number time ratchets up on our individual mileometers in terms of days and years, whatever we dream and dread, every person who has ever lived adds the solitaire of their precious life to the great sum of humans there have been. We are all spurs on the species' wheel clicking round its numbers.

≈

Despite the torrent of lives to which we each contribute the single droplet of ourselves, we lack the seamlessness of liquid. Instead we're marooned in our own quiet pool, the inalienable, detached solitude that rings our person giving us space to be the individuals we are. However much we're part of stupefying measures of time and number, there is about us an aura of private singularity, workable specificity, the impregnable fastness of the individual psyche. Montaigne speaks out of, and into, precisely that nerve of solitude.

According to Graham Good, "At heart, the essay is the voice of the individual." That, I think, is why we listen to it. Individual voices are pitched at a level we can savor, whereas the full chorus of the human swarm would be overwhelming. In *Middlemarch*, George Eliot famously speculated about what it might be like if we could hear grass grow and the beat of squirrels' hearts. Such heightened perception would, she warned, be more than we could bear, "and we should die of that roar which lies on the other side of silence." The sound of seven billion voices is a daunting prospect. Yet, contained in what Richard Chadbourne, writing in the *Encyclopedia of the Essay*, calls "the most famous" of Montaigne's assertions—that "Each person carries the entire form of the human condition" ("Of Repentance")—there's a suggestion that, through any life, we can eavesdrop on every life.

My boyhood cycling companions staring fixedly at their speedometers, Montaigne's short-lived infants, the Lascaux artists, those in plague times whom Montaigne witnessed digging their own graves and pulling the earth over themselves in mortal desperation, George Eliot, Graham Good, whoever now looks upon this sentence, any of the billions of us swarming across the globe—*everyone*—acts as a kind of portal. Discover how to open us, and you're led into panoramas that are incredible in what they can reveal. Explore our story even just a little way and you're soon taken into astonishing vistas. This is what conjures essays. Like philosophy, they begin with wonder. Montaigne, the masterful originator of the genre, was adept at opening the portal of the seemingly ordinary and seeing the extraordinary dimensions just behind it. He may have had a simpler outlook than the one confronting us today, but he had a keen understanding of the way "all subjects are linked with one another." That being the case, he laid down a dictum that resonates through the history of the essay: "Any topic is fertile for me. A fly will serve my purpose" ("On Some Verses of Virgil").

Montaigne's essays provide images as compelling as any Lascaux bison. Reading them, we tap into the same vein of human endeavor that led our Stone Age precursors to blow colored pigment through hollow bones, creating art that still moves us. Such diverse efforts connect us to one of our most fundamental urges: to seek meaning, to understand ourselves. In that connection we may, perhaps, find some comfort to blow through our own mortal bones as we face up to what we can't evade "When the time comes to lose them."

CODA

"Solitude" isn't the kind of thing I normally think about, at least not directly. My writing stems from specific objects and events; it's firmly anchored in the particular. I'm wary of the approach taken by previous generations of essayists where—preceded by "on" or "of"—some wide-ranging topic is announced and readers are treated to a few pages of amiable enough reflection, but pitched at a level of such generality as to be close to vacuous. I find a few such pieces perceptive, some of historical significance, but the majority of no interest whatsoever. It amuses me—though not enough to compensate for reading what's tedious— that their prepositional "on" is so far off the mark. In terms of my attention, this kind of "on" triggers a swift turning off.

I was uneasy, therefore, to find myself writing under precisely such a title for this book. The cyclometer was an intuitive, preemptive countermove against being drawn into the kind of essay whose day, I think, is done. Some part of my psyche, seeing me poised to plunge into dubious waters, threw me the memory-nugget lifebelt of the cyclometer—something hard, specific, definite, rooted in the particularities of time and place that define me; an antidote to any breezy abstractions that "on" might tempt me into making.

Of course the way that "on" means "off" rarely applies to Montaigne. He's an exception to this—as to so many—rules. In any case, you can't judge his essays by their titles. The relationship between them and what he says is loose, tangential, vague, sometimes close to nonexistent. (In part this is due to what Patrick Henry calls "façade titles," titles "designed to trick the censor into missing the hidden, heterodox, or otherwise subversive subject.")

Although it's tempting to present this essay as an echo of Montaigne's of the same title, that would be misleading. An echo suggests a mirror image, something that paces out the same essential shape, albeit at a distance. It is a kind of aural shadow. Echoes wear the livery of repetition, even mimicry; they carry only the residue of a sound already made, rather than making their own original contribution. Although my musings on solitude were occasioned by reading Montaigne, I hope what I've written does more than echo what he says. An echo would be poor homage to a writer I esteem.

Why "Of Solitude"? It's not one of Montaigne's great essays, nor does it reflect a principal characteristic of his personality. Montaigne is the most convivial of men, "born for company and friendship" as he asserts himself ("Of Three Kinds of Association"). In "A Consideration upon Cicero"—which is, in effect, the second part of his essay "On solitude"—he says that he would have preferred letters to essays as the "form to publish my sallies," if only he had "had someone to talk to." The sense of the man that comes across in his writing is of someone genial and talkative who relishes company. Despite his retirement from the affairs of the world, it would be a mistake to see him as a recluse recording his thoughts in lonely isolation. Terence Cave is right to stress the conversational mode of the essays. "Although Montaigne often depicts himself thinking and writing in solitude," says Cave, "he always imagines his writing directed towards others." The essays aren't soliloquies. Rather, they're attempts to reach out and engage others in his ruminations. The sense of conversation, rather than monologue, is enhanced by the frequency with which Montaigne refers to, and quotes from, other writers. Nonetheless, despite all this chatty congeniality, solitude is an essential characteristic of Montaigne—as it is of every individual. How the unique torques and contours of our personality are shaped to form the gradients that make us is clearly a complicated matter. But however the quintessence of the self is calculated, whatever the individual sum may be that makes us who we are, it's held in solution by the water of our solitude.

The quote I've chosen to head this piece is taken from a section in Montaigne's essay where he recommends marriage, family, material possessions, and above all health—but also counsels awareness of the fact that we shall, inevitably, have to part from them. The passage is too long to quote in its entirety for an epigraph. But I hope the haunting resonance of these seven words embedded in it—"When the time comes to lose them . . ." (the ellipsis pointing to our inevitable fate)—will act as reminders of our essential solitariness and our need to clad it, albeit temporarily, in the kind of warm reflective apparel that Montaigne provides so richly.

24

Of Age

MARCIA ALDRICH

We call that only a natural death; as if it were contrary
to nature to see a man break his neck with a fall.
MONTAIGNE, "OF AGE"

I was teaching for a month in San Miguel de Allende, a colonial city of steep cobblestone streets and florid gates in the state of Guanajuato, central Mexico. My students, who ranged in age from just out of college to retirees, were enrolled in a low-residency program that offered, in addition to instruction in writing, day trips to local attractions. For the most part these outings were benign fare, though not always—perhaps because it was Mexico, the country, as André Breton is reported to have said, *le plus surréaliste* in the world. Climbing the hill back to our charter bus after a visit to therapeutic hot springs, the husband of one of the students suffered a heart attack, dropped on his path, and died.

One of these scheduled day trips was an opportunity for horseback riding at a rancho outside San Miguel. This was an unofficial event, for after an unfortunate incident the year before—rumor was that the Americans got drunk and reckless—our sponsoring institution had deemed the undertaking too unsafe to insure. Stepping into the breach, one of the veterans of that prior ride took it upon himself to organize this year's freelance venture on a Saturday.

Before committing myself, I assayed a bit of informal research to find out who was going. At a banquet in our hotel courtyard I asked a group of veteran faculty, "Who's game for an unscripted experience?"

Their reluctant silence suggested they knew something that I did not. A poet whom time had denied his flashing eyes and floating hair, who shuffled at a precarious angle whenever he crossed the courtyard to refill his wine glass, said, "At our age it isn't prudent to undertake the ride."

I was taken aback. What did he mean, at our age? I hadn't lost my hair, my face hadn't fallen onto my chest, and I didn't shuffle. *My* best days were not behind me!

The next morning I asked my students if anyone was riding, and every head around the oblong table shook a vehement no. There was a general air of trepidation. I was incensed by such defeatism—middle-aged people, even the young, galloping toward retirement, gathering it into their open arms as if it were a precious cargo! Now I was determined to go. Students in some of the other classes were also bold, and nine of us signed up, paying our $75. I was the only faculty member.

I had ridden often from the age of seven and had my own horse from age twelve. I rode every day, lived and breathed the animals, felt no separation between myself and my horse, between heart and body. I took jumps at a gallop, was thrown, rolled to save my bones, and climbed back on. I hadn't been on a serious ride for decades, but I felt a kinship with that earlier girl, an intimacy; she was alive inside me, and I was not planning to say goodbye anytime soon. I didn't suppose I would ease into the saddle with the lightness of a sixteen-year-old practiced in the ways of mounting. But the feel of a horse beneath me would come back—it was there waiting in the story of my bones. In my years away from riding, I had often driven by a nearby stable when the horses were set out to pasture, and wondered how I had turned away.

I assumed my body would be up to the challenge. Were a physical examination required, I would pass. I thought of myself as physically tough. I had no thought that my body, the house I lived in, was a vulnerability.

About the specifics of the outing I knew next to nothing. I imagined we'd be riding along trails through the open scrub terrain I'd seen around San Miguel. We were to wear long pants, long-sleeved shirt, and hat, bring sunscreen, and be at the pickup spot by 9:00 a.m. We assembled at Calle Cardo, a twenty-minute walk downhill from the hacienda where I was boarding (the hike back uphill had earned the street its nickname, Calle Cardio). It was the designated meeting place for field trips, and for a congregation of stray dogs that gathered on the grounds of the Episcopal church there.

The people waiting with me for departure were indeed a nonindigenous bunch, none in proper riding clothes. I wore hiking shoes, a T-shirt, thin pants more appropriate for kayaking, and no hat. My backpack carried a water bottle, camera, long-sleeved shirt, sunblock, wallet, glasses, and lip balm. (In my former riding life, a hard hat was obligatory, complete with a chin strap to keep it on through jolts and bounces. I wore stiff boots that ran up to my knees. There were good reasons for such apparel. If you fell off, you wanted to protect your head, and the boots prevented the chafing of flesh.) I was twenty years older than any of the other adventurers, and I recalled lines the director of the program had recited the evening before:

> The night is young.
> You are not.

When the SUVs arrived, we boarded and drove out of San Miguel into grazing land and cactus plains. Outside town there was little human development. Forty minutes along the road we turned off onto a dirt and stone track that cut through terrain rutted with rocks and cactus, impossible to cultivate. We lurched more than rolled, stopping to let wandering cows and sheep cross in front of us.

For four generations the same family had owned the 400-acre ranch, now broken into tracts held by three brothers. I knew better than to imagine a grand hacienda and magnificent stables set on well-groomed grounds. Indeed, the ranch house was small, presiding over an empire of dirt. The guides for our ride were Tomás, Félix, and Roberto, the brothers who owned Rancho Xotolar. The horses, part mustang and part quarter horse, stood in angles of boredom in the dirt, already saddled. They were smaller and stringier than the mounts of my youth. These were workhorses, ridden hard and kept outdoors all year long.

The first task for our guides was to match rider to horse. The brothers applied rules of affinity that were in some cases mysterious. They did not see in me a fearless equestrian ready to be matched with a hard-to-handle beast. Give her a sweet horse, they judged, a slow and gentle one. I was waved over to a little chestnut mare, finely built, fifteen hands high, her neck short and thin, her head small. The white markings on her face and legs were dirty, her tail and mane unlustrous. I doubted she was ever brushed. She was underwhelming in all ways— no gloss or sheen, no magnificence to her carriage. I looked into her eyes, trying to elevate the moment: *Will you take me across a river where I must go? You will, for you have forded it a thousand times.* Her eyes said nothing in response. Her name was Mariposa—*mariposa*, the transforming butterfly. Mariposa was my last ride.

We rode out over the untouched terrain that began outside the stables. Except for one stop at a tiny store, we encountered no human beings and nothing of what humans make, no roads, train tracks, telephone lines, cars, tractors, sounds of engines of any kind. Just land, scruffy land, dotted with the paddles of nopal cactus, grasses, scrubland cut by arroyos, steep and rocky, with a river trickling through. We scrambled up and down ragged trails at the precipices, where if any creature lost its footing, both horse and rider would hurtle over the cliff. The guides had faith in the horses' steadiness, enough to carry an unskilled group such as ours. We gripped the horn of the saddle and went slowly, trusting our mounts more than ourselves. The three brothers, however, were cowboy show-offs, charging down the hillsides, scattering rocks underfoot. When the rest of us neared the bottom of an arroyo, we'd rocket forward as the brothers shouted and rode up and down the line, slapping the horses' flanks to make them gallop. The air was filled with high laughter and gusto as we barreled along a river, plunging in and then emerging on the other side.

Mariposa couldn't have been a sweeter ride. She did what I asked, responded when I lifted my reins to the left or right, stopped when I lightly pulled back on the bit. When I talked to her, she turned her head to listen like a fond companion. Aware of how thin she was, I squeezed her sides gently. I held my rope reins high off her neck and did not yank them. Even so, I felt sorry that she had to carry me. I was not a queen of the horse. I was not accustomed to the Mexican saddle, with its large horn and cantle, to sitting straight and long in the saddle, not posting. I couldn't get the hang of it. Hunter style is what I had ridden, with shorter stirrups, body angled forward, hands resting slightly up on the horse's neck. I knew I should be pushing down on the stirrups, and keeping my back straight. I knew these things, but I jangled and jostled, I bounced. I was not in sync with my horse, and this was not the return to riding I had imagined. It was not like the lost fields of my youth, not a riding out of my body. For the first hour or two I felt sad pity for Mariposa, how hard for her to encounter a clumsy rider like me. I didn't consider what all this bouncing was doing to the bones of my back.

I have no idea how many miles we covered. Branches slapped my face as I angled through thickets, thorny shrubs pricked my uncovered arms, mud and river water splattered my pants. I fell forward, I fell back. I bounced in the unfamiliar saddle. Before long every step, every stumble hurt. The ride lasted four or five hours; I can't say exactly because around midway I felt such pain that I was no longer conscious of what was going on around me. I was partially upright in the saddle, and Mariposa and I were still with the group. For that I credit her instincts, not mine. We cantered through the brush when everyone cantered through the brush, slowing down on the steep inclines. Mariposa was in charge, and I held on the best I could. I felt as if I were splitting open from inside. Cracking.

We stopped in a beautiful grove of trees for our last break. I slithered out of my saddle and leaned against Mariposa's curved neck. Why this pain? I hadn't been dashed against the rocks in the river; no horse had kicked me or pinned me against a tree. After a few minutes we remounted for the final segment. I didn't know if I could make it back. Yet I had to do it—there was no other option. I slumped forward in the saddle and on Mariposa's neck, without the pretense of sitting straight up. Finally Roberto noticed. He took my backpack, but it made no difference.

As a last hurrah the cowboys led us to a wide plateau high above the river and ran the group in wild sprints back and forth. Mariposa and I stood apart, at the edge of the bluff, waiting. This would be my future, I sensed, a spectator rather than a participant.

The ending was a long cooling-down walk back to the house, where I could finally slide to the ground—my last dismount, and a ragged one it was. I slumped to the dirt and didn't get up. One of my companions fished extra-strength Advils out of her pack and brought me a beer to wash them down. I leaned against the trunk of a tree and sat with my legs stretched out in the dirt, which crawled with red ants. I didn't care—let them bite me. Mariposa stood alongside until someone came to lead her away. Her ride for the day was over, and another would come tomorrow.

One of the brothers asked me to lie on my stomach—he was sure I needed a good massage. Before I could manage a no, he was sitting on my back. He was wiry and small, but still it was not good to have him sitting on me. Broken ribs seemed more likely than muscle strain, and no massage would repair the breakage.

The others went into the ranch house for a meal. Now the medicine, beer, and fatigue kicked in, and I slipped away. Where was I again? Where was this place without power or towns, with its vast uninterrupted horizon? I had gone as far from the familiar as I could. In this unknown land and language I had found a river, but it wasn't the one I thought I'd ford. I sat up and waited for the event to be over, for the drive back to San Miguel, for the pain to lift and fly away, for me to return to what I was.

Tomás emerged from the house and came over to me, squinting into my eyes. "I have not seen this before," he said. "You have already much pain, one you do not know about, that the horse show you."

I remember little of the drive back to the hacienda. They dropped me off in front of the gates, and someone helped me to my room. I took to my bed and tried to lie in a position that wouldn't hurt. Kind people came to see how I was.

We were midway through the one-month program. On a cold Monday morning I showed up for my class and continued. At night I'd arrange the pillows to prop myself up in bed, finding some minutes of comfort before moving to another position. Standing on the roof garden in the evenings, looking out over the abandoned bullring down the hill, I sensed an ending. A limit had been reached. I hoped that whatever had happened to me would heal, that I would return to who I had been. But the hope was faint. Pain and melancholy were much stronger. A horse had always been under me, but I would never saddle up, scramble down the arroyo into the river again. I would never feel the rawness of a ride again, be in the grips of it. I let the truth of this hit me. I said to my youth, "I let you go. Go from me." The pulse of romance had died.

I did accompany the others on the last field trip, a return to the thermal springs. I swam along a sunlit channel into the cave where the waterfall spilled. I stood under the pulse of the stream and let it pummel my back where I was old and hurt. Once back home in the States, I saw my doctor and told him the story of my ride. A bone density test revealed little fractures all along my spine. Bouncing roughly in the saddle over rocky terrain for hours had exposed the fissures under the cradle of my skin.

The pain has since dwindled, is not too much to bear, except when a friend of mine posts photos of her rides through the oak hills of California. They stab me like a sharp rib. Sometimes she says we'll go out riding together one day, but I tell her it is finished for me. *Inside I am turning to dust, like the wing of a broken butterfly.* Says the counselor Montaigne of my dead life of riding, "We should acknowledge that so extraordinary a fortune as that which has hitherto rescued us from those eminent perils, and kept us alive beyond the ordinary term of living, is not like to continue long."

CODA

In the centuries since Montaigne wrote "Of Age," the expected span of a human life spent in the wealthy portion of the world has doubled, like a dining table pulled open and fitted with additional leaves. This enlarged banquet has thrown out of alignment his judgments upon specific ages, as if the chairs had stayed in place while the table was extended. The woman of forty who now dines at the middle of life was in Montaigne's time supping toward the end.

But our sequence of growth, maturity, decline, and death remains the same, and Montaigne's gimlet assessments of these stages have an enduring sharpness:

> As to my own particular, I do certainly believe that since that age [thirty], both my understanding and my constitution have rather decayed than improved, and retired rather than advanced. 'Tis possible, that with those who make the best use of their time, knowledge and experience may increase with their years; but vivacity, promptitude, steadiness, and other pieces of us, of much greater importance, and much more essentially our own, languish and decay.

It is this retrospective view, back toward one's own prior strength, that I have taken up in my essay "Of Age." Montaigne's skeptical wisdom is sobering, even tragic, and I have tried to carry forward his frank temper, reminded that the essayist must grapple with what pricks her, riding the horse of her thought into strange terrain, from which there can be no return.

25

Of Practice

PATRICK MADDEN

> I hold that a man should be cautious in making an estimate
> of himself—whether he rates himself high or low makes no
> difference. . . . To say less of yourself than is true is stupidity, not
> modesty. . . . To say more of yourself than is true is not always
> presumption; it too is often stupidity. . . . No particular quality
> will make a man proud who balances it against the many
> weaknesses and imperfections that are also in him.
> MONTAIGNE, "OF PRACTICE"

Tuesday and Thursday evenings after dinner, I gather my daughters and their friends at the park, set up the net, toss out the balls, and teach them the basics of serving and bumping and setting and, recently, spiking. For some this is habit, and their skills are quite refined for their ages, but for others it is a first encounter with volleyball, and they struggle to train their bodies to crouch and their legs to propel them and their arms to stay together and not to swing. The drills are sometimes tedious in their repetitiveness, but all the girls are eager and teachable, and every simple volley elicits their joyous cheers, as well as mine. We play until the wind whips up with the fading light of day.

I myself learned volleyball relatively late in life, having caught the bug from my friend Chris Petitto, who ran an all-night charity fundraiser tournament during high school. We gathered our tall friends from the track team, took second place my junior year, won the next, and bought portable nets and professional balls to play doubles all summer in my backyard. Concurrently with this long-term mania, I graduated and went off to Notre Dame, where I tried out for the men's volleyball team and failed to make the cut. A kindly PE teacher there allowed me to attend all her volleyball classes throughout the day and across the semester, and my old high school added girls' volleyball for the first time in its history, hiring a cagey old stork of a baller named Pat Hall to coach the players, including my sister. My mother mentioned to him my budding interest, and that summer, when I was home, he took me to the beach and drilled me at the park with all the basic, uncomfortable skills until they felt comfortable and we began winning B- and then A-level tournaments, and in the fall I tried out again and made the Notre Dame team.

From then on I majored in volleyball, keeping my knee pads in my backpack and playing every chance I got, not only with the team three nights a week and at matches and tournaments, but on the quad whenever the weather was nice, and at home all summer, with friends and Coach Hall, in my backyard, at the local school, on the beach. Although I sat on the bench my entire sophomore year, the incessant, callous drilling at the hands of the coach and the goading from my teammates molded me into a more aggressive, better skilled player, who could use his height and jumping ability quite well. By my junior year I was a starter and able to cover three different positions when necessary (primarily I played opposite, but also outside and middle), and I contributed to a successful team ranked nationally among all collegiate club teams. My senior year I was the team's president and captain. Each year we flew or drove to collegiate club nationals, where we tended to do well, though never as well as we'd hoped. I dreamed of playing beyond college, perhaps professionally, as my teammate Brian Ceponis did in Norway, or on the beach, taking to the next level what I'd been doing all summer already.

Thanks primarily to Malcolm Gladwell, most of us are aware of K. Anders Ericsson's "ten-thousand-hour rule," which states, basically, that to become expert in an endeavor, a person must put in about ten thousand hours honing the skill. In addition to citing the research, Gladwell refers to the Beatles' years playing steady gigs in Hamburg and Bill Gates's precocious computer programming to anecdotally prove the point.

I mention this because I've recently done some estimates, summing the time I suppose I spent on the court across, say, those years between ages seventeen and

twenty-two, and I think I was nowhere even close to ten thousand hours. That's
a *lot* of time. There are 8,765 hours in a year, but we spend about a third of them
sleeping, and since volleyball for me was something to do outside of school and
other obligations, I'd guess I might have made it a third of the way there. Add in
all my playing after college, on club teams and in graduate school and at picnics
with friends, and I'm beyond halfway but still short of the mark. So I got good,
far better than I was when I had only an inkling and a desire, but my aspiration
to play with the elite was, ultimately, a delusion.

I mention it also because I've begun to think of my middle life as plateau
and decline. I can recall clearly times when my capacity was on the rise, when I
met every new challenge with a shrug, when I absorbed difficulty into my general routine and felt energized by tasks, especially if they required me to learn
something new. I felt this prominently when I was a missionary and every few
months brought a new calling with greater responsibility than the one before,
and even though I constantly felt maxed out, the new work simply took me
to a new maximum, including my final five months, when I was traveling the
mission to do training and staying up late to write talks and running an area
with visiting companions much of the time. I felt great. *Bring it on!* I thought.
Then, later, when I was finishing my PhD, with two young children, Patrick
and Adriana, friends would ask almost daily, "How do you do it?" to which I'd
reply that Karina was a big support, but also I thought, *What's the big deal?* They
meant, I'm sure, where did I find the time to stay abreast of all they were doing
(reading, writing, studying, teaching) in addition to managing the chaos of family life (and, it should be noted, playing on the Ohio University men's volleyball
club team, practicing often and traveling for matches during several months of
the year). I found it by working efficiently, dedicating hours to particular tasks,
minimizing distractions, and sleeping very little. I always felt energized. Later,
once I started working at BYU, my friend Steve asked if I wanted to help him
translate a Uruguayan-Mexican poet he knew, and though I was writing essays
and shopping a book around and building a website by learning the backend
coding and designing the CSS myself, I could handle it all, not just *handle* it but
actually master it, along with a fair share of cleaning and cooking and parenting,
not just the two children I've already mentioned but also Sara and Daniel, who'd
arrived in the meantime.

Of course, Karina was my full partner in everything at home—she's that
still—and yet now that I'm no longer young, and now that Marcos and James

have rounded out the tribe, I can barely find the energy to read student papers, let alone maintain a website or translate poems or finish overdue essays and books. I find my mind pulled every which way by interruptions both external and internal. On the rare occasion when I stay up late to finish grading or writing, I pay for it dearly the next day. Now when people ask, as they still do with fair regularity, "How do you do it?" I stumble and mutter. I have no answer to give them. I want to ask, "What do you mean by *it*?"

I must be cautious in my self-estimation. I harbor no illusions about my talent or skill—I think myself no great essayist nor professor nor father nor great anything—but I can honestly say that while I worked hard when I was younger and sometimes felt fatigued, I also felt that busyness was part of the program. I was fine. Now I feel none of that. I feel harried. Hobbled. Hemmed and hawed. Fully aware that that last one is not typically a transitive verb, yet unwilling to change them to something more accurate or suitable. You know what I mean, right?

Perhaps I am destined to always be obsessed by something or other. Over the past twenty-five years, the place that volleyball occupied in my hierarchy was gradually supplanted by essaying, as I took stock of my capabilities and capacities, realizing that my body wouldn't sustain a high level of play, nor would my interest. I learned, instead, that what I loved to do more than anything was to think: widely, wildly. From there it was a short step to realizing that I could create for myself a life full of thinking by writing essays, which would permit me to explore a subject for as long as it held my interest, to learn as much as I could through study and memory, and to make artful associations toward a new creation. I was right, or lucky. So far, the process has not disappointed me. I still find essaying exhilarating.

But the essays have never been easy. For years I honed my craft and increased my understanding in workshop after workshop and in consultation with friends and mentors. I read voraciously, trying to learn how essays were written, and I wrote wrote wrote, grabbing at every stray idea that flitted across my consciousness, sometimes creating a paragraph, sometimes a completed essay. Whenever I thought I *had it*, thought I had made enough progress that the next essay would be a simple matter, I inevitably learned that there was nothing to be had, that each essay was a new endeavor, that even though I could tick off certain writing skills and techniques, I could never learn a formula for writing a good essay. So I don't know if I ever crested. I hope not. What I see now, though, is that while I can still write a halfway decent essay when I put my mind to it, I've become a monument to inefficiency. With Hazlitt I feel inclined to lament, "What abortions are these Essays! What errors, what ill-pieced transitions, what crooked reasons, what lame conclusions! How little is made out, and that little how ill! Yet they are the best I can do."

This (camaraderie, advice) may be the best consolation I can achieve when even writing has become so difficult for me, when lately I've been taking years to complete some pieces to my satisfaction. I've come to believe that I am always just practicing. I often recall that the Spanish word for essay, *ensayo*, means, most commonly, "rehearsal." And that's okay. Essays are inherently practice. Essays equal practice.

But let me not get away with affirmation here, nor with any suggestion that my darling little boys pushed me over the edge (with only two children, I seemed to be saying, life was a breeze; with four, I was still in my prime; but Marcos and James, with their indefatigable mischief-making, have finally been the end of productive, balanced me). Life feels heavier, that's all. Its yoke is not easy, its burden no longer light.

Enough of this self-pity. Instead, here is a story, of volleyball, from the past:

Among the most memorable matches I ever played was a Notre Dame preseason home game against Michigan in my senior year. With both teams consistently losing to Michigan State but no one else, we'd formed a kind of respectful rivalry, vying for second in the Midwest Intercollegiate Volleyball Association, always hoping for a surge of luck to carry us into first over the Spartans. Things were never overly heated between us, but the matches were spirited and always well played.

We handily took the first game in our best-of-three match, but then in the second, an out-of-control Michigan middle crashed through the net and slid underneath P. J. Stettin, who landed on the Wolverine's foot and fell to the court writhing and holding his ankle. Later, doctors would confirm a compound fracture of the fibula. (Oh, how we watched our video of the match, cringing and squinting at the break, pausing and rewinding and replaying, lamenting our friend's shattered senior season and our team's decreased chances for the championship.) But that day, after the shock of losing our starting middle and reeling to a second-game loss, we rallied under the cry "For P.J." and pieced together a solid enough performance to bring the match to 14–13, match point, our serve. I was in the front row, right side, a position that set me to block against their outside hitter, their best and most likely attacker.

When I pray I can often feel again that match-winning block: the tracking eyes darting from setter's hands to hitter's, Brian Ceponis planting next to me and our simultaneous liftoff, the clenching calves, shrugging shoulders, the pike over the net, fanning fingers, rotating wrists, then the crack of the hit and instantaneous block, as if *I* had hit the ball, as if the ball's momentum transferred upward motion to me, lifted me aloft for longer than my leap would allow, for longer than the ball, so that I'm still in the air, watching, as the ball bounces just inside the line and the team and crowd erupt with joy of vindication. Then my feet return to earth and spring me back upward and around to embrace my friends.

As should be obvious, I look to the past for companions and examples, not only of how to write but how to live. I measure myself against my forebears. When I read eyewitness accounts of Samuel Johnson dashing off his essays while the printer's boy waited (and even Johnson's own mention of such in *Rambler* #134, on procrastination), I am dismayed at my own dammed creativity. Certainly I have a busy life, with the aforementioned six children and two teaching jobs and, recently, glorious international travel directing study abroad programs, not to mention a house to maintain and a companion to share my joys and burdens with and to whom I never give enough of my time or my self. Every year, I calculate, I write enough criticism and commentary on students' essays to fill two books. It's no wonder I'm so slow writing my own work. But I'm not making excuses (or not wanting to, at least); instead I'm asking myself what's wrong, or *if* anything is wrong. How did Johnson (not a young man at the time, with a wife in failing health, and grown-up children) do it?

So I revel in his fellowship and feel a tinge of joy when I read that he, too, lacked confidence in his abilities and felt himself slipping (thirty years before his death), as he states plainly in the last of his *Rambler* essays, where he admits having often brought to his task

> an attention dissipated, a memory embarrassed, an imagination
> overwhelmed, a mind distracted with anxieties, [having labored] on a barren
> topick, till it is too late to change it; or, in the ardour of invention, diffus[ing]
> his thoughts into wild exuberance, which the pressing hour of publication
> cannot suffer judgment to examine or reduce.

It seemed to me as if I had myself written the essay, as Emerson (and so many others in so many words) said of Montaigne.

Because I still play volleyball, and some of my clothing advertises the fact that I played on a college team, I sometimes find myself answering questions about my past. I try to self-deprecate, or to give people an accurate sense of what Notre Dame Men's Volleyball meant, and even here I've tried to clarify in a way I usually cannot when in conversation, either because of lack of time or my own willingness to let people believe that it means something more than it really means. Yes, I played volleyball in college. It was a club team with fine players, but by and large we were not as skilled as the varsity teams out west. Title IX's imposed gender equality in sports would not allow a school like Notre Dame, with dozens of football scholarships, to add a varsity men's sport. So we did the best we could with no recruiting, no scholarships, very little budget. It all brought me great joy, gave me frivolous purpose, allowed me an escape from the buzzing in my mind. When I played, I played wholly. I focused on the ball's bounces, felt the rhythms of the game, subverted my ego to the team's will to win. Through many many hours, my muscles memorized the sport's movements, so that now, when I am still, I can still feel the swing and lift or thrust and dive, can still drive my forearms together or place my open hands above my head at ball's width. In this way, perhaps, I have beaten Hazlitt. "What is there that I can do as well as this?" he asked upon seeing an Indian juggler. I can play volleyball.

The last time I played good volleyball was two years ago, on an intramural team gathered by my friend Jesse and consisting of several former BYU players, a pair of current students, and me. Of the eight men on the roster, I was the oldest and nearly the feeblest. Save the one student who seemed never to have learned the rotations, I was the biggest liability, but the other fellows treated me well, accepting my limitations and including me in the plays with an adequate number of sets and high fives after every successful block or kill. Everyone knew how trivial the whole championship was, especially compared to the glory days nearly everyone had lived in the past, but we still wanted to win, and we ran simple combination plays and double- and triple-blocked far weaker players who, you could tell, were just out to have a good time. We were, too. Just that, for us, a good time was every guy playing his position and acting predictably in the best possible way on each play, and even if it was a weak echo of everyone's youth playing on well-trained cohesive teams, we sometimes flashed with speed and power, and the smiles were plentiful. As the weeks progressed, we met successively stronger teams until we were playing in the upper-division double-elimination tournament on a night when Jesse, the fulcrum, the guy who knew everybody and had brought us all together, was busy at church meetings, and we were stuck with only six guys, including me and the one guy worse than me, with no subs to hide us or give us a rest. We lost our first match to a young, scrappy team that dug most of our hits, and I can't imagine an engaging prose re-creation of a volleyball match, so I will spare us all and cut to the reason I brought it up in the first place: Early in our second match of the night, as I was blocking the right side of the net, an overexuberant young hitter threw himself at a too-low, too-tight set and came crashing under the net, sliding right under my feet just before I landed on him. He was whistled for the violation, but this was small consolation. My foot, failing to find firm floor, wrenched outward, tearing my ligaments and spraining my ankle. The kid didn't even have the decency to help me up or apologize.

And that was that. While my healthy contribution to the team might not have been enough to help us win the match, my absence was certainly enough to give the match to the opponents, and we never played together again.

I said that the last time I played good volleyball was two years ago, but that's not quite true. Just this past summer, I played some beach quadruples with my brothers and their friends, a few of whom play professionally. As it was early in the morning and we were unevenly matched in skill and endurance, we invented variations on the sport—only left-handed underhand hits, only bumps, only overhand spikes, you have to jump every time you contact the ball—which transformed what might have become tedious into joyous silliness. Eventually we played a full-fledged game, but even before then, I could see something utterly unattainable in Billy Allen, whose effortless motions seemed like an emanation from the poles and net and sand. He was one with the game, moving with such grace and fluidity that you'd think he'd played each volley before and memorized its actions. While my brothers and I (most of all) were huffing with effort, sweating profusely, shake-and-baked with sand everywhere but our faces, Billy was at leisure. I knew again what I had long known: that even though I had once been a pretty decent player, certainly could jump higher and swing harder and last longer than I could now, I was never in that elite category, nor could I have been, even if I'd practiced my life away.

So I don't mind practice now that I'm the coach and the players are young and distracted, sometimes goofy, doing cheers and dances while I'm trying to explain things. I don't even mind when I have to go over for the hundredth time please don't swing your arms did you see what just happened when you swung your arms at the ball it sailed sideways out of bounds and that's not going to help us win so please just trust me I know it sounds counterintuitive but you want to pass with your legs lift your legs and use your arms as a platform to direct the ball where you want it to go please concentrate just trust me if you do what I'm saying it will work every time please okay hey no swinging! Those dusk hours are sweet to me now, and I think I care more deeply for the results of the girls' games than I ever cared about the ones I played in, which is a lie, I know, but what I mean is that I can no longer care about the frivolity of winning and losing for myself. I scarcely know who that was who screamed a profanity at the referee when she ended a close match by calling Brian Ceponis for a lift off the block when he'd clearly popped the ball off his fist. Or who stormed into the storage room when his coach accidentally pulled him out for the final allowable substitution in a game that was nowhere near over. Or who overdosed on ibuprofen to combat acute Achilles tendinitis after two weeks of injury kept him from playing important matches that his team was losing (I tell this story often: how the nine Advils *cured* me and my heel never hurt again, though just that morning I'd been *unable to wear shoes* for the stabbing pain).

I'm always telling people how volleyball is a lifelong sport, the kind of thing you can casually enjoy into your golden years, and I still believe that, though I rarely show up for Wednesday night pickup games at church, and when I set up the net at a picnic, I feel more like I'm doing service than enjoying myself, and my knee pads (not any of the many pairs I destroyed through my youth, but a new pair that Karina thoughtfully bought me a few Christmases ago) are often lost for long months or hidden in my closet wedged between two piles of T-shirts, but just this morning, as I was writing, Marcos and James interrupted, asking me to give them horsey rides. Of course, I said, as I am always keen to recognize the spirit's whisper, and we had a rollicking time galloping around the family room until my knees began to ache against the thin carpet, and I thought, no doubt because I was dwelling in this essay at the time, *my knee pads!* and traipsed up the stairs to pull them from their resting place and slide them over my creaky knees to once more shuffle and swing beneath my overexuberant sons. It was a repurposing, an improvement, a little more time with my young sons before they are no longer so young or so light.

CODA

Like many people I've met, I struggled to *get* Montaigne the first time I read his *Essays*. I found him a bit dry and, having been raised surrounded by narrative, I wondered where the stories were. But with time and patience, I grew not only to understand him but to love him, as I saw the shape of his mind laid out on the page, and I wanted to adopt his method of literary exploration.

So in a way, I've been writing Montaignean essays for more than a decade, and many times I have assigned my students to borrow his titles and mimic his form, but I'd never done such a tightly bound Montaignean essay as this one. At first I thought of writing "Of the Affection of Fathers for Their Children," for obvious reasons, and then "Our Feelings Reach Out Beyond Us," for reasons that now escape me. One fine fall evening, after a particularly pleasant volleyball practice with my daughters, my mind turned to my undecided essay project. Montaigne's "Of Practice" showed up, too, and the idea of writing about volleyball practice suggested itself. This was doubly appealing, because although I'd loved volleyball for all of my adult life, I'd never written a volleyball essay. The match seemed fated. After finally settling on "Of Practice," but (predictably) struggling with the actual writing, I felt a flash of inspiration and began writing "Of Names" but realized that I had often written "of names" elsewhere, and wondered what more I might have to say. So I returned to "Of Practice," one of my favorite Montaignean essays, and I began to understand that my current life experience beyond volleyball also seemed to align well with an attempt at refiguring it (for Montaigne, it was practice for death; for me, it was subversion to suggest a much more pedestrian kind of practice, and to hook into his thinking on self-appraisal). Montaigne's essay is one of the few that narrates an extraordinary event from his life (his near-death experience upon being knocked from a horse), and it includes some of his best, most extensive meta-essaying, or instructions for would-be essayists. I began with his idea of self-assessment and let myself consider the ways my youthful hopes had changed into something more realistic, how I'm far from the volleyball player I once was, and how I'm making peace with my decreasing capacities. In short, against my intentions, the essay may have become "Of Age."

26

The Ceremony of the Interview of Princes

ELENA PASSARELLO

It is much better to offend him once than myself
every day, for it would be a perpetual slavery.
MONTAIGNE, "THE CEREMONY OF THE INTERVIEW OF PRINCES"

If I can't do what I want 2 do, what am I?
When U stop a man from dreaming, he becomes a slave.

Do not call him on the telephone. He often insists he does not own one, or that he does not know its number. He is permitted to call you anytime (on a phone he presumably borrowed or just found lying around somewhere), and Lord knows you will answer him whenever he does. But if you try to call him first, you will not be successful. Even if you're an employee, even if you are married to him, the custom is that *he* first reaches out, and he does so at his leisure. So wait by the telephone.

First, a woman will call and advise you to make yourself ready. She will call back to say you can expect him in twenty-five more minutes. In a half-hour, she will call again and ask that you wait another nineteen minutes. Then she will call to say he'd rather call you at your home and would you give her that number? When you arrive at your house, you'll find a message from her to wait five more minutes. Ninety seconds later, your phone will ring, and there will be his voice.

You will never be permitted to record his voice, but you will feel fiercely compelled to describe it. You'll want to report its dusky smallness and its simple modulation—a massive contrast to the three octaves it runs so nimbly in larger arenas. But in a private phone conversation, he offers no pyrotechnics, and the vertigo is palpable. There is something unnerving about a majestic voice presenting itself as the sound of an intimate.

He can offer several reasons for forbidding tape recorders. Verbatim conversation creates an unjust covenant—that is one reason. *Some in the past have taken my voice and sold it*—that is another. A third reason is somehow connected to *The Matrix*, as are several other dicta.

All this resonates with his penchant for redefinition. Though born a Prince, he grew up a Skipper. His coquettish soprano was christened Camille before anyone but him knew of it. When in the service of others, he is often credited as others: Jamie Starr, Joey Coco, Alexander Nevermind. At his most irritable, he wore an oversized top hat and veil and refused to speak; his name then was Tora Tora. And of course, there was his decade as the glyph, the symbol, a half-round and half-pointy character in the shape of his most famous guitar. His staff called him Boss, Bro, the Dude, while the rest of us called him nothing, or put a passive phrase before the name we'd always used. This was when the ceremony of addressing him was a discomfort.

Perhaps he wants no reminder of how little his early decrees jibe with his present thoughts. Maybe he does not see the same Prince from one interview to the next. One cannot be a Prince for this long without some contradiction. If so, all this might be to tell us that we have spent thirty years chasing a singular Prince to set in oil and to frame—one voice, one name, one interview—and that has been a mistake.

Count yourself lucky if, after he calls you, he sends an invitation to fly out to his residence. A few airport cabbies already know the way to Audubon Road. Memorize your preapproved questions during the thirty-minute drive, as he has been known to confiscate pencils. Scan the list of off-limits topics as well, for they are legion. He will have sent you a lyrics sheet, or a Matt Damon film, or a fan blog along with his invitation—make sure you've done your homework. Do not arrive without the four-page confidentiality agreement, sealed in an envelope.

His boxy gray building is unmissable—several times larger than the Small World day care center, the Kingdom Hall of Jehovah's Witnesses, or anything else on Audubon Road. Ask the cabbie to keep the meter running, as it is usually freezing out and it often takes several minutes for the gates to open. There's a chance he'll send the attendant to dismiss you at the gate. If this is the case, the

Holiday Inn Express is a mile down Arboretum; wait out the night and return tomorrow, when a member of his staff might admit you out of pity.

When you are finally inside, you will see that the carpets are embossed with galaxies and the walls are mottled with clouds. He too is all over the walls, in various exposures of midriff. Dozens of people in his service move along the spiral staircase to the four recording studios, the mirrored rehearsal halls, the cavernous soundstage. If they have been given clearance to speak to you, his people will be friendly, but guarded. They might only refer to the Prince as He and Him.

Do not ask them if they, too, get a weird vibe from the place. It is absolutely dustless, and all of the rooms have been both wired and soundproofed. There could be two doves, caged, in the hallway. The doves might be named Divinity and Majesty. Or maybe Divinity and Majesty are the names of two ex-lovers, or maybe they are members of a sexy girl band he oversaw in 1986. Maybe all these things. You will not be able to confirm any of this, though, because the hallway you're standing in will have started to vibrate.

If he sends you away on Wednesday and allows you back in to wander the building on Thursday, it's likely you'll first see him on Friday or Saturday, but it could be as late as Sunday before he invites you into a small room for a chat. It could also be that, come Sunday, he has you ushered into a room with nothing but a phone in it, and you will have your ten-minute interview with only his off-putting voice. If you then step out to the Perkins restaurant on Arboretum for lunch, you will not be permitted reentry. You will be told that you got your interview, and now a cab has been called. You will get the impression you have done something wrong, but no one will be able to tell you what. So it's crucial to stay put, to follow protocol throughout every beat of this ceremony.

When he walks the halls, it is important to keep a distance. He knows you're there. You might pass him in the atrium or spy on a few meetings in his all-glass conference room. Each time, he will wear a new ensemble. He changes outfits nearly every mealtime, though he rarely eats meals. A paisley jumpsuit with an oversized gold crucifix. A white linen hat, white linen tunic, and white bell-bottoms. Lace tights and a sweater with a neck of cowl or turtle. Ice skating pants with the boots sewn in. Cuban heels, red hi-tops, silver wedges that light when he walks (to set off the sparkles in his cane). He will be tinier than you could ever imagine, and you have already imagined him tiny. When he passes by, he will smell absolutely fucking incredible.

There is something you must know before you end up alone with him. The rumor that he is magical is completely true. It is the only constant in these thirty years of interviews (save the rule about taping his voice). Pray that he retains his sunglasses, because once they come off, you will be done for. His brown eyes, expertly rimmed into almonds, are festooned with lashes like two dancers with four fans. He has the slowest eyelids this side of Abishag. There, in that gaze, is what allows him to compose God and fornication into a befuddling chiasmus. The steel bar that joins Jesus with sex comes to us through those eyes. You will try to bar from your conscious his overheated breathing in "Lady Cab Driver" and "Do Me," but you will fail, and now it will be in the room, behind his eyes, as well. How can one take notes when locked in a room with *that*? Nothing compares to it. Your own sexuality is irrelevant; or perhaps it is crucial. No one is immune, not even Oprah. She shuffled her papers, her voice tight in her throat, and said, "Oooh, you're pretty."

He might ask you not to report any of the *words* of your meeting, but to instead *just write down the vibes*. But you have all these questions about TR-808's and legalese and the bass line in "Let's Work." *U will remember the things that r important*, he has been known to say. But you don't trust your dirty mind, struck into buzzing like a tuning fork. *The mind is perfect*, he has replied. But if you could just have your pencil back, things would go so much more smoothly. He might permit this, but only if he never catches you scribbling when he speaks. *That would be just like U were texting.*

You will trust him, and you will want to eat him. You would like him to murder you. Because he will still be looking at you and the interview will not even have begun yet and you will long to be back in the hallway with those doves.

He might be munching on something—a Tootsie Pop or a hunk of bread wrapped in a napkin. A gentle belch is not out of the question. On occasion, he will spontaneously veto the asking of *any* questions, which will paralyze you. You will wait for him, frozen, as he paces or flops about in his chair, sighing audibly. If you could move your arms, perhaps you would try pantomiming the questions. You might feel that your interview has ceased to be an interview and has instead become a riddle to solve. This will never be far from the truth.

There is an expression he may don in the silence that is very reminiscent of a cat forced to wear a sweatshirt. It will somehow confirm for you that the Q&A is permitted to begin. And now, when he opens up the gates to himself, that list of verboten topics will fall out of your head like stars.

Do not refer to his fans as fans.

Do not refer to his vices as vices.

Do not refer to his work as his business.

Do not refer to any of his dreams as nightmares.

Do not refer to his wives, even if one sits next to him as he speaks.

Do not ask if he knows what a ringtone is.

Do not ask if he feels normal. Ever.

Do not call him weird.

Do not call him by his last name, because he does not understand it.

Do not grab the heel of his disco-ball boot, even if he has propped the boot up on your armrest.

Do not wonder if he ever just chillaxes in a pair of sweatpants.

Do not wonder what happened to the baby he said was coming but who never appeared.

He would prefer not to be asked about nostalgia.

He would prefer that you avoid feeling any nostalgia while you speak to him.

He would prefer just to talk to you, *just 2 have an Xperience.*

He would prefer no questions between 1985 and 1990.

He would prefer to stop the interview when his hotel TV makes noises like it is haunted.

You will be permitted to ask about his hair, but only if you are a former supermodel.

You will be permitted to say you've never heard of him, but only if you are a Muppet.

You will be permitted to ask his age, but if you are Dick Clark, he will lie to you.

If you tell him you've wanted to make love to him your whole life, he will get up and leave.

If he has not yet had breakfast, he will address your questions with a mouth full of crackers.

If you challenge him to a game of one-on-one, he'll take you to the hoop and whup your ass.

If you ask for career advice, he will say never to eat things with parents *bcuz u will inherit their dreams.*

He will not tell you why he opted out of "We Are the World."

He will not tell you if that was Kate Bush on the phone just now.

He will not admit to ever hearing a 2LiveCrew song.

He will not confirm that Kim Basinger is the whiny sex voice in "Peach."

He will not play "Friend, Lover, Sister, Mother/Wife" at your daughter's wedding.

He will not reveal if "Computer Blue" has anything to do with computers.

He will not allow profanity, but he will allow a substitute expletive, like "artichoke."

He will not explain why he condemns covers of his own songs but covers the artichoke out of that Radiohead song and that Foo Fighters song and that Sheryl Crow song, and these songs are all so much artichoking better when he covers them.

He will not discuss the fact that, after all these years, you still believe he would die 4U.

You will have forgotten that he does not look at you this way at all.

You will have forgotten that he is only here to make something that doesn't concern you.

You will have forgotten that you were only to pay attention to that making.

You will have forgotten that he does not want to make sound for you; he wants to be sound.

You will not believe that his huge building, his staff, the white linen and Cuban heels, the control of time and space—it's all an effort to become the sounds that he makes.

You will refuse to admit this is not the same thing as performance. That his voice is quiet until he reaches into music and the music makes him loud.

We think the Prince is reaching to us, but he is not. *It* reaches through *him* like a prophetic dream, one he will never reward us for interpreting. When we reach to him, we are only in his way. So he reschedules us, confuses us, stares us down. And occasionally, for reasons none of us understand, he appeases us: *I am ready 4 ur ?stions, but I cannot give U what U want.* All his answers will either be too dully practical or too lofty for us to imagine:

Because what will U want, really?

You will want to know that the Prince is good, that he is badass, that he is rich.

Will U not want 2 B entertained?

Yes you will, by loud scenes of his idiosyncrasy.

But don't U think there is more 4U 2C?

You just want to see behind the curtain of the sounds.

But Y?

Because they seem so impossible when he presents them to you, polished and buckled, tight like a Bible.

You will want the Prince to be impossible because this is what is desired of princes. When the Prince is impossible, he becomes a vessel for impossible feelings, as well as the impossible questions you find yourself asking whether he is present or not. So throw those questions into the air like prayers; chuck them out like messages in bottles. This is the only option for a ceremony worth memorializing—an interview with him in which you interview without him.

Q: Does knowing how 2B funky help U feel less lonesome?

Q: Does sensational spelling make U unafraid of language?

Q: Can U dress me, Baby? I mean pick out my clothes before we go out.

Q: Is it OK that I am getting older and that sometimes it hurts 2 much 2 party?

Q: That I am interested in total control, but someone taught me that power = shame?

Q: I have tried 2 imagine what silence looks like. I think U know it looks terrible.

Q: It looks like the butterflies all tied up.

Q: It looks like an elevator trying 2 break U down.

Q: It looks like when Daniel awoke on the banks of the Tigris and a gr8 man was in the sky, dressed in gold and white linen. His eyes burned outward like torches and his mouth had a choir inside it. He opened a book that told Daniel all of the future days, three and a half times' worth, and in those times were the rise and fall of princes, and their successors were not given the honor of royalty. And many names were in it, and images of the destruction from which all the names would try 2 run.

And when Daniel tried 2 ask him questions, the man in linen did not answer them fully. So Daniel asked again, though he knew 2 do so might anger him. The man in linen touched his face and answered *U go ur way till the end.*

And after he shut the book and sealed it, Daniel opened his eyes and he was alone. And he sat up, put forward both his hands, and sang in2 the river *I was dreaming when I wrote this, 4give me if it goes astray.*

CODA

I've always loved how unafraid Montaigne is to leave the beginning of an essay in the dust. I revel in the twists and turns of his inquiries—getting caught up in the fervor of his references, his examples, and the live-feed of his thoughts, and then ending in places I never thought I'd be. When I turn back through the piece, I can't believe how much the landscape around me has changed. Sometimes even the title is a distant memory. Every essay that I write teaches me more about what a brave and skilled practice this is on Montaigne's part.

I also, like Emerson and many others, am very taken with how Montaigne presents himself, quite unapologetically, as a man of contradictions. His gleeful refusal to present a consistent persona is hilarious to me. In reading his essays, you meet a multitude of Montaignes. Perusing thirty years of interviews with the musician Prince produces a similar effect.

Prince R. Nelson, like Michel E. de Montaigne, is not a cat interested in staying on one message. The same goes for Prince's albums, really, which slam into the holy and the filthy, the elegiac and the underground, the macho and the prissy—and this is why we love him. Not to mention, Prince, like Montaigne, knows his way around an aphorism (though Prince's spelling can be a little more sensational). They both like to hole up in their respective towers and make stuff, and neither dude is much for standing on ceremony. I just wonder which of the two men was taller.

Anyway, when I saw the title "The Ceremony of the Interview of Princes" among the *Essais*, I thought it would be fun to score one man's persona to the other man's "music." I read several hundred pages of interviews with the Purple One and tried to piece together a manual of etiquette for the practice. Very little could be generalized, aside from the rule that Prince's voice should never be recorded, but a motley portrait emerged that I think Montaigne would dig, if you will.

In these interviews, Prince emerges as a challenging, unreliable, generous, and, more than anything, thoughtful subject. He often rattles his interviewers so significantly that they leave the conversation with their heads spinning, not quite sure how they ended up where they did, much like me at the end of a righteous Montaigne trip. This was the major task of the essay—to fuse these two men together and to give a wild Montaignean structure to the disorientation (and exaltation!) so many have experienced when they asked Prince, "How do you live"?

27

We Can Savour Nothing Pure

MAGGIE NELSON

> The feebleness of our condition means that we can make
> habitual use of nothing in its natural unsophisticated purity.
> MONTAIGNE, "WE CAN SAVOUR NOTHING PURE"

The phrase "toxic maternal" refers to a mother whose milk delivers poison along with nourishment. If you turn away from the poison, you also turn away from the nourishment. Given that human breast milk now contains literal poisons, from paint thinners to dry-cleaning fluid to toilet deodorizers to rocket fuel to DDT to flame retardants, there is literally no escape. Toxicity is now a question of degree, of acceptable parts per unit. Infants don't get to choose—they take what they can get, in their scramble to stay alive.

I had never thought much about this dilemma until after I had been working for many years in a bar that was regularly voted "a smoker's paradise" in an NYC guidebook. I had quit smoking a few months before taking the job, primarily because cigarettes made me feel so completely awful, and now I was spending hundreds, if not thousands, of dollars on an acupuncturist to help me with swollen glands and difficulty breathing as a result of inhaling smoke that wasn't even mine. (I ended up quitting the job about a month before Mayor Bloomberg's ban took effect; in my final hours, I secretly allowed myself to be interviewed by the antismoking crusaders, to advance their cause.) Anyone to whom I complained at the time said, wisely, *Why don't you just get a different job? There are hundreds upon hundreds of restaurants and bars in New York City.* My therapist—I had taken on yet another choking shift in order to keep seeing her—suggested I help rich kids study for the SAT instead, which made me want to sock her. How could I explain? I had already had a hundred restaurant jobs in New York City, and finally I had found one at which I made more in a week than I would have in an entire semester as an adjunct instructor (the other discernible option). I also thought—a larval Karen Silkwood—*If they, whoever "they" are, let me work here, it couldn't be that bad, could it?*

But it was that bad. The bills I stashed under my mattress were almost wet with smoke, and stayed that way until rent time. And it's only now that I see that the job assured me something else I needed: the constant company of alcoholics apparently worse off than I was. I can still see them all: the silent owner who had to be carried into the back of a taxi at dawn after he'd blacked out from Rolling Rocks and shots of Stoli that we'd served him, raking in his Wall Street–derived tips; the punk Swedes who drank shot after shot of jalapeno-pickled vodka dissolved in iced coffee (the Swedeball, we called it); the woman who left her baby in a car seat under the bar one night and forgot about it; the rotted teeth of a successful Foley editor; the man who inexplicably took off his belt after a few Hurricanes and started whipping a fellow diner with it . . . Their example, and the ease with which I deemed myself together by comparison, purchased me a few more years of believing alcohol more precious than toxic to me. "The self without sympathetic attachments is either a fiction or a lunatic. Yet dependence is scorned even in intimate relationships, as though dependence were incompatible with self-reliance rather than the only thing that makes it possible" (Adam Philips and Barbara Taylor, *On Kindness*).

I learned this scorn from my own mother; perhaps it laced my milk. I therefore have to be on the alert for a tendency to treat other people's needs as repulsive. Corollary habit: deriving the bulk of my self-worth from a feeling of hyper-competence, an irrational but fervent belief in my near total self-reliance.

You're a great student because you don't have any baggage, a teacher once told me, at which moment the subterfuge of my life felt complete.

One of the gifts of recognizing oneself in thrall to a substance is the perforation of such subterfuge. In place of an exhausting autonomy, there is the blunt admittance of dependence, and its subsequent relief. I will always aspire to contain my shit as best I can, but I am no longer interested in hiding my dependencies in an effort to appear superior to those who are more visibly undone or aching. Most people decide at some point that it is better "to be enthralled with what is impoverished or abusive than not to be enthralled at all and so to lose the condition of one's being and becoming" (Judith Butler, *Precarious Life*). I'm glad not to be there right now, but I'm also glad to have been there, to know how it is.

CODA

The first line of "We Can Savour Nothing Pure"—"The feebleness of our condition means that we can make habitual use of nothing in its natural unsophisticated purity"—instantly reminded me of breast-feeding, which often has a sentimental aura of "purity" wafting around it, whereas it is really ground zero for the hot problem of contaminated nourishment. In saying that, I don't mean to invoke a lamentable contamination of milk by pollutants or drugs—my piece starts there, but moves on. I mean that nourishing of all kinds must get done by and for real people who are blessedly impure, corrupt, laced with all the ambivalences and melancholias and joys that Montaigne here describes. Whereas Montaigne relates such impurity to the "feebleness" of our condition, my piece hopes to imbue such mixed inheritances and complex attachments with a different color: it ends in gratitude, for example.

28

Experience Necessary

PHILLIP LOPATE

> There is nothing so beautiful and legitimate as to play the man well
> and properly, no knowledge so hard to acquire as the knowledge of
> how to live this life well and naturally; and the most barbarous of
> our maladies is to despise our being.
> MONTAIGNE, "OF EXPERIENCE"

"Of Experience" is Montaigne's last and, I insist, greatest essay. It inspires us with its wisdom and balance. Montaigne, like Goethe, had the knack—some would say the bad taste—of benefiting from his experience at every stage of life and achieving a calm, benign perspective with age. Which I can't entirely seem to do. I am approaching my seventieth birthday: three score and ten, the alleged fulfillment of a life span. I am still agitated, perplexed. I look back at all that has happened to me and it seems as though it were practically nothing. To quote the last line of Borges's poem on Emerson: "I have not lived. I want to be someone else."

On the other hand, I want to be only myself. I think I know what I am about, am comfortable with that person, can distinguish good writing from bad, and decent human beings from jerks. Less and less do I feel the need to justify my conclusions. I carry myself in public with impervious self-confidence. (In private is another story.) My students look to me for answers, and I improvise—something that passes for adequate. Most of the dilemmas that shake these young people, their existential, religious, or romantic doubts, their future professional prospects, their worries that someone won't like them, roll off my back. It could be that I am just numbed, unable to summon the urgency behind what to them constitutes a crisis. Mine is the questionable wisdom of passivity. What I cannot change, I no longer let myself be insanely bothered by. Even the latest political folly elicits from me only a disgruntled shrug. I am more upset when my favorite sports team loses; but then I remind myself that it wasn't, technically, my fault since I lacked magical powers to alter the outcome.

"Are you experienced?" asked Jimi Hendrix, tauntingly. Does he mean: have I slept with fifty groupies, humped a guitar onstage before adulating thousands, taken so many drugs that I risked dying from an overdose? In that sense, no, I am not experienced.

Otherwise, are you experienced? Hell, yes. I know the score. I wasn't born yesterday. I've been around the block a few times. I can tell which way is up. You can't pull a fast one on me. You can't pull the wool over my eyes. I'm from Missouri; show me. I know a thing or two. I know which side my bread is buttered on. I'm hip. I'm sadder but wiser. I'm no fool. I have eyes in the back of my head. I can tell my left from my right. I know my ass from my elbow. I can see which way the wind blows. I have a pretty good idea. I've been through the mill. I've been around the world in a plane. I've seen it all. *Now* I've seen it all.

"Detachment . . . is one of the forms that engagement with experience can take: things seen at a remove, appearing strange and so more clearly seen," writes the art historian Svetlana Alpers. Experience can mean plunging into dangerous war zones, witnessing tragedies under fire, like George Orwell at the Spanish front and Susan Sontag in Bosnia, or it can mean staying on the sidelines, exercising watchful prudence. Then there is the experience of ordinary humdrum life, what Virginia Woolf calls cotton wool, those moments of "nonbeing." Bring it on. As

Bartleby might say, I prefer not to live at the highest pitch. I have always been a fan of bemused detachment. I am rather attached to the notion of detachment. I accept in advance the guilt for being detached, should any such guilt attach.

"Of Experience" was, as I said, Montaigne's last essay. I wonder if this will be my last essay. I am running out of things to say. Moreover, I feel I have done my life's work as a writer. I have nothing more to prove. It is strange to have come to such a pass and be surrounded by friends and colleagues still pressing on, unsure whether they will have time enough to fulfill their appointed destinies. I have fulfilled a modest destiny modestly. I have done what I set out to do, and now linger on past my assignment. I can still visit museums and relish new movies or old books, can still enjoy a walk through unfamiliar parts of the city, can still participate in the delights, follies, and chagrins of family life, can still teach the young and hold forth in AWP panel discussions, but I don't want to work so hard at writing anymore. It's as if I have a form of post-traumatic stress disorder: all those years trying to meet the challenge of writing well have left me trembling, with a desire for peace and inactivity.

There is an abundance of things I can't do now, and so probably will never do. I can't change a tire to save my life (although if it were a matter of life and death perhaps I could). I can't read sheet music or play the piano. I used to be able to read Hebrew, but now I can't without committing lots of errors. I am a poor swimmer and can barely stay alive in the water. I don't run marathons, not because I couldn't, physically speaking, but because I can't *make* myself run a marathon. What I can't do and what I don't care to do are connected at the hip. I don't know Latin. I can't tell one tree or flowering shrub from another. I am at a loss as to how to identify the stars; in fact, my grasp of astronomy is so scant that I could say, with Charles Lamb, "I guess at Venus only by her brightness— and if the sun on some portentous morn were to make his first appearance in the West, I verily believe, that, while all the world were gasping in apprehension about me, I alone should stand unterrified, from sheer incuriosity and want of observation." My understanding of the way things work, including the laws of physics, is so pathetic it's a wonder I can navigate the world at all. I specialize in ignorance. "What *do* I know?" as Michel would say. It looks as though I won't have sex with a man in this lifetime. Experience has taught me to honor my indifference and my cowardice both. Put it this way: Experience has finally proved to be a school that trains me to limit my concerns and tolerate my limitations.

One privilege of growing older is that you do not have to adjust to the new, or even wax excited about it. I remain a man of the twentieth century. Reluctantly dragged into the new millennium, I stay loyal to the previous one, hewing to the patterns I established then. For instance, I still read the print versions of newspapers and magazines, and dress respectably when I take an airplane. I avoid thinking about Facebook, Twitter, or texting or any such innovations—not that I deplore them, I have no high-minded objections to the new technology, I simply refuse to engage mentally with it. When I happen to glance at op-ed essays about the evolutionary danger these new forms of communication pose to humanist values, I stop reading the article forthwith, because I don't want to care enough about the phenomena even to be alarmed by them. I refuse to be topical. I am thus spared much wasted effort trying to write ingenious think pieces about the latest splash or gizmo.

Experience has also taught me to recognize that much of what passes for innovation is simply puffery, the product of public relations and short memories. In pop or high culture, the "edgy" turns out usually to be the recycling of a tired trope. Take androgyny: Marlene Dietrich wore her tux and kissed a woman on the lips; now Madonna or Lady Gaga does the same. Similarly S/M and black leather, fragmentation, jettisoning of narrative, scrambling of chronology, self-reflexive loops, Artaudian stage ritual, Khlebnikovian nonsense syllables, Neo-Dadaist anti-art, Brechtian-Marxist alienation effects, and politically correct consciousness-raising of all stripes.

In my youth I would read the pages of the *New York Times* Arts & Leisure section (it was called something different then, but no matter) with avid credulity, thinking I must make it a point to catch up with this filmmaker, painter, opera conductor, or theater production. Now I scan the bylines, and, knowing most of these arts journalists, whose opinions I don't particularly trust nor do I value their prose styles, hardworking though they may be, I spend more time musing about how they got the assignment than reading through their articles. Does that sound merely snotty, or qualify as a sign of experience?

I have experienced enough in the way of people's strange behaviors not to be surprised by sudden breakouts of kindness, brutality, tenderness, betrayal, inconsistency, vanity, rigidity, schadenfreude, and its opposite. What does surprise me is current events. When 9/11 happened, I was taken aback by such a freakish thing. (It was, to me, no accident that 9/11 occurred on the other side of the millennium, in 2001: no good, I thought, can come of the twenty-first century. Not that the twentieth did not have its share of nasty surprises.) I continue to marvel at Republicans' seeming willingness to shut down the federal government, and allow the United States to default rather than negotiate with the president. I don't understand my country anymore: how, after a century of federal programs such as the New Deal, social security, bank regulation, public housing, and food stamps, a large swath of the population can still take umbrage at the government's minimal efforts to protect the weak and the poor, or indeed to have a presence in any aspect of life beyond the maintenance of a military force. Nothing prior has prepared me for this frightening swerve. I grew up in the postwar atmosphere of a modestly progressive welfare state, where problems such as racial segregation and poverty were expected to be addressed at the governmental level, and I assumed naively that we were marching at best or creeping at worst toward a more just society. What I took for an inevitable historical progression turned out to be an anomalous blip. I might better have looked to Nietzsche's theory of eternal recurrence. Today I am less experienced, less able to adapt to this harshly selfish environment than the average twenty-year-old, who has grown up without my New Deal–Great Society set of expectations.

Newspapers were once enormously important; now they're not. I am a creature of newspaper culture, therefore I'm no longer important. I'm redundant. I must learn to accept my redundancy, like Turgenev's superfluous man. Fortunately,

I've had plenty of practice. I always anticipated I would be redundant, a cultural throwback, which is why I prepared by steeping myself in the antiquarian tomes of ages past, whose authors' names I suspected would mean next to nothing to future generations. When my writer-friends in college were reading Beckett, Burroughs, and Pynchon, I was poring over Fielding, Machado de Assis, and Lady Murasaki. Later, when I discovered the joys of the personal essay, I clung to the fustian charms of Lamb, Hazlitt, Stevenson, and Beerbohm, with scarcely a side glance at Sedaris, Wallace, and Vowell. I have cheerfully morphed into the type whose idea of a fun movie, as my teenage daughter scoffingly reminds me, is a restored black-and-white silent film.

So what good is experience if the experience I have managed to acquire no longer applies to the new era's challenges, except as the contrarian stiffening of my stubbornness in the face of novelty, and the embrace of the antedated and rarefied?

Emerson rebukes me:

> But the man and woman of seventy assume to know all, they have outlived their hope, they renounce aspiration, accept the actual for the necessary, and talk down to the young. Let them, then, become organs of the Holy Ghost; let them be lovers; let them behold truth; and their eyes are uplifted, their wrinkles smoothed, they are perfumed again with hope and power. This old age ought not to creep on a human mind. In nature every moment is new; the past is always swallowed and forgotten; the coming only is sacred. Nothing is secure but life, transition, the energizing spirit.... People wish to be settled; only as far as they are unsettled is there any hope for them.
>
> "Circles"

Yeah, yeah; so you say. I *do* wish to be settled; perhaps I *have* outlived my hope. When Emerson wrote this passage, it must have sounded fresh, rebellious, positively electric. Now it sounds dated. I realize that even in choosing to let Ralph Waldo Emerson rebuke me, I am indulging in an antiquarian longing.

These are the last six lines of that beautiful Borges poem about Emerson:

> He thinks: I have read the essential books
> And written others which oblivion
> Will not efface. I have been allowed
> That which is given mortal man to know.
> The whole continent knows my name.
> I have not lived. I want to be someone else.

Well, the whole continent does not know my name, but I am . . . respected. I have read a good many essential books (alas, forgetting most of what was in them, so that I find I have to read them again from scratch) and have written more than a dozen books which, if not guaranteed to escape oblivion, have given some pleasure to some readers. More than that I will not, must not, ask: the gods get angry at ingratitude. I am not grandiose enough, like Emerson or Borges, to think it even my place to want to be someone else. (This reminds me of the old Jewish joke: The rabbi and the synagogue bigwigs are beating their breasts on Yom Kippur, the Day of Atonement, and crying out, "I'm a worm, I'm nothing, I'm nobody." The janitor, a goy, decides it looks like a good idea, and starts beating his chest too and moaning, "I'm nobody, I'm nobody!" They stare at him with alarmed disdain until one of them says: "Look who thinks he's Nobody!") So who am I to think myself a nobody, a failure, when the planet itself is slinking off to darkness and extinction from mankind's sheer incapacity to correct its gluttony?

What is the nature of experience? What is the connection, if any, between experience and knowledge? What is the relationship between knowledge and wisdom? Can one acquire wisdom passively? Can one live and *not* acquire experience? Is experience only "experience" if it has been converted into self-conscious thought, or do we count the unconscious in our stock of experience? Our dreams, for instance; are they not part of our experience? By the way, is there really such a thing as the unconscious? Is wisdom principally an intellectual or an emotional property? Can wisdom bypass the heart and lodge only in the brain? Or does it ever work vice versa? What is the difference in value between a shady experience consciously undertaken and one prudently avoided?

Does prudence, meaning the wise avoidance of certain sketchy paths, result in a shallower or deeper soul? Is there even such a thing as the soul? If not, what is the point of gaining experience?

> We are great fools. "He has spent his life in idleness," we say; "I have done nothing today." What, have you not lived? That is not only the fundamental but the most illustrious of your occupations. "If I had been placed in a position to manage great affairs, I would have shown what I could do." Have you been able to think out and manage your own life? You have done the greatest task of all. . . . To compose our character is our duty, not to compose books, and to win, not battles and provinces, but order and tranquility in our conduct. Our great and glorious masterpiece is to live appropriately.

So said Montaigne, who wrote "Of Experience" at fifty-six, and died when he was fifty-nine. We'll say sixty, for the sake of rounded numbers. Since seventy is the new sixty, I should be reaching that point of ripe wisdom that Montaigne attained at the end of his life, no? But since the average young person today has so protracted an adolescence, compared to a youth in sixteenth-century France (see Philippe Ariès's *Centuries of Childhood*, which demonstrated that children were treated as little adults and expected to work from age seven on), we would have to subtract an additional twenty years from my maturity index, bringing me down to age forty. Then take another ten years off for the syndrome that Hemingway contemptuously called the "American boy-man," meaning that there was something uniquely arrested-development about the males in this particular land, which would reduce my emotional age even further, so I should probably be considered the equivalent of a thirty-year-old. No wonder I am still blinking my eyes like a hatched chick and pondering what's what.

The problem of solipsism: not believing that others are as real as you are would seem to put a lid on acquiring wisdom. On the other hand, maybe we are all narcissists, and if narcissism proves to be the universal law, then we need to reexamine all the high-minded inveighing against narcissism and ask if it is a hypocritical form of social coercion. Why should we feel guilty about something we cannot avoid?

I don't think I'm really a narcissist of the first order. Unlike Montaigne, I'm not even terribly interested in myself. When I'm alone, in my study or walking the streets, I am usually thinking not about me but about other people, trying to figure them out, though that could just be another form of narcissistic self-protection: trying to anticipate what they might do, so as to parry it effectively when the situation arises. In any case, I am something of a literalist when it comes to reality. I assume that the people around me *are* real, the tree outside my window is real, et cetera. I have never understood that notion put forward by Jean Baudrillard or David Shields, that we less and less feel our lives to be real, that the simulacra incessantly produced by the media have robbed us of the sense of our own authenticity, and therefore we hunger for the real. I don't hunger for the real. I don't have the foggiest notion what that means. I just want to get by, I just want to enjoy what years are left to me on earth, and most of all, I want to watch my daughter Lily turn into the amazing adult she is fast becoming, want to watch her embrace her full potential and her destiny. I worry about her fretting too much. *Amor fati*, I want to tell her. Love your fate—which I also tell myself constantly, for all the good it does.

I wake up between six and six-thirty each morning, having to pee. My cats know this about me and begin to rummage about the bed at that hour, to make sure I will get up and feed them. I put glaucoma-controlling drops in my eyes the first thing in the morning and the last thing at night. I have no problem dropping off to sleep, but I wake up in the night more often than I used to, sometimes roused by noisy neighbors, sometimes by snoring (mine or my wife's), sometimes by a dream, or for no discernible reason whatsoever. I wake up and start picking my nose, to clear the breathing passageways. This is particularly true in winter, when the heat goes on at night and dries out the bedroom air. Because I don't get enough sleep, in the late afternoon I find my eyes drooping when I read, and many times when I am at the movies or listening to an opera I start nodding off. It's outrageous to pay so much for opera tickets and then doze, but I can't help myself. Sometimes, just to keep awake, I rub my scalp above my forehead where there used to be hair, and often I find scabs or bumps that I try to smooth out by picking off the indentations. When I am in a public place such as the subway or at the movies, I am always worrying about bedbugs latching onto me, ever since we had an infestation of them a few years back and had to take extreme measures to rid ourselves, hauling all our clothing off to the dry cleaners and wrapping the books. Every time my skin itches, I think it must be bedbugs returning.

I hate to lie, and will do almost anything to avoid telling a lie, even if it means sneaking out of a poetry reading the moment it's over or, if directly accosted, blurting out something undiplomatic and giving offense. This resistance to lying stems not so much from an ethical principle as a superstitious dread, as though, if I ever started to lie glibly, my core self would dissolve and I would become a creature of multiple personalities. When you lie you split yourself into two selves, and then a third self has to keep watch and adjudicate the first two. Hence, adultery has never been much of an option for me. Of course I have lied, on some occasions, but I am not going to tell you where or when. *That* experienced I am. Most of my lies are sins of omission, like keeping my mouth shut when I could get in trouble by saying what I actually thought. If someone tells me that he loved a movie I found abysmal, I smile and nod enthusiastically, though with a slight catch of the head, so that if God is watching, He will understand and forgive my deception. Why should we be transparent, though? Is art transparent? Better to honor the mysteries. There is so much we will never be able to understand that we do not need to go in search of mystery, it will come to us regardless.

CODA

In responding to Montaigne's great last essay, I attempted to gather my own notions and hunches about experience. I began writing my piece before rereading Montaigne's, telling myself that I would get a head start in this way; but in the end I could not bring myself to reread his text carefully—though I skimmed it for underlined passages—because it was too depressing. I felt too inadequate next to his bold, life-embracing manner. He was the master, he was the Father, and I could not engage him in Oedipal struggle because I owed him everything as an essayist, and knew it. The most I could do in the way of resisting his domination was to evade rereading his essay while writing my own. Mind you, I had read "Of experience" at least fifteen times before, having taught it often over the years; and it was during one of these readings that I came to the definitive conclusion that it was his best, so much so that I second-guessed myself for including "On Some Verses from Virgil," his sexual meditation which I hoped would be popular with young readers, in my anthology *The Art of the Personal Essay*, instead of his more conclusive one on experience.

This was my third attempt to use Montaigne self-consciously as an influence. I had tried to appropriate his aphoristic manner in my essay "Against Joie de Vivre," and his listing of anatomical quirks in "Portrait of My Body." But when it came to approximating his robust final summations on life experience, I could not. I found my own grasp on experience much more tentative. And here we come to my apprehensions about the unitary self. I have been maintaining for quite a while that personal essayists assert a cohesive self and, in this respect, are more traditional than the postmodernists or French theorists who question the whole idea of the individual self. Now the fact is that I don't know whether my self is unitary, cohesive, or even that it exists—only that it profits me in my essay-writing to proceed according to the assumption that it is. I *pretend* that I have a unitary self, and that is good enough to get me started. Montaigne, for all his proclamations about doubt and the ever-changeable, undulating inconstancy of the human animal, does have, it seems to me, a single, self-confident, fracture-proof self. Or maybe it is his voice that seems so all-of-a-piece to me. He manages to sustain that self, that drily mellifluous voice, through lengthy essays that digress and return to the main matter over and over. I, on the other hand, could only sustain an essay on experience that came to fewer than twenty pages by breaking it into seventeen measly sections. I did the mosaic thing, wrote it in fragments with space breaks surrounding each discontinuous piece, which is not the way I usually compose essays. Usually I get a good head of steam up and follow it to the end. But I found myself fragmenting in the face of the Gascon's cliff-like certitude. Actually, what brought him to his nobly stoical awareness that "We must learn to endure what we cannot avoid," and what held together that last essay of his, was his kidney stones. That disease was the central teacher of his final years: "But is there anything so sweet as that sudden change, when from extreme pain, by the voiding of my stone, I come to recover as if by lightning the beautiful light of health, so free and so full, as happens in our sudden and sharpest attacks of colic?" No, thanks. I will take my prolonged, unresolved immaturity over his enlightenment via kidney stones.

Notes

CAPPELLO (30–36):

For classical references I have relied on Anthony Corbeill's fluent, learned study *Nature Embodied: Gesture in Ancient Rome* (Princeton, N.J.: Princeton University Press, 2004), especially chapter 2, "The Power of Thumbs," 40–66. Other sources include e-Hand.com, the Electronic Textbook of Hand Surgery, eatonhand.com/hw/facts.htm, and David Ignatow, "Cockroaches," in *The Party Train: A Collection of North American Prose Poetry*, ed. Robert Alexander, Mark Vinz, and C. W. Truesdale (Minneapolis: New Rivers Press, 1996), 192–93.

CHURCH (91–103):

Sic. Excerpted passages taken from the Moving Sound Technologies website, movingsoundtech.com, have been edited and arranged by the author.

ATWAN (162–174):

1. Trans. Florio. For this essay I relied on three translations: *The Complete Essays* by M. A. Screech (1991), *The Complete Essays of Montaigne* by Donald M. Frame (1958), and *Montaigne's Essays* by John Florio (1603–13) in the Everyman's Library edition (1910). For the original French I used the Bibliothèque de la Pléiade edition *Montaigne: Oeuvres complètes* (1962). For each citation I used the translation I preferred after checking against the original; when I felt I could render a passage better, I did so. The epigraph and most quotations are from Screech. My Latin is rustier than my French, so for the Latin translations I'm indebted to my son, Gregory Atwan.

2. The word "embarrassment" appears relatively late in English; Shakespeare, for example, wrote all his plays without once using it. Montaigne tends almost always to

use the common French word *honte*, which can best be translated as "shame." Many psychologists today distinguish between shame and embarrassment, and that strikes me as correct: see Rowland S. Miller, *Embarrassment* (1966).

3. "But when all is said and done, you never speak about yourself without loss. Your self-condemnation is always accredited, your self-praise discredited" ("Of the Art of Discussion"). Except of course in modern memoir, where self-condemnation is so often self-congratulatory.

4. I have avoided the important issue of Montaigne's attitude toward women, primarily because it deserves—especially in this particular essay—far more attention to detail than I can provide in a limited, largely personal, response. In a 1939 essay for the *Yale Review*, André Gide claimed he noted every passage in the essays in which Montaigne speaks of women, and "there is not one that is not insulting." Yet Montaigne's alleged misogyny is complicated by many remarks in the Virgil essay that suggest he believes women are the equal of men, and both sexes are "cast in the same mold." An interesting feminist perspective on the essay is Julia Watson's "En-gendering the Essays," in *Approaches to Teaching Montaigne's "Essays,"* ed. Patrick Henry (1993). I also recommend chapter 8 of Sarah Bakewell's *How to Live* (2010).

ARTHUR (183–194):

As I was working on my contribution to this book, two of the great contemporary authorities on the essay died—Lydia Fakundiny on March 31, 2013, and Richard Chadbourne on June 8, 2013. I will miss the communication I was privileged to enjoy with these exceptional scholars. This essay is dedicated to their memory.

A Note on the Translations

We know of eight full English translations of Montaigne's *Essays*. They are, in order of first publication:

John Florio (1603)
Charles Cotton (1685)
George Ives (1925)
E. J. Trechmann (1927)
Jacob Zeitlin (1934)
Donald Frame (1943)
John M. Cohen (1958)
M. A. Screech (1991)

There have also been several editions and revisions of the Cotton translation, most notably by William Carew Hazlitt (sometimes called just William Hazlitt), grandson of the great essayist. The most widely used nowadays, in general and in this book, are Cotton, Frame, and Screech. And while most translators have used identical or identifiably similar titles for the essays, in some cases ("De l'exercitation" became both "Use Makes Perfect" and "Of Practice") the titles are quite different. Here we settled on Donald Frame's list, because Frame seems close to Montaigne in spirit and makes sense grammatically (essays beginning with "De" are translated as "Of" and not "On"). But we have gathered, as well, for your information and inspiration, all of Montaigne's titles in the various English versions at www.aftermontaigne.org.

Frame's translations:

BOOK I

I.1. By diverse means we arrive at the same end (1578–80)
I.2. Of sadness (1572–74)

Contributors

MARCIA ALDRICH is the author of the free memoir *Girl Rearing*, published by W. W. Norton and part of the Barnes and Noble Discover New Writers Series. She has been the editor of *Fourth Genre: Explorations in Nonfiction*. In 2010 she was the recipient of the Distinguished Professor of the Year Award for the State of Michigan. *Companion to an Untold Story* won the AWP Award in Creative Nonfiction. She is at work on *Haze*, a narrative of marriage and divorce during her college years.

CHRIS ARTHUR is author of five essay collections, most recently *On the Shoreline of Knowledge* (Iowa/Sightline, 2012). His work has appeared in a range of journals, including the *American Scholar, Hotel Amerika, Irish Pages, North American Review, Orion, Southern Humanities Review,* and *Threepenny Review*. A member of Irish PEN, he has been the recipient of a number of awards, including the Akegarasu Haya International Essay Prize and the Theodore Christian Hoepfner Award. His work has been included in *The Best American Essays* (and frequently mentioned in the Notable Essays lists of this annual series). He has recently become a Fellow in the Royal Literary Fund's Fellowships scheme and advises the Open College of the Arts on their creative writing degree course. For further information see www.chrisarthur.org.

ROBERT ATWAN is the series editor of *The Best American Essays*, which he founded in 1985. He has edited numerous anthologies and written on a wide variety of subjects that include the interpretation of dreams in ancient literature, photography, Shakespeare, literary nonfiction, and the cultural history of American advertising. His essays, criticism, humor, reviews, and poetry have appeared in many periodicals, including the *Atlantic Monthly, Denver Quarterly, Image, Iowa Review, Kenyon Review, Creative Nonfiction, River Teeth, Los Angeles Times,* and *New York Times*.

BARRIE JEAN BORICH is the author of *Body Geographic*, published in the American Lives Series of the University of Nebraska Press and winner of a Lambda Literary Award in Memoir, an IPPY Gold Medal in Essay/Creative Nonfiction, and *Foreword*

Review's 2013 IndieFab Bronze Award for Essays. Her previous book, *My Lesbian Husband*, won the American Library Association Stonewall Book Award, and her work has been named Notable in *The Best American Essays* and *The Best American Nonrequired Reading*. She is a faculty member of the English Department and the MA in Writing & Publishing program at Chicago's DePaul University, where she edits *Slag Glass City*, a creative nonfiction and new media journal focused on sustainability, identity, and art in urban environments. She teaches courses in creative nonfiction writing, literary journals, and the future of the book.

MARY CAPPELLO's four books of literary nonfiction include *Awkward: A Detour* (a *Los Angeles Times* best seller) and, following Maya Deren, a ritual in transfigured time titled *Called Back*. Her most recent book, *Swallow*, emerges from the Chevalier Jackson Foreign Body Collection in Philadelphia's Mütter Museum. A recipient of the Bechtel Prize for Educating the Imagination, the Dorothea Lange–Paul Taylor Prize, and a Guggenheim Fellowship, Cappello is a former Fulbright lecturer at the Gorky Literary Institute (Moscow) and currently professor of English and creative writing at the University of Rhode Island. She is currently writing a book-length essay on mood.

STEVEN CHURCH is the author of *The Guinness Book of Me: A Memoir of Record*, *Theoretical Killings: Essays and Accidents*, and *The Day after the Day After: My Atomic Angst*. His fourth book, *Ultrasonic: Soundings*, a collection of essays, will be released in 2015 by Lavender Ink. His essays have been published recently in *River Teeth*, *Brevity*, *Passages North*, *Creative Nonfiction*, *Fourth Genre*, *Agni*, *Diagram*, Salon.com, and the *Rumpus*. He is a founding editor of the literary magazine *Normal School*.

JUDITH ORTIZ COFER is the author of *If I Could Fly* (2011), a novel; the children's books *Animal Jamboree: Latino Folktales* (2012), *The Poet Upstairs* (2012), and *¡A Bailar!* (2011); *Call Me Maria* (2006), a young adult novel; *A Love Story Beginning in Spanish: Poems* (2005); *The Meaning of Consuelo* (2003), a novel; *Woman in Front of the Sun: On Becoming a Writer* (2000), a collection of essays; *An Island Like You: Stories of the Barrio* (1995), a collection of short stories; *The Line of the Sun* (1989), a novel; *Silent Dancing* (1990), a collection of essays and poetry; two books of poetry, *Terms of Survival* (1987) and *Reaching for the Mainland* (1987); and *The Latin Deli: Prose and Poetry* (1993). *The Cruel Country*, a cultural memoir, is forthcoming from the University of Georgia Press in 2015. In 2010 Judith Ortiz Cofer was inducted into the Georgia Writers Hall of Fame. She is the Regents' and Franklin Professor of English and Creative Writing, Emerita, at the University of Georgia. For further information see judithortizcofer.english.uga.edu.

DANIELLE CADENA DEULEN is an assistant professor at the University of Cincinnati. Her poetry collection *Lovely Asunder* (University of Arkansas Press) won the Miller Williams Arkansas Poetry Prize, the Utah Book Award, and an Ohio Arts Council

Award. Her memoir *The Riots* (University of Georgia Press) won the AWP Prize in Creative Nonfiction and the GLCA New Writers Award. Her poetry chapbook *American Libretto* will be published by Sow's Ear Press in 2015. Her second poetry collection, *Our Emotions Get Carried Away Beyond Us*, won the Barrow Street Press Book Contest award and will also appear in 2015. She was a 2007 Jay C. and Ruth Halls Poetry Fellow at the University of Wisconsin–Madison.

BRIAN DOYLE is the editor of *Portland Magazine* at the University of Portland, in Oregon. He is the author of many books of essays and fiction, most recently the "whopping sea novel" *The Plover* (St. Martin's Press).

LINA M. FERREIRA C.-V. graduated with both creative nonfiction writing and literary translation MFAs from the University of Iowa. Her fiction, nonfiction, and translation work has been featured in journals including the *Bellingham Review*, *Drunken Boat*, and *Rio Grande Review*. Her 2015 book *Don't Come Back* is published by Sarabande Books. She was the recipient of Best of the Net and *Iron Horse Review*'s Discovered Voices awards and has been nominated for two Pushcart Prizes. She currently lives in China; no one is quite sure why.

VIVIAN GORNICK is an American critic, essayist, and memoirist. For many years she wrote for the *Village Voice*. Among her books are *Fierce Attachments*, *Approaching Eye Level*, *The Situation and the Story*, *The End of the Novel of Love*, and *The Men in My Life* (National Book Critics Circle Award finalist for criticism).

ROBIN HEMLEY directs the Writing Program at Yale-NUS College in Singapore and is the author of eleven books of nonfiction and fiction and the winner of many awards including a 2008 Guggenheim Fellowship, as well as three Pushcart Prizes in both fiction and nonfiction, an Independent Press Book of the Year Award, the American Library Association's Editor's Choice Award, and the Washington State Book Award. He is a graduate of the Iowa Writers' Workshop and directed the Nonfiction Writing Program at the University of Iowa from 2004 to 2013. His memoir *NOLA: A Memoir of Faith, Art, and Madness* was reissued by the University of Iowa Press in 2013. He is the founder and organizer of NonfictioNow, a biennial conference that will convene next at Northern Arizona University in October of 2015.

WAYNE KOESTENBAUM is a poet, critic, and artist. He has published nine books of nonfiction, on such subjects as hotels, Harpo Marx, humiliation, Jackie Onassis, opera, and Andy Warhol. His latest book of prose is *My 1980s & Other Essays* (Farrar, Straus & Giroux, 2013). His six books of poetry include *Blue Stranger with Mosaic Background* (Turtle Point, 2012) and *Best-Selling Jewish Porn Films* (Turtle Point, 2006). His first solo exhibition of paintings was at White Columns gallery in New York in 2012.

SHANNON LAKANEN teaches nonfiction writing at Otterbein University. Her writing has been published in *Tusculum Review, Fourth Genre, North Dakota Quarterly, Indiana Review*, and *Quarter After Eight*, among other publications. She is currently writing a collection of essays evolving out of her travels through Eastern Europe and Southeast Asia.

DAVID LAZAR's most recent book is *Occasional Desire: Essays* (University of Nebraska Press). His other books include *The Body of Brooklyn* and *Truth in Nonfiction* (both University of Iowa Press), *Michael Powell: Interviews* and *Conversations with M.F.K. Fisher* (both University Press of Mississippi), and *Powder Town* (Pecan Grove). He has been awarded an Ohio Individual Artist Grant and a Guggenheim Fellowship in nonfiction. He is the founding editor of *Hotel Amerika* and professor of creative writing at Columbia College Chicago.

E. J. LEVY's debut story collection, *Love, in Theory*, won the 2012 Flannery O'Connor Award, a 2013 ForeWord Book of the Year Award, and the 2014 Great Lakes Colleges Association New Writers Award, and is being released in French by Éditions Payot & Rivages. Her essays and stories have appeared in *The Best American Essays*, the *New York Times*, and the *Paris Review* and have received a Pushcart Prize. Her anthology *Tasting Life Twice: Literary Lesbian Fiction by New American Writers* won a Lambda Literary Award.

PHILLIP LOPATE is the author of five essay collections (*Bachelorhood, Against Joie de Vivre, Portrait of My Body, Portrait Inside My Head, To Show and To Tell*), the editor of the anthology *The Art of the Personal Essay*, and the director of graduate nonfiction at Columbia University. He has also written fiction (*The Rug Merchant, Two Marriages*) and poetry (*At the End of the Day*).

BRET LOTT is the bestselling author of fourteen books, most recently the nonfiction collection *Letters and Life: On Being a Writer, On Being a Christian* (Crossway, 2013) and the novel *Dead Low Tide* (Random House, 2012). He has served as Fulbright Senior American Scholar and writer in residence at Bar-Ilan University in Tel Aviv, spoken on Flannery O'Connor at the White House, and been a member of the National Council on the Arts from 2006 to 2012. He teaches at the College of Charleston and lives in Hanahan, South Carolina.

PATRICK MADDEN's first book, *Quotidiana* (University of Nebraska Press, 2010), won an Independent Publisher Book of the Year award, and his essays have been published widely in journals and anthologies including *The Best American Spiritual Writing* and *The Best Creative Nonfiction*. Nebraska will publish his second book, *Sublime Physick*, in 2015. A two-time Fulbright Fellow to Uruguay, he teaches at Brigham Young University and Vermont College of Fine Arts and curates the online anthology of classical essays at www.quotidiana.org.

DESIRAE MATHERLY teaches writing at Tusculum College and serves as nonfiction editor for the *Tusculum Review*. Her most recent essays appear in *Hotel Amerika, Descant*, and *Red Holler: An Anthology of Contemporary Appalachian Literature*. Four of her essays have made the Notable list in *The Best American Essays*, and one essay was anthologized in *The Best Creative Nonfiction*. Desirae earned a PhD in creative nonfiction from Ohio University in 2004 and was a Harper Fellow at the University of Chicago.

MAGGIE NELSON is the author of five books of nonfiction, *The Argonauts* (Graywolf, 2015), from which her piece here is excerpted; *The Art of Cruelty: A Reckoning* (Norton, 2011); *Bluets* (Wave Books, 2009); *Women, the New York School, and Other True Abstractions* (University of Iowa Press, 2007); and *The Red Parts* (Free Press, 2007), as well as four books of poetry, *Something Bright, Then Holes* (Soft Skull, 2007), *Jane: A Murder* (Soft Skull, 2005), *The Latest Winter* (Hanging Loose, 2003), and *Shiner* (Hanging Loose, 2001). Since 2005 she has been a member of the faculty of the School of Critical Studies at CalArts in Valencia, California. She lives in Los Angeles.

JOSÉ ORDUÑA is a recent graduate of the University of Iowa's Nonfiction Writing Program. He was born in Córdoba, Veracruz, and immigrated to Chicago with his mother at the age of one and a half. When he was in fourth grade, he and his parents traveled by bus from their home in Chicago to Ciudad Juárez in order to file for permanent residency under section 245(i) of the Immigration and Nationality Act. In December of 2010, while in graduate school, he applied for naturalization, and he was sworn in as a United States citizen the following year. He currently lives in Iowa City, where he is at work on his forthcoming book from Beacon Press, *The Naturalization: Notes on the Browning of America*.

ELENA PASSARELLO is an actor, a writer, and the first female winner of the Stella! Shout-Out screaming contest in New Orleans. Her book *Let Me Clear My Throat*, a collection of essays on the voice in pop culture, won the gold medal for creative nonfiction at the 2013 Independent Publisher Book Awards. Her essays have appeared in the *Oxford American, Slate, Iowa Review, Creative Nonfiction*, the *Normal School*, and the music writing anthology *Pop When the World Falls Apart*. She teaches creative writing at Oregon State University.

LIA PURPURA is the author of seven collections of essays, poems, and translations, most recently *Rough Likeness* (essays) and *King Baby* (poems). Her honors include a Guggenheim Foundation Fellowship, National Book Critics Circle Award finalist,

National Endowment for the Arts and Fulbright Fellowships, three Pushcart Prizes, the Associated Writing Programs Award in Nonfiction, and the Beatrice Hawley and Ohio State University Press awards in poetry. Recent work appears in *The Best American Essays* and in *Agni, Field, Georgia Review, Orion, New Republic, New Yorker, Paris Review*, and elsewhere. She is writer in residence at the University of Maryland, Baltimore County.

KRISTEN RADTKE's first book, a graphic memoir, is forthcoming from Pantheon Books. She is the marketing and publicity director for Sarabande Books and the film and video editor of *TriQuarterly* magazine. She has an MFA from the University of Iowa's Nonfiction Writing Program.

AMY LEE SCOTT received an MFA from the University of Iowa's Nonfiction Writing Program. Her essays have appeared in various literary magazines, as well as on the Notable lists for *The Best American Essays 2009* and *2013*, and *The Best American Travel Writing 2013*. She lives in Dearborn, Michigan, where she is working on a collection of essays about loss, memory, and adoption. Her writing can be found at amyleescott.com.

JERALD WALKER is the author of *Street Shadows: A Memoir of Race, Rebellion, and Redemption*, recipient of the 2011 PEN New England/L. L. Winship Award for Nonfiction. His essays have appeared in numerous periodicals and anthologies, including four times in *The Best American Essays*, and his memoir about growing up in a doomsday cult will be published in 2015. Walker is an associate professor of creative writing at Emerson College.

NICOLE WALKER's *Quench Your Thirst with Salt* won the Zone 3 Award for Creative Nonfiction and was released in June 2013. She is the author of a collection of poems, *This Noisy Egg* (Barrow Street, 2010), and has edited, with Margot Singer, *Bending Genre: Essays on Creative Nonfiction* (Bloomsbury, 2013) and, with Rebecca Campbell, *7 Artists, 7 Rings—An Artist's Game of Telephone* for the *Huffington Post*. She is nonfiction editor at *Diagram* and associate professor at Northern Arizona University in Flagstaff.

Index

Whitman, Walt, 7, 40
wisdom, 22, 31, 85, 87, 131, 154, 186, 201,
    224–25, 230–31
writing, 35, 74–75; advice, 94, 115, 154,
    204–7; creative, 7, 177; dream of,
    152; essays, 2–3, 7, 82–83, 234;
    memories of, 118, 119, 125, 128;
    Montaigne's, 28, 84, 171, 181, 185,

188, 194; personal, 78, 193; process of,
5, 44, 71, 78–79, 116, 127, 187, 193,
207, 211, 226, 233; about self, 8, 140;
stories, 72–73, 81; teachers, 115, 177;
thinking about, 94; voice, 7; writing
about, 154

Yogananda, Paramahansa, 132, 139